EXCURSIONS

BY

HENRY DAVID THOREAU

BOSTON AND NEW YORK
HOUGHTON, MIFFLIN AND COMPANY
The Riverside Press, Cambridge

The Riverside Press, Cambridge, Mass., U. S. A.
Electrotyped and Printed by H. O. Houghton & Company.

CONTENTS

PAGE

INTRODUCTORY NOTE vii

A YANKEE IN CANADA 1

   I. Concord to Montreal 3

   II. Quebec and Montmorenci 24

   III. St. Anne 49

   IV. The Walls of Quebec 85

   V. The Scenery of Quebec; and the River St.
      Lawrence 105

NATURAL HISTORY OF MASSACHUSETTS . . . 127

A WALK TO WACHUSETT 163

THE LANDLORD 187

A WINTER WALK 199

THE SUCCESSION OF FOREST TREES 225

WALKING 251

AUTUMNAL TINTS 305

WILD APPLES 356

NIGHT AND MOONLIGHT 397

MAY DAYS 410

DAYS AND NIGHTS IN CONCORD 438

3878

INTRODUCTORY NOTE

THE title given to this volume is the same as that used in 1863 when, shortly after Thoreau's death, his sister collected for Messrs. Ticknor & Fields a number of his fugitive pieces and prefaced the volume with a biographical sketch by Ralph Waldo Emerson. The contents of the two volumes are with a few exceptions the same, the chief differences being that Mr. Emerson's sketch precedes the final volume of the series, and *A Yankee in Canada*, formerly published in a volume with *Anti-Slavery and Reform Papers*, is made here the first in the series of *Excursions*.

Thoreau made this excursion with his friend Ellery Channing, and sent his narrative to Mr. Greeley, who wrote him regarding it, March 18, 1852, "I shall get you some money for the articles you sent me, though not immediately. As to your long account of a Canadian tour, I don't know. It looks unmanageable. Can't you cut it into three or four, and omit all that relates to time? The cities are described to death, but I know you are at home with Nature, and that *she* rarely and slowly changes. Break this up, if you can, and I will try to have it swallowed and digested." Thoreau appears to have taken Greeley's advice, and the narrative was divided into chapters. But after it had been begun in *Putnam's* in January, 1853, where it was entitled *Excursion to Canada*, the author and the editor, who appears from the following letter to have been Mr. G. W. Curtis, disagreed regarding the expediency of including certain passages, and Thoreau withdrew all after the third chapter. The letter is as follows: —

NEW YORK, *January* 2, 1853.

FRIEND THOREAU. . . . I am sorry you and C. cannot agree so as to have your whole *MS.* printed. It will be worth nothing elsewhere after having partly appeared in *Putnam's.* I think it is a mistake to conceal the authorship of the several articles, making them all (so to speak) *editorial;* but *if* that is done, don't you see that the elimination of very flagrant heresies (like your defiant Pantheism) becomes a necessity? If you had withdrawn your *MS.* on account of the abominable misprints in the first number, your ground would have been far more tenable. However, do what you will. Yours,

HORACE GREELEY.

Natural History of Massachusetts was contributed to *The Dial*, July, 1842, nominally as a review of a recent state report. *A Walk to Wachusett* was printed in *The Boston Miscellany*, 1843. Mr. Sanborn, in his volume on Thoreau, prints a very interesting letter written by Margaret Fuller in 1841, in criticism of the verses which stand near the beginning of the paper offered at that time for publication in *The Dial*. *The Landlord* was printed in *The Democratic Review* for October, 1843. *A Winter Walk* appeared in *The Dial* in the same month and year. Emerson in a letter to Thoreau, September 8, 1843, says : "I mean to send the *Winter's Walk* to the printer to-morrow for *The Dial*. I had some hesitation about it, notwithstanding its faithful observation and its fine sketches of the pickerel-fisher and of the woodchopper, on account of *mannerism*, an old charge of mine, — as if, by attention, one could get the trick of the rhetoric; for example, to call a cold place sultry, a solitude public, a wilderness *domestic* (a favorite word), and in the woods to insult over cities, armies, etc. By pretty free omissions, however, I have removed my principal objections." The address, *The Succession of Forest Trees*, was printed first in *The New York Weekly Tribune*, October 6,

1860, and was perhaps the latest of his writings which Thoreau saw in print.

After his death the interest which had already been growing was quickened by the successive publication in *The Atlantic Monthly* in 1862 of *Autumnal Tints* (October), *Wild Apples* (November), and *Night and Moonlight* (November, 1863). The last named appeared just before the publication of the volume *Excursions* which collected the several papers, but, as Channing remarks, though the contents of the volume had all been printed before, and some had been used also as lectures, they "are really descriptions drawn from his journals."

May Days has appeared before only in *The Atlantic* for May, 1878. *Days and Nights in Concord* was published in *Scribner's Monthly*, September, 1878. The time of the year covered by these last named extracts is that of August and September, and falls for the most part between the two volumes *Summer* and *Autumn*. Other extracts from the journal occur in a somewhat mosaic form in *Thoreau, the Poet Naturalist*, by W. Ellery Channing.

A YANKEE IN CANADA

"New England is by some affirmed to be an island, bounded on the north with the River Canada (so called from Monsieur Cane)." — JOSSE-LYN'S RARITIES.

And still older, in Thomas Morton's "New English Canaan," published in 1632, it is said, on page 97, "From this Lake [Erocoise] Northwards is derived the famous River of Canada, so named, of Monsier de Cane, a French Lord, who first planted a Colony of French in America."

A YANKEE IN CANADA

CHAPTER I

CONCORD TO MONTREAL

I FEAR that I have not got much to say about
Canada, not having seen much; what I got by
going to Canada was a cold. I left Concord,
Massachusetts, Wednesday morning, September
25th, 1850, for Quebec. Fare, seven dollars
there and back; distance from Boston, five hundred and ten miles; being obliged to leave Montreal on the return as soon as Friday, October
4th, or within ten days. I will not stop to tell
the reader the names of my fellow-travelers;
there were said to be fifteen hundred of them.
I wished only to be set down in Canada, and
take one honest walk there as I might in Concord woods of an afternoon.

The country was new to me beyond Fitchburg.
In Ashburnham and afterward, as we were
whirled rapidly along, I noticed the woodbine
(*Ampelopsis quinquefolia*), its leaves now
changed, for the most part on dead trees, drap-
ing them like a red scarf. It was a little excit-

ing, suggesting bloodshed, or at least a military life, like an epaulet or sash, as if it were dyed with the blood of the trees whose wounds it was inadequate to stanch. For now the bloody autumn was come, and an Indian warfare was waged through the forest. These military trees appeared very numerous, for our rapid progress connected those that were even some miles apart. Does the woodbine prefer the elm? The first view of Monadnock was obtained five or six miles this side of Fitzwilliam, but nearest and best at Troy and beyond. Then there were the Troy cuts and embankments. Keene Street strikes the traveler favorably, it is so wide, level, straight, and long. I have heard one of my relatives, who was born and bred there, say that you could see a chicken run across it a mile off. I have also been told that when this town was settled they laid out a street four rods wide, but at a subsequent meeting of the proprietors one rose and remarked, "We have plenty of land, why not make the street eight rods wide? and so they voted that it should be eight rods wide, and the town is known far and near for its handsome street. It was a cheap way of securing comfort, as well as fame, and I wish that all new towns would take pattern from this. It is best to lay our plans widely in youth, for then land is cheap, and it is but too easy to contract our views afterward.   Youths so laid out, with broad avenues and parks, that they may make handsome and liberal old men!   Show me a youth whose mind is like some Washington city of magnificent distances, prepared for the most remotely successful and glorious life after all, when those spaces shall be built over and the idea of the founder be realized.   I trust that every New England boy will begin by laying out a Keene Street through his head, eight rods wide.   I know one such Washington city of a man, whose lots as yet are only surveyed and staked out, and, except a cluster of shanties here and there, only the Capitol stands there for all structures, and any day you may see from afar his princely idea borne coachwise along the spacious but yet empty avenues.   Keene is built on a remarkably large and level interval, like the bed of a lake, and the surrounding hills, which are remote from its street, must afford some good walks.   The scenery of mountain towns is commonly too much crowded.   A town which is built on a plain of some extent, with an open horizon, and surrounded by hills at a distance, affords the best walks and views.

As we travel northwest up the country, sugar-maples, beeches, birches, hemlocks, spruce, butternuts, and ash trees prevail more and more. To the rapid traveler the number of elms in a

town is the measure of its civility. One man
in the cars has a bottle full of some liquor.
The whole company smile whenever it is exhibited. I find no difficulty in containing myself.
The Westmoreland country looked attractive.
I heard a passenger giving the very obvious derivation of this name, West-more-land, as if it
were purely American, and he had made a discovery; but I thought of "my cousin Westmoreland" in England. Every one will remember
the approach to Bellows Falls, under a high cliff
which rises from the Connecticut. I was disappointed in the size of the river here; it appeared
shrunk to a mere mountain stream. The water
was evidently very low. The rivers which we
had crossed this forenoon possessed more of the
character of mountain streams than those in the
vicinity of Concord, and I was surprised to see
everywhere traces of recent freshets, which had
carried away bridges and injured the railroad,
though I had heard nothing of it. In Ludlow,
Mount Holly, and beyond, there is interesting
mountain scenery, not rugged and stupendous,
but such as you could easily ramble over, —
long, narrow, mountain vales through which to
see the horizon. You are in the midst of the
Green Mountains. A few more elevated blue
peaks are seen from the neighborhood of Mount
Holly, perhaps Killington Peak is one. Some-

times, as on the Western Railroad, you are whirled over mountainous embankments, from which the scared horses in the valleys appear diminished to hounds. All the hills blush; I think that autumn must be the best season to journey over even the *Green* Mountains. You frequently exclaim to yourself, what *red* maples! The sugar-maple is not so red. You see some of the latter with rosy spots or cheeks only, blushing on one side like fruit, while all the rest of the tree is green, proving either some partiality in the light or frosts, or some prematurity in particular branches. Tall and slender ash-trees, whose foliage is turned to a dark mulberry color, are frequent. The butternut, which is a remarkably spreading tree, is turned completely yellow, thus proving its relation to the hickories. I was also struck by the bright yellow tints of the yellow birch. The sugar-maple is remarkable for its clean ankle. The groves of these trees looked like vast forest sheds, their branches stopping short at a uniform height, four or five feet from the ground, like eaves, as if they had been trimmed by art, so that you could look under and through the whole grove with its leafy canopy, as under a tent whose curtain is raised.

As you approach Lake Champlain you begin to see the New York mountains. The first view

of the Lake at Vergennes is impressive, but
rather from association than from any peculiarity in the scenery. It lies there so small (not
appearing in that proportion to the width of the
State that it does on the map), but beautifully
quiet, like a picture of the Lake of Lucerne on
a music-box, where you trace the name of Lucerne among the foliage; far more ideal than
ever it looked on the map. It does not say,
"Here I am, Lake Champlain," as the conductor
might for it, but having studied the geography
thirty years, you crossed over a hill one afternoon and beheld it. But it is only a glimpse
that you get here. At Burlington you rush to
a wharf and go on board a steamboat, two hundred and thirty-two miles from Boston. We
left Concord at twenty minutes before eight in
the morning, and were in Burlington about six
at night, but too late to see the lake. We got
our first fair view of the lake at dawn, just before reaching Plattsburg, and saw blue ranges
of mountains on either hand, in New York and
in Vermont, the former especially grand. A
few white schooners, like gulls, were seen in the
distance, for it is not waste and solitary like a
lake in Tartary; but it was such a view as
leaves not much to be said; indeed, I have post-
poned Lake Champlain to another day.

The oldest reference to these waters that I

have yet seen is in the account of Cartier's discovery and exploration of the St. Lawrence in
1535. Samuel Champlain actually discovered
and paddled up the lake in July, 1609, eleven
years before the settlement of Plymouth, accompanying a war-party of the Canadian Indians
against the Iroquois. He describes the islands
in it as not inhabited, although they are pleasant, — on account of the continual wars of the
Indians, in consequence of which they withdraw
from the rivers and lakes into the depths of the
land, that they may not be surprised. "Con-
tinuing our course," says he, "in this lake, on
the western side, viewing the country, I saw on
the eastern side very high mountains, where
there was snow on the summit. I inquired of
the savages if those places were inhabited.
They replied that they were, and that they were
Iroquois, and that in those places there were
beautiful valleys and plains fertile in corn, such
as I have eaten in this country, with an infinity
of other fruits." This is the earliest account of
what is now Vermont.

The number of French Canadian gentlemen
and ladies among the passengers, and the sound
of the French language, advertised us by this
time that we were being whirled towards some
foreign vortex. And now we have left Rouse's
Point, and entered the Sorel River, and passed

the invisible barrier between the States and
Canada. The shores of the Sorel, Richelieu, or
St. John's River are flat and reedy, where I
had expected something more rough and mountainous for a natural boundary between two nations. Yet I saw a difference at once, in the
few huts, in the pirogues on the shore, and as
it were, in the shore itself. This was an interesting scenery to me, and the very reeds or
rushes in the shallow water and the tree-tops in
the swamps have left a pleasing impression.
We had still a distant view behind us of two or
three blue mountains in Vermont and New York.
About nine o'clock in the forenoon we reached
St. John's, an old frontier post three hundred
and six miles from Boston, and twenty-four
from Montreal. We now discovered that we
were in a foreign country, in a station-house of
another nation. This building was a barn-like
structure, looking as if it were the work of the
villagers combined, like a log-house in a new
settlement. My attention was caught by the
double advertisements in French and English
fastened to its posts, by the formality of the
English, and the covert or open reference to
their queen and the British lion. No gentle-
manly conductor appeared, none whom you
would know to be the conductor by his dress
and demeanor; but erelong we began to see

here and there a solid, red-faced, burly-looking Englishman, a little pursy perhaps, who made us ashamed of ourselves and our thin and nervous countrymen, — a grandfatherly personage, at home in his great-coat, who looked as if he might be a stage proprietor, certainly a railroad director, and knew, or had a right to know, when the cars did start. Then there were two or three pale-faced, black-eyed, loquacious Canadian French gentlemen there, shrugging their shoulders; pitted as if they had all had the small-pox. In the mean while some soldiers, red-coats, belonging to the barracks near by, were turned out to be drilled. At every important point in our route the soldiers showed themselves ready for us; though they were evidently rather raw recruits here, they manœuvred far better than our soldiers; yet, as usual, I heard some Yankees talk as if they were no great shakes, and they had seen the Acton Blues manœuvre as well. The officers spoke sharply to them, and appeared to be doing their part thoroughly. I heard one suddenly coming to the rear, exclaim, "Michael Donouy, take his name!" though I could not see what the latter did or omitted to do. It was whispered that Michael Donouy would have to suffer for that. I heard some of our party discussing the possibility of their driving these troops off the field with their umbrellas. I thought that the Yankee, though undisciplined, had this advantage at least, that he especially is a man who, everywhere and under all circumstances, is fully resolved to better his condition essentially, and therefore he could afford to be beaten at first; while the virtue of the Irishman, and to a great extent the Englishman, consists in merely maintaining his ground or condition. The Canadians here, a rather poor-looking race, clad in gray homespun, which gave them the appearance of being covered with dust, were riding about in caleches and small one-horse carts called charettes. The Yankees assumed that all the riders were racing, or at least exhibiting the paces of their horses, and saluted them accordingly. We saw but little of the village here, for nobody could tell us when the cars would start; that was kept a profound secret, perhaps for political reasons; and therefore we were tied to our seats. The inhabitants of St. John's and vicinity are described by an English traveler as "singularly unprepossessing," and before completing his period he adds, "besides, they are generally very much disaffected to the British crown." I suspect that that "besides" should have been a because.

At length, about noon, the cars began to roll towards La Prairie. The whole distance of fifteen miles was over a remarkably level country, resembling a Western prairie, with the mountains about Chambly visible in the northeast. This novel but monotonous scenery was exciting. At La Prairie we first took notice of the tinned roofs, but above all of the St. Lawrence, which looked like a lake; in fact it is considerably expanded here; it was nine miles across diagonally to Montreal. Mount Royal in the rear of the city, and the island of St. Helen's opposite to it, were now conspicuous. We could also see the Sault St. Louis about five miles up the river, and the Sault Norman still farther eastward. The former are described as the most considerable rapids in the St. Lawrence; but we could see merely a gleam of light there as from a cobweb in the sun. Soon the city of Montreal was discovered with its tin roofs shining afar. Their reflections fell on the eye like a clash of cymbals on the ear. Above all the church of Notre Dame was conspicuous, and anon the Bonsecours market-house, occupying a commanding position on the quay, in the rear of the shipping. This city makes the more favorable impression from being approached by water, and also being built of stone, a gray limestone found on the island. Here, after traveling directly inland the whole breadth of New England, we had struck upon a city's har-

bor, — it made on me the impression of a sea-
port, — to which ships of six hundred tons can
ascend, and where vessels drawing fifteen feet
lie close to the wharf, five hundred and forty
miles from the Gulf; the St. Lawrence being
here two miles wide.   There was a great crowd
assembled on the ferry-boat wharf and on the
quay to receive the Yankees, and flags of all
colors were streaming from the vessels to celebrate their arrival.   When the gun was fired,
the gentry hurrahed again and again, and then
the Canadian caleche-drivers, who were most
interested in the matter, and who, I perceived,
were separated from the former by a fence, hurrahed their welcome; first the broadcloth, then
the homespun.

It was early in the afternoon when we stepped
ashore.   With a single companion, I soon found
my way to the church of Notre Dame.   I saw
that it was of great size and signified something.
It is said to be the largest ecclesiastical structure in North America, and can seat ten thousand.   It is two hundred and fifty-five and a
half feet long, and the groined ceiling is eighty
feet above your head.   The Catholic are the
only churches which I have seen worth remembering, which are not almost wholly profane.
I do not speak only of the rich and splendid like
this, but of the humblest of them as well.   Com-

ing from the hurrahing mob and the rattling carriages, we pushed aside the listed door of this church, and found ourselves instantly in an atmosphere which might be sacred to thought and religion, if one had any. There sat one or two women who had stolen a moment from the concerns of the day, as they were passing; but, if there had been fifty people there, it would still have been the most solitary place imaginable. They did not look up at us, nor did one regard another. We walked softly down the broad aisle with our hats in our hands. Presently came in a troop of Canadians, in their homespun, who had come to the city in the boat with us, and one and all kneeled down in the aisle before the high altar to their devotions, somewhat awkwardly, as cattle prepare to lie down, and there we left them. As if you were to catch some farmer's sons from Marlboro, come to cattle-show, silently kneeling in Concord meeting-house some Wednesday! Would there not soon be a mob peeping in at the windows? It is true, these Roman Catholics, priests and all, impress me as a people who have fallen far behind the significance of their symbols. It is as if an ox had strayed into a church and were trying to bethink himself. Nevertheless, they are capable of reverence; but we Yankees are a people in whom this sentiment has nearly died out, and in this respect we cannot bethink ourselves even as oxen. I did not mind the pictures nor the candles, whether tallow or tin. Those of the former which I looked at appeared tawdry. It matters little to me whether the pictures are by a neophyte of the Algonquin or the Italian tribe. But I was impressed by the quiet, religious atmosphere of the place. It was a great cave in the midst of a city; and what were the altars and the tinsel but the sparkling stalactics, into which you entered in a moment, and where the still atmosphere and the sombre light disposed to serious and profitable thought? Such a cave at hand, which you can enter any day, is worth a thousand of our churches which are open only Sundays, — hardly long enough for an airing, — and then filled with a bustling congregation, — a church where the priest is the least part, where you do your own preaching, where the universe preaches to you and can be heard. I am not sure but this Catholic religion would be an admirable one if the priest were quite omitted. I think that I might go to church myself sometimes some Monday, if I lived in a city where there was such a one to go to. In Concord, to be sure, we do not need such. Our forests are such a church, far grander and more sacred. We dare not leave *our* meeting-houses open for fear they would be profaned. Such a cave, such a shrine, in one of our groves, for instance, how long would it be respected? for what purposes would it be entered, by such baboons as we are? I think of its value not only to religion, but to philosophy and to poetry; besides a reading-room, to have a thinking-room in every city! Perchance the time will come when every house even will have not only its sleeping-rooms, and dining-room, and talking-room or parlor, but its thinking-room also, and the architects will put it into their plans. Let it be furnished and ornamented with whatever conduces to serious and creative thought. I should not object to the holy water, or any other simple symbol, if it were consecrated by the imagination of the worshipers.

I heard that some Yankees bet that the candles were not wax, but tin. A European assured them that they were wax; but, inquiring of the sexton, he was surprised to learn that they were tin filled with oil. The church was too poor to afford wax. As for the Protestant churches, here or elsewhere, they did not interest me, for it is only as caves that churches interest me at all, and in that respect they were inferior.

Montreal makes the impression of a larger city than you had expected to find, though you may have heard that it contains nearly sixty thousand inhabitants. In the newer parts, it appeared to be growing fast like a small New York, and to be considerably Americanized. The names of the squares reminded you of Paris, — the Champ de Mars, the Place d'Armes, and others, and you felt as if a French revolution might break out any moment. Glimpses of Mount Royal rising behind the town, and the names of some streets in that direction, make one think of Edinburgh. That hill sets off this city wonderfully. I inquired at a principal bookstore for books published in Montreal. They said that there were none but school-books and the like; they got their books from the States. From time to time we met a priest in the streets, for they are distinguished by their dress, like the *civil* police. Like clergymen generally, with or without the gown, they made on us the impression of effeminacy. We also met some Sisters of Charity, dressed in black, with Shaker-shaped black bonnets and crosses, and cadaverous faces, who looked as if they had almost cried their eyes out, their complexions parboiled with scalding tears; insulting the daylight by their presence, having taken an oath not to smile. By cadaverous I mean that their faces were like the faces of those who have been dead and buried for a year, and then untombed, with the life's grief upon them, and yet, for some unaccountable reason, the process of decay arrested.

> " Truth never fails her servant, sir, nor leaves him
> With the day's shame upon him."

They waited demurely on the sidewalk while a truck laden with raisins was driven in at the seminary of St. Sulpice, never once lifting their eyes from the ground.

The soldier here, as everywhere in Canada, appeared to be put forward, and by his best foot. They were in the proportion of the soldiers to the laborers in an African ant-hill. The inhabitants evidently rely on them in a great measure for music and entertainment. You would meet with them pacing back and forth before some guard-house or passage-way, guarding, regarding, and disregarding all kinds of law by turns, apparently for the sake of the discipline to themselves, and not because it was important to exclude anybody from entering that way. They reminded me of the men who are paid for piling up bricks and then throwing them down again. On every prominent ledge you could see England's hands holding the Canadas, and I judged by the redness of her knuckles that she would soon have to let go. In the rear of such a guard-house, in a large graveled square or parade ground, called the

Champ de Mars, we saw a large body of soldiers
being drilled, we being as yet the only spectators. But they did not appear to notice us any
more than the devotees in the church, but were
seemingly as indifferent to fewness of spectators
as the phenomena of nature are, whatever they
might have been thinking under their helmets
of the Yankees that were to come. Each man
wore white kid gloves. It was one of the most
interesting sights which I saw in Canada. The
problem appeared to be how to smooth down all
individual protuberances or idiosyncrasies, and
make a thousand men move as one man, animated by one central will; and there was some
approach to success. They obeyed the signals
of a commander who stood at a great distance,
wand in hand; and the precision, and prompt-
ness, and harmony of their movements could not
easily have been matched. The harmony was
far more remarkable than that of any choir or
band, and obtained, no doubt, at a greater cost.
They made on me the impression, not of many
individuals, but of one vast centipede of a man,
good for all sorts of pulling down; and why not
then for some kinds of building up? If men
could combine thus earnestly, and patiently,
and harmoniously to some really worthy end,
what might they not accomplish? They now
put their hands, and partially perchance their

heads together, and the result is that they are the imperfect tools of an imperfect and tyrannical government. But if they could put their hands and heads and hearts and all together, such a coöperation and harmony would be the very end and success for which government now exists in vain, — a government, as it were, not only with tools, but stock to trade with.

I was obliged to frame some sentences that sounded like French in order to deal with the market-women, who, for the most part, cannot speak English. According to the guide-book the relative population of this city stands nearly thus: two fifths are French Canadian; nearly one fifth British Canadian; one and a half fifth English, Irish, and Scotch; somewhat less than one half fifth Germans, United States people, and others. I saw nothing like pie for sale, and no good cake to put in my bundle, such as you can easily find in our towns, but plenty of fair-looking apples, for which Montreal Island is celebrated, and also pears, cheaper, and I thought better than ours, and peaches, which, though they were probably brought from the South, were as cheap as they commonly are with us. So imperative is the law of demand and supply that, as I have been told, the market of Montreal is sometimes supplied with green apples from the State of New York some weeks

even before they are ripe in the latter place.   I
saw here the spruce wax which the Canadians
chew, done up in little silvered papers, a penny
a roll; also a small and shriveled fruit which
they called *cerises* mixed with many little stems
somewhat like raisins, but I soon returned what
I had bought, finding them rather insipid, only
putting a sample in my pocket.   Since my return, I find on comparison that it is the fruit of
the sweet viburnum (*Viburnum lentago*), which
with us rarely holds on till it is ripe.

I stood on the deck of the steamer John
Munn, late in the afternoon, when the second
and third ferry-boats arrived from La Prairie,
bringing the remainder of the Yankees.   I
never saw so many caleches, cabs, charettes, and
similar vehicles collected before, and doubt if
New York could easily furnish more.   The
handsome and substantial stone quay, which
stretches a mile along the river-side, and pro-
tects the street from the ice, was thronged with
the citizens who had turned out on foot and in
carriages to welcome or to behold the Yankees.
It was interesting to see the caleche drivers dash
up and down the slope of the quay with their
active little horses.   They drive much faster
than in our cities.   I have been told that some
of them come nine miles into the city every
morning and return every night, without chang-

ing their horses during the day. In the midst
of the crowd of carts, I observed one deep one
loaded with sheep with their legs tied together,
and their bodies piled one upon another, as if
the driver had forgotten that they were sheep
and not yet mutton. A sight, I trust, peculiar
to Canada, though I fear that it is not.

CHAPTER II

QUEBEC AND MONTMORENCI

ABOUT six o'clock we started for Quebec, one hundred and eighty miles distant by the river; gliding past Longueil and Boucherville on the right, and *Pointe aux Trembles*, "so called from having been originally covered with aspens," and *Bout de l'Isle*, or the end of the island, on the left. I repeat these names not merely for want of more substantial facts to record, but because they sounded singularly poetic to my ears. There certainly was no lie in them. They suggested that some simple, and, perchance, heroic human life might have transpired there. There is all the poetry in the world in a name. It is a poem which the mass of men hear and read. What is poetry in the common sense, but a string of such jingling names? I want nothing better than a good word. The name of a thing may easily be more than the thing itself to me. Inexpressibly beautiful appears the recognition by man of the least natural fact, and the allying his life to it. All the world reiterating this slender truth, that aspens once grew there; and the swift inference is, that men were there to see them. And so it would be with the names of our native and neighboring villages, if we had not profaned them.

The daylight now failed us, and we went below; but I endeavored to console myself for being obliged to make this voyage by night, by thinking that I did not lose a great deal, the shores being low and rather unattractive, and that the river itself was much the more interesting object. I heard something in the night about the boat being at William Henry, Three Rivers, and in the Richelieu Rapids, but I was still where I had been when I lost sight of *Pointe aux Trembles*. To hear a man who has been waked up at midnight in the cabin of a steamboat, inquiring, "Waiter, where are we now?" is as if, at any moment of the earth's revolution round the sun, or of the system round its centre, one were to raise himself up and inquire of one of the deck hands, "Where are we now?"

I went on deck at daybreak, when we were thirty or forty miles above Quebec. The banks were now higher and more interesting. There was an "uninterrupted succession of whitewashed cottages," on each side of the river. This is what every traveler tells. But it is not

to be taken as an evidence of the populousness
of the country in general, hardly even of the
river banks. They have presented a similar
appearance for a hundred years. The Swedish
traveler and naturalist, Kalm, who descended
the river in 1749, says, "It could really be
called a village, beginning at Montreal and end-
ing at Quebec, which is a distance of more than
one hundred and eighty miles; for the farm-
houses are never above five arpents, and sometimes but three asunder, a few places excepted."
Even in 1684 Hontan said that the houses were
not more than a gunshot apart at most. Erelong we passed Cape Rouge, eight miles above
Quebec, the mouth of the Chaudière on the opposite or south side; New Liverpool Cove with
its lumber rafts and some shipping; then Sillery
and Wolfe's Cove and the Heights of Abraham
on the north, with now a view of Cape Diamond, and the citadel in front. The approach
to Quebec was very imposing. It was about six
o'clock in the morning when we arrived. There
is but a single street under the cliff on the south
side of the cape, which was made by blasting
the rocks and filling up the river. Three-story
houses did not rise more than one fifth or one
sixth the way up the nearly perpendicular rock,
whose summit is three hundred and forty-five
feet above the water. We saw, as we glided

past, the sign on the side of the precipice, part way up, pointing to the spot where Montgomery was killed in 1775. Formerly it was the custom for those who went to Quebec for the first time to be ducked, or else pay a fine. Not even the Governor General escaped. But we were too many to be ducked, even if the custom had not been abolished.[1]

Here we were, in the harbor of Quebec, still three hundred and sixty miles from the mouth of the St. Lawrence, in a basin two miles across, where the greatest depth is twenty-eight fathoms, and though the water is fresh, the tide rises seventeen to twenty-four feet, — a harbor "large and deep enough," says a British traveler, "to hold the English navy." I may as well state that, in 1844, the county of Quebec contained about forty-five thousand inhabitants (the city and suburbs having about forty-three thousand); about twenty-eight thousand being Canadians of French origin; eight thousand British; over seven thousand natives of Ireland;

[1] Hierosme Lalemant says in 1648, in his relation, he being Superior: "All those who come to New France know well enough the mountain of Notre Dame, because the pilots and sailors, being arrived at that part of the Great River which is opposite to those high mountains, baptize ordinarily for sport the new passengers, if they do not turn aside by some present the inundation of this baptism which one makes flow plentifully on their heads."

one thousand five hundred natives of England; the rest Scotch and others. Thirty-six thousand belong to the Church of Rome.

Separating ourselves from the crowd, we walked up a narrow street, thence ascended by some wooden steps, called the Break-neck Stairs, into another steep, narrow, and zigzag street, blasted through the rock, which last led through a low, massive, stone portal, called Prescott Gate, the principal thoroughfare into the Upper Town. This passage was defended by cannon, with a guard-house over it, a sentinel at his post, and other soldiers at hand ready to relieve him. I rubbed my eyes to be sure that I was in the nineteenth century, and was not entering one of those portals which sometimes adorn the frontispieces of new editions of old black-letter volumes. I thought it would be a good place to read Froissart's Chronicles. It was such a reminiscence of the Middle Ages as Scott's novels. Men apparently dwelt there for security! Peace be unto them! As if the inhabitants of New York were to go over to Castle William to live! What a place it must be to bring up children! Being safe through the gate we naturally took the street which was steepest, and after a few turns found ourselves on the Durham Terrace, a wooden platform on the site of the old castle of St. Louis, still one

hundred and fifteen feet below the summit of
the citadel, overlooking the Lower Town, the
wharf where we had landed, the harbor, the
Isle of Orleans, and the river and surrounding
country to a great distance. It was literally a
splendid view. We could see six or seven
miles distant, in the northeast, an indentation
in the lofty shore of the northern channel, apparently on one side of the harbor, which marked
the mouth of the Montmorenci, whose celebrated
fall was only a few rods in the rear.

At a shoe-shop, whither we were directed for
this purpose, we got some of our American
money changed into English. I found that
American hard money would have answered as
well, excepting cents, which fell very fast before
their pennies, it taking two of the former to
make one of the latter, and often the penny,
which had cost us two cents, did us the service
of one cent only. Moreover, our robust cents
were compelled to meet on even terms a crew of
vile half-penny tokens, and bung-town coppers,
which had more brass in their composition, and
so perchance made their way in the world.
Wishing to get into the citadel, we were directed to the Jesuits' Barracks, — a good part
of the public buildings here are barracks, — to
get a pass of the Town Major. We did not
heed the sentries at the gate, nor did they us,

and what under the sun they were placed there
for, unless to hinder a free circulation of the air,
was not apparent. There we saw soldiers eating their breakfasts in their mess-room, from
bare wooden tables in camp fashion. We were
continually meeting with soldiers in the streets,
carrying funny little tin pails of all shapes, even
semicircular, as if made to pack conveniently.
I supposed that they contained their dinners, —
so many slices of bread and butter to each, perchance. Sometimes they were carrying some
kind of military chest on a sort of bier or hand-
barrow, with a springy, undulating, military
step, all passengers giving way to them, even
the charette drivers stopping for them to pass,
— as if the battle were being lost from an inadequate supply of powder. There was a regiment
of Highlanders, and, as I understood, of Royal
Irish, in the city; and by this time there was a
regiment of Yankees also. I had already observed, looking up even from the water, the
head and shoulders of some General Poniatow-
sky, with an enormous cocked hat and gun,
peering over the roof of a house, away up where
the chimney caps commonly are with us, as it
were a caricature of war and military awfulness;
but I had not gone far up St. Louis Street before my riddle was solved, by the apparition of
a real live Highlander under a cocked hat, and

with his knees out, standing and marching sentinel on the ramparts, between St. Louis and
St. John's Gate. (It must be a holy war that
is waged there.) We stood close by without
fear and looked at him. His legs were somewhat tanned, and the hair had begun to grow
on them, as some of our wise men predict that
it will in such cases, but I did not think they
were remarkable in any respect. Notwithstanding all his warlike gear, when I inquired of him
the way to the Plains of Abraham, he could not
answer me without betraying some bashfulness
through his broad Scotch. Soon after, we
passed another of these creatures standing sen-
try at the St. Louis Gate, who let us go by
without shooting us, or even demanding the
countersign. We then began to go through the
gate, which was so thick and tunnel-like, as to
remind me of those lines in Claudian's Old
Man of Verona, about the getting out of the
gate being the greater part of a journey; — as
you might imagine yourself crawling through an
architectural vignette *at the end* of a black-letter volume. We were then reminded that we
had been in a fortress, from which we emerged
by numerous zigzags in a ditch-like road, going
a considerable distance to advance a few rods,
where they could have shot us two or three times
over, if their minds had been disposed as their

guns were. The greatest, or rather the most prominent, part of this city was constructed with the design to offer the deadest resistance to leaden and iron missiles that might be cast against it. But it is a remarkable meteorological and psychological fact, that it is rarely known to rain lead with much violence, except on places so constructed. Keeping on about a mile we came to the Plains of Abraham, — for having got through with the Saints, we came next to the Patriarchs. Here the Highland regiment was being reviewed, while the band stood on one side and played, — methinks it was *La Claire Fontaine*, the national air of the Canadian French. This is the site where a real battle once took place, to commemorate which they have had a sham fight here almost every day since. The Highlanders manœuvred very well, and if the precision of their movements was less remarkable, they did not appear so stiffly erect as the English or Royal Irish, but had a more elastic and graceful gait, like a herd of their own red deer, or as if accustomed to stepping down the sides of mountains. But they made a sad impression on the whole, for it was obvious that all true manhood was in the process of being drilled out of them. I have no doubt that soldiers well drilled are, as a class, peculiarly destitute of originality and independence. The officers appeared like men dressed above their condition. It is impossible to give the soldier a good education, without making him a deserter. His natural foe is the government that drills him. What would any philanthropist, who felt an interest in these men's welfare, naturally do, but first of all teach them so to respect themselves, that they could not be hired for this work, whatever might be the consequences to this government or that; — not drill a few, but educate all. I observed one older man among them, gray as a wharf-rat, and supple as the Devil, marching lock-step with the rest, who would have to pay for that elastic gait.

We returned to the citadel along the heights, plucking such flowers as grew there. There was an abundance of succory still in blossom, broad - leaved golden - rod, buttercups, thorn-bushes, Canada thistles, and ivy, on the very summit of Cape Diamond. I also found the bladder-campion in the neighborhood. We there enjoyed an extensive view, which I will describe in another place. Our pass, which stated that all the rules were "to be strictly enforced," as if they were determined to keep up the semblance of reality to the last gasp, opened to us the Dalhousie Gate, and we were conducted over the citadel by a bare-legged Highlander in cocked hat and full regimentals. He told us that he had been here about three years, and had formerly been stationed at Gibraltar. As if his regiment, having perchance been nestled amid the rocks of Edinburgh Castle, must flit from rock to rock thenceforth over the earth's surface, like a bald eagle, or other bird of prey, from eyrie to eyrie. As we were going out, we met the Yankees coming in, in a body headed by a red-coated officer called the commandant, and escorted by many citizens, both English and French Canadian. I therefore immediately fell into the procession, and went round the citadel again with more intelligent guides, carrying, as before, all my effects with me. Seeing that nobody walked with the red-coated commandant, I attached myself to him, and though I was not what is called well-dressed, he did not know whether to repel me or not, for I talked like one who was not aware of any deficiency in that respect. Probably there was not one among all the Yankees who went to Canada this time, who was not more splendidly dressed than I was. It would have been a poor story if I had not enjoyed some distinction. I had on my "bad-weather clothes," like Olaf Trygesson the Northman, when he went to the Thing in England, where, by the way, he won his bride. As we stood by the thirty-two-pounder on the summit of Cape Dia-

mond, which is fired three times a day, the commandant told me that it would carry to the Isle
of Orleans, four miles distant, and that no hostile vessel could come round the island. I now
saw the subterranean or, rather, "casemated
barracks" of the soldiers, which I had not noticed before, though I might have walked over
them. They had very narrow windows, serving
as loop-holes for musketry, and small iron chimneys rising above the ground. There we saw
the soldiers at home and in an undress, split-
ting wood, — I looked to see whether with
swords or axes, — and in various ways endeavoring to realize that their nation was now at
peace with this part of the world. A part of
each regiment, chiefly officers, are allowed to
marry. A grandfatherly, would-be witty Englishman could give a Yankee whom he was pa-
tronizing no reason for the bare knees of the
Highlanders, other than oddity. The rock
within the citadel is a little convex, so that
shells falling on it would roll toward the circumference, where the barracks of the soldiers
and officers are; it has been proposed, therefore, to make it slightly concave, so that they
may roll into the centre, where they would be
comparatively harmless; and it is estimated
that to do this would cost twenty thousand
pounds sterling. It may be well to remember

this when I build my next house, and have the roof "all correct" for bombshells.

At mid-afternoon we made haste down *Sault-au-Matelot* Street, towards the Falls of Mont-morenci, about eight miles down the St. Law-rence, on the north side, leaving the further examination of Quebec till our return. On our way, we saw men in the streets sawing logs pit-fashion, and afterward, with a common wood-saw and horse, cutting the planks into squares for paving the streets. This looked very shift-less, especially in a country abounding in water-power, and reminded me that I was no longer in Yankee land. I found, on inquiry, that the excuse for this was, that labor was so cheap; and I thought, with some pain, how cheap men are here! I have since learned that the English traveler, Warburton, remarked, soon after land-ing at Quebec, that everything was cheap there but men. That must be the difference between going thither from New and from Old England. I had already observed the dogs harnessed to their little milk-carts, which contain a single large can, lying asleep in the gutters regardless of the horses, while they rested from their la-bors, at different stages of the ascent in the Upper Town. I was surprised at the regular and extensive use made of these animals for drawing, not only milk, but groceries, wood,

etc. It reminded me that the dog commonly is
not put to any use. Cats catch mice; but dogs
only worry the cats. Kalm, a hundred years
ago, saw sledges here for ladies to ride in,
drawn by a pair of dogs. He says, "A middle-
sized dog is sufficient to draw a single person,
when the roads are good;" and he was told by
old people, that horses were very scarce in their
youth, and almost all the land-carriage was then
effected by dogs. They made me think of the
Esquimaux, who, in fact, are the next people
on the north. Charlevoix says that the first
horses were introduced in 1665.

We crossed Dorchester Bridge, over the St.
Charles, the little river in which Cartier, the
discoverer of the St. Lawrence, put his ships,
and spent the winter of 1535, and found ourselves on an excellent macadamized road, called
Le Chemin de Beauport. We had left Concord
Wednesday morning, and we endeavored to
realize that now, Friday morning, we were taking a walk in Canada, in the Seigniory of Beauport, a foreign country, which a few days before
had seemed almost as far off as England and
France. Instead of rambling to Flint's Pond
or the Sudbury Meadows, we found ourselves,
after being a little detained in cars and steam-
boats, — after spending half a night at Burlington, and half a day at Montreal, — taking a

walk down the bank of the St. Lawrence to the Falls of Montmorenci, and elsewhere. Well, I thought to myself, here I am in a foreign country; let me have my eyes about me, and take it all in. It already looked and felt a good deal colder than it had in New England, as we might have expected it would. I realized fully that I was four degrees nearer the pole, and shuddered at the thought; and I wondered if it were possible that the peaches might not be all gone when I returned. It was an atmosphere that made me think of the fur-trade, which is so interesting a department in Canada, for I had for all head covering a thin palm-leaf hat without lining, that cost twenty-five cents, and over my coat one of those unspeakably cheap, as well as thin, brown linen sacks of the Oak Hall pattern, which every summer appear all over New England, thick as the leaves upon the trees. It was a thoroughly Yankee costume, which some of my fellow-travelers wore in the cars to save their coats a dusting. I wore mine, at first, because it looked better than the coat it covered, and last, because two coats were warmer than one, though one was thin and dirty. I never wear my best coat on a journey, though perchance I could show a certificate to prove that I have a more costly one, at least, at home, if that were all that a gentleman required. It is not wise for a traveler to go dressed. I should no more think of it than of putting on a clean dicky and blacking my shoes to go a-fishing; as if you were going out to dine, when, in fact, the genuine traveler is going out to work hard, and fare harder, — to eat a crust by the wayside whenever he can get it. Honest traveling is about as dirty work as you can do, and a man needs a pair of overalls for it. As for blacking my shoes in such a case, I should as soon think of blacking my face. I carry a piece of tallow to preserve the leather and keep out the water; that's all; and many an officious shoeblack, who carried off my shoes when I was slumbering, mistaking me for a gentleman, has had occasion to repent it before he produced a gloss on them.

My pack, in fact, was soon made, for I keep a short list of those articles which, from frequent experience, I have found indispensable to the foot-traveler; and, when I am about to start, I have only to consult that, to be sure that nothing is omitted, and, what is more important, nothing superfluous inserted. Most of my fellow-travelers carried carpet-bags, or valises. Sometimes one had two or three ponderous yellow valises in his clutch, at each hitch of the cars, as if we were going to have another rush for seats; and when there was a rush in earnest,

and there were not a few, I would see my man
in the crowd, with two or three affectionate
lusty fellows along each side of his arm, between
his shoulder and his valises, which last held them
tight to his back, like the nut on the end of a
screw. I could not help asking in my mind,
What so great cause for showing Canada to
those valises, when perhaps your very nieces had
to stay at home for want of an escort? I should
have liked to be present when the custom-house
officer came aboard of him, and asked him to
declare upon his honor if he had anything but
wearing apparel in them. Even the elephant
carries but a small trunk on his journeys. The
perfection of traveling is to travel without bag-
gage. After considerable reflection and experience, I have concluded that the best bag for
the foot-traveler is made with a handkerchief,
or, if he study appearances, a piece of stiff
brown paper, well tied up, with a fresh piece
within to put outside when the first is torn.
That is good for both town and country, and
none will know but you are carrying home the
silk for a new gown for your wife, when it may
be a dirty shirt. A bundle which you can carry
literally under your arm, and which will shrink
and swell with its contents. I never found the
carpet-bag of equal capacity, which was not a
bundle of itself. We styled ourselves the

Knights of the Umbrella and the Bundle; for, wherever we went, whether to Notre Dame or Mount Royal or the Champ de Mars, to the Town Major's or the Bishop's Palace, to the Citadel, with a bare-legged Highlander for our escort, or to the Plains of Abraham, to dinner or to bed, the umbrella and the bundle went with us; for we wished to be ready to digress at any moment. We made it our home nowhere in particular, but everywhere where our umbrella and bundle were. It would have been an amusing circumstance, if the Mayor of one of those cities had politely asked us where we were staying. We could only have answered, that we were staying with his Honor for the time being. I was amused when, after our return, some green ones inquired if we found it easy to get accommodated; as if we went abroad to get accommodated, when we can get that at home.

We met with many charettes, bringing wood and stone to the city. The most ordinary looking horses traveled faster than ours, or perhaps they were ordinary looking because, as I am told, the Canadians do not use the curry-comb. Moreover, it is said that on the approach of winter their horses acquire an increased quantity of hair, to protect them from the cold. If this be true, some of our horses would make you think winter were approaching,

even in midsummer. We soon began to see
women and girls at work in the fields, digging
potatoes alone, or bundling up the grain which
the men cut. They appeared in rude health,
with a great deal of color in their cheeks, and,
if their occupation had made them coarse, it
impressed me as better in its effects than making shirts at fourpence apiece, or doing nothing
at all,— unless it be chewing slate pencils, with
still smaller results. They were much more
agreeable objects, with their great broad-
brimmed hats and flowing dresses, than the men
and boys. We afterwards saw them doing
various other kinds of work; indeed, I thought
that we saw more women at work out of doors
than men. On our return, we observed in this
town a girl, with Indian boots nearly two feet
high, taking the harness off a dog.

The purity and transparency of the atmosphere
were wonderful. When we had been walking
an hour, we were surprised, on turning round, to
see how near the city, with its glittering tin roofs,
still looked. A village ten miles off did not appear to be more than three or four. I was convinced that you could see objects distinctly there
much farther than here. It is true the villages
are of a dazzling white, but the dazzle is to be
referred, perhaps, to the transparency of the atmosphere as much as to the whitewash.

We were now fairly in the village of Beauport, though there was still but one road. The
houses stood close upon this, without any front
yards, and at an angle with it, as if they had
dropped down, being set with more reference to
the road which the sun travels. It being about
sundown, and the Falls not far off, we began to
look round for a lodging, for we preferred to
put up at a private house, that we might see
more of the inhabitants. We inquired first at
the most promising looking houses, if, indeed,
any were promising. When we knocked, they
shouted some French word for come in, perhaps
entrez, and we asked for a lodging in English;
but we found, unexpectedly, that they spoke
French only. Then we went along and tried
another house, being generally saluted by a rush
of two or three little curs, which readily distinguished a foreigner, and which we were prepared now to hear bark in French. Our first
question would be, *Parlez-vous Anglais?* but
the invariable answer was, *Non, monsieur;*
and we soon found that the inhabitants were exclusively French Canadians, and nobody spoke
English at all, any more than in France; that,
in fact, we were in a foreign country, where the
inhabitants uttered not one familiar sound to
us. Then we tried by turns to talk French
with them, in which we succeeded sometimes

pretty well, but for the most part pretty ill. *Pouvez-vous nous donner un lit cette nuit?* we would ask, and then they would answer with French volubility, so that we could catch only a word here and there. We could understand the women and children generally better than the men, and they us; and thus, after a while, we would learn that they had no more beds than they used.

So we were compelled to inquire *Y a-t-il une maison publique ici?* (*auberge* we should have said, perhaps, for they seemed never to have heard of the other), and they answered at length that there was no tavern, unless we could get lodgings at the mill, *le moulin*, which we had passed; or they would direct us to a grocery, and almost every house had a small grocery at one end of it. We called on the public notary or village lawyer, but he had no more beds nor English than the rest. At one house there was so good a misunderstanding at once established through the politeness of all parties, that we were encouraged to walk in and sit down, and ask for a glass of water; and having drank their water, we thought it was as good as to have tasted their salt. When our host and his wife spoke of their poor accommodations, meaning for themselves, we assured them that they were good enough, for we thought that they were

only apologizing for the poorness of the accommodations they were about to offer us, and we
did not discover our mistake till they took us up
a ladder into a loft, and showed to our eyes
what they had been laboring in vain to commu-
nicate to our brains through our ears, that they
had but that one apartment with its few beds
for the whole family. We made our *a-dieus*
forthwith, and with gravity, perceiving the lit-
eral signification of that word. We were finally
taken in at a sort of public-house, whose master worked for Patterson, the proprietor of the
extensive saw-mills driven by a portion of the
Montmorenci stolen from the fall, whose roar
we now heard. We here talked, or murdered,
French all the evening, with the master of the
house and his family, and probably had a more
amusing time than if we had completely understood one another. At length they showed us
to a bed in their best chamber, very high to get
into, with a low wooden rail to it. It had no
cotton sheets, but coarse, home-made, dark-col-
ored, linen ones. Afterward, we had to do with
sheets still coarser than these, and nearly the
color of our blankets. There was a large open
buffet loaded with crockery in one corner of the
room, as if to display their wealth to travelers,
and pictures of Scripture scenes, French, Italian, and Spanish, hung around. Our hostess

came back directly to inquire if we would have brandy for breakfast. The next morning, when I asked their names, she took down the temperance pledges of herself and husband, and children, which were hanging against the wall. They were Jean Baptiste Binet, and his wife, Geneviève Binet. Jean Baptiste is the sobriquet of the French Canadians.

After breakfast we proceeded to the fall, which was within half a mile, and at this distance its rustling sound, like the wind among the leaves, filled all the air. We were disappointed to find that we were in some measure shut out from the west side of the fall by the private grounds and fences of Patterson, who appropriates not only a part of the water for his mill, but a still larger part of the prospect, so that we were obliged to trespass. This gentleman's mansion house and grounds were formerly occupied by the Duke of Kent, father to Queen Victoria. It appeared to me in bad taste for an individual, though he were the father of Queen Victoria, to obtrude himself with his land titles, or at least his fences, on so remarkable a natural phenomenon, which should, in every sense, belong to mankind. Some falls should even be kept sacred from the intrusion of mills and factories, as water privileges in another than the millwright's sense. This small

river falls perpendicularly nearly two hundred
and fifty feet at one pitch. The St. Lawrence
falls only one hundred and sixty-four feet at
Niagara. It is a very simple and noble fall,
and leaves nothing to be desired; but the most
that I could say of it would only have the force
of one other testimony to assure the reader that
it is there. We looked directly down on it
from the point of a projecting rock, and saw far
below us, on a low promontory, the grass kept
fresh and green by the perpetual drizzle, looking like moss. The rock is a kind of slate, in
the crevices of which grew ferns and golden-
rods. The prevailing trees on the shores were
spruce and arbor-vitæ, — the latter very large
and now full of fruit, — also aspens, alders, and
the mountain-ash with its berries. Every emigrant who arrives in this country by way of the
St. Lawrence, as he opens a point of the Isle of
Orleans, sees the Montmorenci tumbling into the
Great River thus magnificently in a vast white
sheet, making its contribution with emphasis.
Roberval's pilot, Jean Alphonse, saw this fall
thus, and described it, in 1542. It is a splendid introduction to the scenery of Quebec. Instead of an artificial fountain in its square,
Quebec has this magnificent natural waterfall,
to adorn one side of its harbor. Within the
mouth of the chasm below, which can be entered

only at ebb tide, we had a grand view at once
of Quebec and of the fall.   Kalm says that the
noise of the fall is sometimes heard at Quebec,
about eight miles distant, and is a sign of a
northeast wind.   The side of this chasm, of soft
and crumbling slate too steep to climb, was
among the memorable features of the scene.   In
the winter of 1829 the frozen spray of the fall,
descending on the ice of the St. Lawrence, made
a hill one hundred and twenty-six feet high.   It
is an annual phenomenon which some think may
help explain the formation of glaciers.

In the vicinity of the fall we began to notice
what looked like our red-fruited thorn bushes,
grown to the size of ordinary apple-trees, very
common, and full of large red or yellow fruit,
which the inhabitants called *pommettes,* but I
did not learn that they were put to any use.

CHAPTER III

ST. ANNE

By the middle of the forenoon, though it was a rainy day, we were once more on our way down the north bank of the St. Lawrence, in a northeasterly direction, toward the Falls of St. Anne, which are about thirty miles from Quebec. The settled, more level, and fertile portion of Canada East may be described rudely as a triangle, with its apex slanting toward the northeast, about one hundred miles wide at its base, and from two to three or even four hundred miles long, if you reckon its narrow northeastern extremity; it being the immediate valley of the St. Lawrence and its tributaries, rising by a single or by successive terraces toward the mountains on either hand. Though the words Canada East on the map stretch over many rivers and lakes and unexplored wildernesses, the actual Canada, which might be the colored portion of the map, is but a little clearing on the banks of the river, which one of those syllables would more than cover. The banks of the St. Lawrence are rather low from Montreal to the

Richelieu Rapids, about forty miles above Quebec. Thence they rise gradually to Cape Diamond, or Quebec. Where we now were, eight
miles northeast of Quebec, the mountains which
form the northern side of this triangle were only
five or six miles distant from the river, gradually departing farther and farther from it, on
the west, till they reach the Ottawa, and making
haste to meet it on the east, at Cape Tourmente,
now in plain sight about twenty miles distant.
So that we were traveling in a very narrow and
sharp triangle between the mountains and the
river, tilted up toward the mountains on the
north, never losing sight of our great fellow-
traveler on our right. According to Bouchette's
Topographical Description of the Canadas, we
were in the Seigniory of the Côte de Beaupré,
in the county of Montmorenci, and the district
of Quebec; in that part of Canada which was
the first to be settled, and where the face of the
country and the population have undergone the
least change from the beginning, where the influence of the States and of Europe is least felt,
and the inhabitants see little or nothing of the
world over the walls of Quebec. This Seigniory
was granted in 1636, and is now the property
of the Seminary of Quebec. It is the most
mountainous one in the province. There are
some half a dozen parishes in it, each contain-

ing a church, parsonage-house, grist-mill, and
several saw-mills. We were now in the most
westerly parish, called Ange Gardien, or the
Guardian Angel, which is bounded on the west
by the Montmorenci. The north bank of the
St. Lawrence here is formed on a grand scale.
It slopes gently, either directly from the shore,
or from the edge of an interval, till, at the distance of about a mile, it attains the height of
four or five hundred feet. The single road runs
along the side of the slope two or three hundred
feet above the river at first, and from a quarter
of a mile to a mile distant from it, and affords
fine views of the north channel, which is about
a mile wide, and of the beautiful Isle of Orleans, about twenty miles long by five wide,
where grow the best apples and plums in the
Quebec District.

Though there was but this single road, it was
a continuous village for as far as we walked this
day and the next, or about thirty miles down
the river, the houses being as near together all
the way as in the middle of one of our smallest
straggling country villages, and we could never
tell by their number when we were on the skirts
of a parish, for the road never ran through the
fields or woods. We were told that it was just
six miles from one parish church to another. I
thought that we saw every house in Ange Gar-

dien. Therefore, as it was a muddy day, we never got out of the mud, nor out of the village, unless we got over the fence; then, indeed, if it was on the north side, we were out of the civilized world. There were sometimes a few more houses near the church, it is true, but we had only to go a quarter of a mile from the road to the top of the bank to find ourselves on the verge of the uninhabited, and, for the most part, unexplored wilderness stretching toward Hudson's Bay. The farms accordingly were extremely long and narrow, each having a frontage on the river. Bouchette accounts for this peculiar manner of laying out a village by referring to "the social character of the Canadian peasant, who is singularly fond of neighborhood," also to the advantage arising from a concentration of strength in Indian times. Each farm, called *terre*, he says, is, in nine cases out of ten, three arpents wide by thirty deep, that is, very nearly thirty-five by three hundred and forty-nine of our rods; sometimes one half arpent by thirty, or one to sixty; sometimes, in fact, a few yards by half a mile. Of course it costs more for fences. A remarkable difference between the Canadian and the New England character appears from the fact that, in 1745, the French government were obliged to pass a law forbidding the farmers or *censitaires* building

on land less than one and a half arpents front
by thirty or forty deep, under a certain penalty,
in order to compel emigration, and bring the
seigneur's estates all under cultivation; and it
is thought that they have now less reluctance to
leave the paternal roof than formerly, "remov-
ing beyond the sight of the parish spire, or the
sound of the parish bell." But I find that in
the previous or seventeenth century, the com-
plaint, often renewed, was of a totally opposite
character, namely, that the inhabitants dispersed and exposed themselves to the Iroquois.
Accordingly, about 1664, the king was obliged
to order that "they should make no more clearings except one next to another, and that they
should reduce their parishes to the form of the
parishes in France as much as possible." The
Canadians of those days, at least, possessed a
roving spirit of adventure which carried them
further, in exposure to hardship and danger,
than ever the New England colonist went, and
led them, though not to clear and colonize the
wilderness, yet to range over it as *coureurs de
bois*, or runners of the woods, or, as Hontan
prefers to call them, *coureurs de risques*, runners
of risks; to say nothing of their enterprising
priesthood; and Charlevoix thinks that if the
authorities had taken the right steps to prevent
the youth from ranging the woods (*de courir les*

bois) they would have had an excellent militia to fight the Indians and English.

The road in this clayey-looking soil was exceedingly muddy in consequence of the night's rain. We met an old woman directing her dog, which was harnessed to a little cart, to the least muddy part of it. It was a beggarly sight. But harnessed to the cart as he was, we heard him barking after we had passed, though we looked anywhere but to the cart to see where the dog was that barked. The houses commonly fronted the south, whatever angle they might make with the road; and frequently they had no door nor cheerful window on the road side. Half the time they stood fifteen to forty rods from the road, and there was no very obvious passage to them, so that you would suppose that there must be another road running by them. They were of stone, rather coarsely mortared, but neatly whitewashed, almost invariably one story high and long in proportion to their height, with a shingled roof, the shingles being pointed, for ornament, at the eaves, like the pickets of a fence, and also one row halfway up the roof. The gables sometimes projected a foot or two at the ridge-pole only. Yet they were very humble and unpretending dwellings. They commonly had the date of their erection on them. The windows opened

in the middle, like blinds, and were frequently
provided with solid shutters. Sometimes, when
we walked along the back side of a house which
stood near the road, we observed stout stakes
leaning against it, by which the shutters, now
pushed half open, were fastened at night; within,
the houses were neatly ceiled with wood not
painted. The oven was commonly out of doors,
built of stone and mortar, frequently on a raised
platform of planks. The cellar was often on
the opposite side of the road, in front of or behind the houses, looking like an ice-house with
us, with a lattice door for summer. The very
few mechanics whom we met had an old-Betty-
ish look, in their aprons and *bonnets rouges*,
like fools' caps. The men wore commonly the
same *bonnet rouge*, or red woolen or worsted
cap, or sometimes blue or gray, looking to us as
if they had got up with their night-caps on, and,
in fact, I afterwards found that they had.
Their clothes were of the cloth of the country,
étoffe du pays, gray or some other plain color.
The women looked stout, with gowns that stood
out stiffly, also, for the most part, apparently
of some home-made stuff. We also saw some
specimens of the more characteristic winter
dress of the Canadian, and I have since frequently detected him in New England by his
coarse gray homespun capote and picturesque

red sash, and his well-furred cap, made to protect his ears against the severity of his climate.

It drizzled all day, so that the roads did not
improve. We began now to meet with wooden
crosses frequently, by the roadside, about a
dozen feet high, often old and toppling down,
sometimes standing in a square wooden platform, sometimes in a pile of stones, with a little
niche containing a picture of the Virgin and
Child, or of Christ alone, sometimes with a
string of beads, and covered with a piece of
glass to keep out the rain, with the words, *pour
la vierge*, or INRI, on them. Frequently, on
the cross-bar, there would be quite a collection
of symbolical knickknacks, looking like an
Italian's board; the representation in wood of
a hand, a hammer, spikes, pincers, a flask of
vinegar, a ladder, etc., the whole, perchance,
surmounted by a weathercock; but I could not
look at an honest weathercock in this walk without mistrusting that there was some covert reference in it to St. Peter. From time to time
we passed a little one-story chapel-like building,
with a tin-roofed spire, a shrine, perhaps it
would be called, close to the pathside, with a
lattice door, through which we could see an altar, and pictures about the walls; equally open,
through rain and shine, though there was no
getting into it. At these places the inhabitants

kneeled and perhaps breathed a short prayer.
We saw one school-house in our walk, and lis-
tened to the sounds which issued from it; but it
appeared like a place where the process, not of
enlightening, but of obfuscating the mind was
going on, and the pupils received only so much
light as could penetrate the shadow of the Catholic Church. The churches were very picturesque, and their interior much more showy than
the dwelling-houses promised. They were of
stone, for it was ordered, in 1699, that that
should be their material. They had tinned
spires, and quaint ornaments. That of l'Ange
Gardien had a dial on it, with the Middle Age
Roman numerals on its face, and some images
in niches on the outside. Probably its counterpart has existed in Normandy for a thousand
years. At the church of Chateau Richer, which
is the next parish to l'Ange Gardien, we read,
looking over the wall, the inscriptions in the
adjacent churchyard, which began with, "*Ici
git*" or "*Repose*," and one over a boy contained, "*Priez pour lui.*" This answered as
well as Père la Chaise. We knocked at the
door of the curé's house here, when a sleek,
friar-like personage, in his sacerdotal robe, appeared. To our *Parlez-vous Anglais?* even he
answered, "*Non, monsieur;*" but at last we
made him understand what we wanted. It was

to find the ruins of the old *chateau*. "*Ah!
oui! oui!*" he exclaimed, and, donning his
coat, hastened forth, and conducted us to a
small heap of rubbish which we had already
examined. He said that fifteen years before,
it was *plus considérable*. Seeing at that moment three little red birds fly out of a crevice
in the ruins, up into an arbor-vitæ tree which
grew out of them, I asked him their names, in
such French as I could muster, but he neither
understood me nor ornithology; he only inquired
where we had *appris à parler Français;* we
told him, *dans les États-Unis;* and so we
bowed him into his house again. I was surprised to find a man wearing a black coat, and
with apparently no work to do, even in that part
of the world.

The universal salutation from the inhabitants
whom we met was *bon jour*, at the same time
touching the hat; with *bon jour*, and touching
your hat, you may go smoothly through all
Canada East.   A little boy, meeting us, would
remark, "*Bon jour, monsieur; le chemin est
mauvais*," Good morning, sir; it is bad walking. Sir Francis Head says that the immigrant
is forward to "appreciate the happiness of living in a land in which the old country's servile
custom of touching the hat does not exist," but
he was thinking of Canada West, of course. It

would, indeed, be a serious bore to be obliged
to touch your hat several times a day. A Yankee has not leisure for it.

We saw peas, and even beans, collected into
heaps in the fields. The former are an important crop here, and, I suppose, are not so much
infested by the weevil as with us. There were
plenty of apples, very fair and sound, by the
roadside, but they were so small as to suggest
the origin of the apple in the crab. There was
also a small, red fruit which they called *snells*,
and another, also red and very acid, whose
name a little boy wrote for me, "*pinbéna.*" It
is probably the same with, or similar to, the
pembina of the voyageurs, a species of viburnum, which, according to Richardson, has given
its name to many of the rivers of Rupert's
Land. The forest trees were spruce, arbor-vitæ,
firs, birches, beeches, two or three kinds of maple, bass-wood, wild-cherry, aspens, etc., but
no pitch pines (*Pinus rigida*). I saw very few,
if any, trees which had been set out for shade
or ornament. The water was commonly running streams or springs in the bank by the roadside, and was excellent. The parishes are commonly separated by a stream, and frequently the
farms. I noticed that the fields were furrowed
or thrown into beds seven or eight feet wide to
dry the soil.

At the *Rivière du Sault à la Puce*, which, I suppose, means the River of the Fall of the Flea, was advertised in English, as the sportsmen are English, "The best Snipe-shooting grounds," over the door of a small public-house. These words being English affected me as if I had been absent now ten years from my country, and for so long had not heard the sound of my native language, and every one of them was as interesting to me as if I had been a snipe-shooter, and they had been snipes. The prunella, or self-heal, in the grass here, was an old acquaintance. We frequently saw the inhabitants washing, or cooking for their pigs, and in one place hackling flax by the roadside. It was pleasant to see these usually domestic operations carried on out of doors, even in that cold country.

At twilight we reached a bridge over a little river, the boundary between Chateau Richer and St. Anne, *le premier pont de St. Anne*, and at dark the church of *La Bonne St. Anne*. Formerly vessels from France, when they came in sight of this church, gave "a general discharge of their artillery," as a sign of joy that they had escaped all the dangers of the river. Though all the while we had grand views of the adjacent country far up and down the river, and, for the most part, when we turned about, of Quebec in the horizon behind us, and we never beheld it without new surprise and admiration; yet, throughout our walk, the Great River of Canada on our right hand was the main feature in the landscape, and this expands so rapidly below the Isle of Orleans, and creates such a breadth of level horizon above its waters in that direction, that, looking down the river as we approached the extremity of that island, the St. Lawrence seemed to be opening into the ocean, though we were still about three hundred and twenty-five miles from what can be called its mouth.[1]

When we inquired here for a *maison publique* we were directed apparently to that private house where we were most likely to find entertainment. There were no guideboards where we walked, because there was but one road; there were no shops nor signs, because there were no artisans to speak of, and the people raised their own provisions; and there were no taverns, because there were no travelers. We here bespoke lodging and breakfast. They had, as

[1] From McCulloch's Geographical Dictionary we learn that " immediately beyond the Island of Orleans it is a mile broad; where the Saguenay joins it, eighteen miles; at Point Peter, upward of thirty; at the Bay of Seven Islands, seventy miles; and at the Island of Anticosti (about three hundred and fifty miles from Quebec), it rolls a flood into the ocean nearly one hundred miles across."

usual, a large, old-fashioned, two-storied box
stove in the middle of the room, out of which,
in due time, there was sure to be forthcoming
a supper, breakfast, or dinner. The lower half
held the fire, the upper the hot air, and as it
was a cool Canadian evening, this was a com-
forting sight to us. Being four or five feet
high it warmed the whole person as you stood
by it. The stove was plainly a very important
article of furniture in Canada, and was not set
aside during the summer. Its size, and the respect which was paid to it, told of the severe
winters which it had seen and prevailed over.
The master of the house, in his long-pointed,
red woolen cap, had a thoroughly antique physi-
ognomy of the old Norman stamp. He might
have come over with Jacques Cartier. His was
the hardest French to understand of any we had
heard yet, for there was a great difference between one speaker and another, and this man
talked with a pipe in his mouth beside, a kind
of tobacco French. I asked him what he called
his dog. He shouted *Brock!* (the name of
the breed). We like to hear the cat called *min*,
— min! min! min! I inquired if we could
cross the river here to the Isle of Orleans, thinking to return that way when we had been to the
falls. He answered, " *S'il ne fait pas un trop
grand vent*," If there is not too much wind.

They use small boats, or pirogues, and the
waves are often too high for them. He wore,
as usual, something between a moccasin and a
boot, which he called *bottes Indiennes*, Indian
boots, and had made himself. The tops were
of calf or sheep-skin, and the soles of cowhide
turned up like a moccasin. They were yellow
or reddish, the leather never having been tanned
nor colored. The women wore the same. He
told us that he had traveled ten leagues due
north into the bush. He had been to the Falls
of St. Anne, and said that they were more beautiful, but not greater, than Montmorenci, *plus
beau, mais non plus grand que Montmorenci.*
As soon as we had retired, the family commenced their devotions. A little boy officiated,
and for a long time we heard him muttering
over his prayers.

In the morning, after a breakfast of tea, maple-sugar, bread and butter, and what I suppose
is called *potage* (potatoes and meat boiled with
flour), the universal dish as we found, perhaps
the national one, I ran over to the Church of
La Bonne St. Anne, whose matin bell we had
heard, it being Sunday morning. Our book
said that this church had "long been an object
of interest, from the miraculous cures said to
have been wrought on visitors to the shrine."
There was a profusion of gilding, and I counted

more than twenty-five crutches suspended on the walls, some for grown persons, some for children, which it was to be inferred so many sick had been able to dispense with; but they looked as if they had been made to order by the carpenter who made the church. There were one or two villagers at their devotions at that early hour, who did not look up, but when they had sat a long time with their little book before the picture of one saint, went to another. Our whole walk was through a thoroughly Catholic country, and there was no trace of any other religion. I doubt if there are any more simple and unsophisticated Catholics anywhere. Emery de Caen, Champlain's contemporary, told the Huguenot sailors that "Monseigneur the Duke de Ventadour (Viceroy) did not wish that they should sing psalms in the Great River."

On our way to the falls, we met the habitans coming to the Church of La Bonne St. Anne, walking or riding in charettes by families. I remarked that they were universally of small stature. The toll-man at the bridge over the St. Anne was the first man we had chanced to meet, since we left Quebec, who could speak a word of English. How good French the inhabitants of this part of Canada speak, I am not competent to say; I only know that it is not made impure by being mixed with English. I

do not know why it should not be as good as is
spoken in Normandy. Charlevoix, who was
here a hundred years ago, observes, "The
French language is nowhere spoken with greater
purity, there being no accent perceptible;" and
Potherie said "they had no dialect, which, indeed, is generally lost in a colony."

The falls, which we were in search of, are
three miles up the St. Anne. We followed for
a short distance a foot-path up the east bank of
this river, through handsome sugar-maple and
arbor-vitæ groves. Having lost the path which
led to a house where we were to get further
directions, we dashed at once into the woods,
steering by guess and by compass, climbing directly through woods a steep hill, or mountain,
five or six hundred feet high, which was, in
fact, only the bank of the St. Lawrence. Beyond this we by good luck fell into another
path, and following this or a branch of it, at
our discretion, through a forest consisting of
large white pines, — the first we had seen in our
walk, — we at length heard the roar of falling
water, and came out at the head of the Falls of
St. Anne. We had descended into a ravine or
cleft in the mountain, whose walls rose still a
hundred feet above us, though we were near its
top, and we now stood on a very rocky shore,
where the water had lately flowed a dozen feet

higher, as appeared by the stones and drift-
wood, and large birches twisted and splintered
as a farmer twists a withe. Here the river, one
or two hundred feet wide, came flowing rapidly
over a rocky bed out of that interesting wilderness which stretches toward Hudson's Bay and
Davis's Straits. Ha-ha Bay, on the Saguenay,
was about one hundred miles north of where we
stood. Looking on the map, I find that the
first country on the north which bears a name is
that part of Rupert's Land called East Main.
This river, called after the holy Anne, flowing
from such a direction, here tumbled over a precipice, at present by three channels, how far
down I do not know, but far enough for all our
purposes, and to as good a distance as if twice
as far. It matters little whether you call it
one, or two, or three hundred feet; at any rate,
it was a sufficient water-privilege for us. I
crossed the principal channel directly over the
verge of the fall, where it was contracted to
about fifteen feet in width, by a dead tree, which
had been dropped across and secured in a cleft
of the opposite rock, and a smaller one a few
feet higher, which served for a hand-rail. This
bridge was rotten as well as small and slippery,
being stripped of bark, and I was obliged to
seize a moment to pass when the falling water
did not surge over it, and mid-way, though at

the expense of wet feet, I looked down probably
more than a hundred feet, into the mist and
foam below. This gave me the freedom of an
island of precipitous rock by which I descended
as by giant steps, — the rock being composed of
large cubical masses, clothed with delicate close-
hugging lichens of various colors, kept fresh and
bright by the moisture, — till I viewed the first
fall from the front, and looked down still deeper
to where the second and third channels fell into
a remarkably large circular basin worn in the
stone. The falling water seemed to jar the very
rocks, and the noise to be ever increasing. The
vista down stream was through a narrow and
deep cleft in the mountain, all white suds at the
bottom; but a sudden angle in this gorge prevented my seeing through to the bottom of the
fall. Returning to the shore, I made my way
down stream through the forest to see how far
the fall extended, and how the river came out of
that adventure. It was to clamber along the
side of a precipitous mountain of loose mossy
rocks, covered with a damp primitive forest,
and terminating at the bottom in an abrupt
precipice over the stream. This was the east
side of the fall. At length, after a quarter of a
mile, I got down to still water, and, on looking
up through the winding gorge, I could just see
to the foot of the fall which I had before exam-

ined; while from the opposite side of the stream, here much contracted, rose a perpendicular wall, I will not venture to say how many hundred feet, but only that it was the highest perpendicular wall of bare rock that I ever saw. In front of me tumbled in from the summit of the cliff a tributary stream, making a beautiful cascade, which was a remarkable fall in itself, and there was a cleft in this precipice, apparently four or five feet wide, perfectly straight up and down from top to bottom, which, from its cavernous depth and darkness, appeared merely as *a black streak.* This precipice is not sloped, nor is the material soft and crumbling slate as at Montmorenci, but it rises perpendicular, like the side of a mountain fortress, and is cracked into vast cubical masses of gray and black rock shining with moisture, as if it were the ruin of an ancient wall built by Titans. Birches, spruces, mountain-ashes with their bright red berries, arbor-vitæs, white pines, alders, etc., overhung this chasm on the very verge of the cliff and in the crevices, and here and there were buttresses of rock supporting trees part way down, yet so as to enhance, not injure, the effect of the bare rock. Take it altogether, it was a most wild and rugged and stupendous chasm, so deep and narrow where a river had worn itself a passage through a moun-

tain of rock, and all around was the comparatively untrodden wilderness.

This was the limit of our walk down the St.
Lawrence.   Early in the afternoon we began to
retrace our steps, not being able to cross the
north channel and return by the Isle of Orleans,
on account of the *trop grand vent*, or too great
wind.   Though the waves did run pretty high,
it was evident that the inhabitants of Montmorenci County were no sailors, and made but
little use of the river.   When we reached the
bridge, between St. Anne and Chateau Richer,
I ran back a little way to ask a man in the field
the name of the river which we were crossing,
but for a long time I could not make out what
he said, for he was one of the more unintelligible Jacques Cartier men.   At last it flashed
upon me that it was *La Rivière au Chien*, or
the Dog River, which my eyes beheld, which
brought to my mind the life of the Canadian
voyageur and *coureur de bois*, a more western
and wilder Arcadia, methinks, than the world
has ever seen; for the Greeks, with all their
wood and river gods, were not so qualified to
name the natural features of a country as the
ancestors of these French Canadians; and if any
people had a right to substitute their own for
the Indian names, it was they.   They have pre-
ceded the pioneer on our own frontiers, and

named the *prairie* for us. *La Rivière au Chien*
cannot, by any license of language, be translated
into Dog River, for that is not such a giving it
to the dogs, and recognizing their place in creation, as the French implies. One of the tributaries of the St. Anne is named *La Rivière de
la Rose ;* and farther east are *La Rivière de la
Blondelle* and *La Rivière de la Friponne.*
Their very *rivière* meanders more than our *river.*

Yet the impression which this country made
on me was commonly different from this. To a
traveler from the Old World, Canada East may
appear like a new country, and its inhabitants
like colonists, but to me coming from New England, and being a very green traveler withal, —
notwithstanding what I have said about Hudson's Bay, — it appeared as old as Normandy
itself, and realized much that I had heard of
Europe and the Middle Ages. Even the names
of humble Canadian villages affected me as if
they had been those of the renowned cities of
antiquity. To be told by a habitan, when I
asked the name of a village in sight, that it is
St. Fereole or *St. Anne*, the *Guardian Angel*
or the *Holy Joseph's ;* or of a mountain, that it
was *Bélange* or *St. Hyacinthe!* As soon as
you leave the States, these saintly names begin.
St. John is the first town you stop at (fortu-
nately we did not see it), and thenceforward,

the names of the mountains, and streams, and
villages reel, if I may so speak, with the intoxi-
cation of poetry, — *Chambly, Longueil, Pointe
aux Trembles, Bartholomy,* etc., etc.; as if it
needed only a little foreign accent, a few more
liquids and vowels perchance in the language, to
make us locate our ideals at once. I began to
dream of Provence and the Troubadours, and of
places and things which have no existence on the
earth. They veiled the Indian and the primitive forest, and the woods toward Hudson's
Bay were only as the forests of France and Ger-
many. I could not at once bring myself to believe that the inhabitants who pronounced daily
those beautiful and, to me, significant names
lead as prosaic lives as we of New England. In
short, the Canada which I saw was not merely a
place for railroads to terminate in and for crim-
inals to run to.

When I asked the man to whom I have referred, if there were any falls on the Rivière au
Chien, — for I saw that it came over the same
high bank with the Montmorenci and St. Anne,
— he answered that there were. How far? I
inquired. *Trois quatres lieue.* How high?
Je pense, quatre-vingt-dix pieds; that is, ninety
feet. We turned aside to look at the falls of
the *Rivière du Sault à la Puce,* half a mile
from the road, which before we had passed in

our haste and ignorance, and we pronounced
them as beautiful as any that we saw; yet they
seemed to make no account of them there, and,
when first we inquired the way to the falls, directed us to Montmorenci, seven miles distant.
It was evident that this was the country for waterfalls; that every stream that empties into the
St. Lawrence, for some hundreds of miles, must
have a great fall or cascade on it, and in its
passage through the mountains was, for a short
distance, a small Saguenay, with its upright
walls. This fall of La Puce, the least remarkable of the four which we visited in this vicinity,
we had never heard of till we came to Canada,
and yet, so far as I know, there is nothing of
the kind in New England to be compared with
it. Most travelers in Canada would not hear of
it, though they might go so near as to hear it.
Since my return I find that in the topographical
description of the country mention is made of
"two or three romantic falls" on this stream,
though we saw and heard of but this one. Ask
the inhabitants respecting any stream, if there
is a fall on it, and they will perchance tell you
of something as interesting as Bashpish or the
Catskill, which no traveler has ever seen, or if
they have not found it, you may possibly trace
up the stream and discover it yourself. Falls
there are a drug; and we became quite dissi-

pated in respect to them. We had drank too
much of them. Beside these which I have referred to, there are a thousand other falls on
the St. Lawrence and its tributaries which I
have not seen nor heard of; and above all there
is one which I have heard of, called Niagara, so
that I think that this river must be the most
remarkable for its falls of any in the world.

At a house near the western boundary of
Chateau Richer, whose master was said to speak
a very little English, having recently lived at
Quebec, we got lodging for the night. As usual,
we had to go down a lane to get round to the
south side of the house where the door was,
away from the road. For these Canadian
houses have no front door, properly speaking.
Every part is for the use of the occupant exclusively, and no part has reference to the traveler
or to travel. Every New England house, on
the contrary, has a front and principal door
opening to the great world, though it may be on
the cold side, for it stands on the highway of
nations, and the road which runs by it comes
from the Old World and goes to the far West;
but the Canadian's door opens into his back-
yard and farm alone, and the road which runs
behind his house leads only from the church of
one saint to that of another. We found a large
family, hired men, wife and children, just eat-

ing their supper. They prepared some for us afterwards. The hired men were a merry crew of short, black-eyed fellows, and the wife a thin-faced, sharp-featured French Canadian woman. Our host's English staggered us rather more than any French we had heard yet; indeed, we found that even we spoke better French than he did English, and we concluded that a less crime would be committed on the whole if we spoke French with him, and in no respect aided or abetted his attempts to speak English. We had a long and merry chat with the family this Sunday evening in their spacious kitchen. While my companion smoked a pipe and par-lez-vous'd with one party, I parleyed and ges-ticulated to another. The whole family was enlisted, and I kept a little girl writing what was otherwise unintelligible. The geography getting obscure, we called for chalk, and the greasy oiled table-cloth having been wiped, — for it needed no French, but only a sentence from the universal language of looks on my part, to indicate that it needed it, — we drew the St. Lawrence, with its parishes, thereon, and thenceforward went on swimmingly, by turns handling the chalk and committing to the table-cloth what would otherwise have been left in a limbo of unintelligibility. This was greatly to the entertainment of all parties. I was

amused to hear how much use they made of the
word *oui* in conversation with one another. After repeated single insertions of it, one would
suddenly throw back his head at the same time
with his chair, and exclaim rapidly, " *Oui ! oui !
oui ! oui !* " like a Yankee driving pigs. Our
host told us that the farms thereabouts were
generally two acres or three hundred and sixty
French feet wide, by one and a half leagues, (?)
or a little more than four and a half of our miles
deep. This use of the word *acre* as long measure arises from the fact that the French acre
or arpent, the arpent of Paris, makes a square
of ten perches, of eighteen feet each on a side, a
Paris foot being equal to 1.06575 English feet.
He said that the wood was cut off about one
mile from the river. The rest was "bush," and
beyond that the "Queen's bush." Old as the
country is, each landholder bounds on the primitive forest, and fuel bears no price. As I had
forgotten the French for *sickle*, they went out in
the evening to the barn and got one, and so
clenched the certainty of our understanding one
another. Then, wishing to learn if they used
the cradle, and not knowing any French word
for this instrument, I set up the knives and
forks on the blade of the sickle to represent
one; at which they all exclaimed that they knew
and had used it. When *snells* were mentioned

they went out in the dark and plucked some.
They were pretty good. They said they had
three kinds of plums growing wild, — blue,
white, and red, the two former much alike and
the best. Also they asked me if I would have
des pommes, some apples, and got me some.
They were exceedingly fair and glossy, and it
was evident that there was no worm in them;
but they were as hard almost as a stone, as if
the season was too short to mellow them. We
had seen no soft and yellow apples by the roadside. I declined eating one, much as I admired
it, observing that it would be good *dans le
printemps*, in the spring. In the morning when
the mistress had set the eggs a-frying she
nodded to a thick-set, jolly-looking fellow, who
rolled up his sleeves, seized the long-handled
griddle, and commenced a series of revolutions
and evolutions with it, ever and anon tossing its
contents into the air, where they turned completely topsy-turvy and came down t'other side
up; and this he repeated till they were done.
That appeared to be his duty when eggs were
concerned. I did not chance to witness this
performance, but my companion did, and he
pronounced it a masterpiece in its way. This
man's farm, with the buildings, cost seven hundred pounds; some smaller ones, two hundred.

In 1827, Montmorenci County, to which the

Isle of Orleans has since been added, was nearly as large as Massachusetts, being the eighth county out of forty (in Lower Canada) in extent; but by far the greater part still must continue to be waste land, lying as it were under the walls of Quebec.

I quote these old statistics, not merely because of the difficulty of obtaining more recent ones, but also because I saw there so little evidence of any recent growth. There were in this county, at the same date, five Roman Catholic churches, and no others, five curés and five presbyteries, two schools, two corn-mills, four saw-mills, one carding-mill, — no medical man, or notary or lawyer, — five shopkeepers, four taverns (we saw no sign of any, though, after a little hesitation, we were sometimes directed to some undistinguished hut as such), thirty artisans, and five river crafts, whose tonnage amounted to sixty-nine tons! This, notwithstanding that it has a frontage of more than thirty miles on the river, and the population is almost wholly confined to its banks. This describes nearly enough what we saw. But double some of these figures, which, however, its growth will not warrant, and you have described a poverty which not even its severity of climate and ruggedness of soil will suffice to account for. The principal productions were wheat, potatoes, oats, hay, peas, flax, maple-sugar, etc., etc.; linen cloth, or *étoffe du pays*, flannel, and homespun, or *petite étoffe*.

In Lower Canada, according to Bouchette, there are two tenures, — the feudal and the socage. Tenanciers, censitaires, or holders of land *en roture* pay a small annual rent to the seigneurs, to which "is added some articles of provision, such as a couple of fowls, or a goose, or a bushel of wheat." "They are also bound to grind their corn at the *moulin banal*, or the lord's mill, where one fourteenth part of it is taken for his use" as toll. He says that the toll is one twelfth in the United States where competition exists. It is not permitted to exceed one sixteenth in Massachusetts. But worse than this monopolizing of mill rents is what are called *lods et ventes*, or mutation fines, — according to which the seigneur has "a right to a twelfth part of the purchase-money of every estate within his seigniory that changes its owner by sale." This is over and above the sum paid to the seller. In such cases, moreover, "the lord possesses the *droit de retrait*, which is the privilege of preëmption at the highest bidden price within forty days after the sale has taken place," — a right which, however, is said to be seldom exercised. "Lands held by Roman Catholics are further subject to the payment to their curates of one twenty-sixth part of all the

grain produced upon them, and to occasional as-
sessments for building and repairing churches,"
etc., — a tax to which they are not subject if the
proprietors change their faith; but they are not
the less attached to their church in consequence.
There are, however, various modifications of the
feudal tenure. Under the socage tenure, which
is that of the townships or more recent settlements, English, Irish, Scotch, and others, and
generally of Canada West, the landholder is
wholly unshackled by such conditions as I have
quoted, and "is bound to no other obligations
than those of allegiance to the king and obedience to the laws." Throughout Canada "a
freehold of forty shillings yearly value, or the
payment of ten pounds rent annually, is the
qualification for voters." In 1846 more than
one sixth of the whole population of Canada
East were qualified to vote for members of Parliament, — a greater proportion than enjoy a
similar privilege in the United States.

The population which we had seen the last
two days — I mean the habitans of Montmorenci County — appeared very inferior, intellectually and even physically, to that of New
England. In some respects they were incredi-
bly filthy. It was evident that they had not
advanced since the settlement of the country,
that they were quite behind the age, and fairly

represented their ancestors in Normandy a thousand years ago. Even in respect to the common arts of life, they are not so far advanced as
a frontier town in the West three years old.
They have no money invested in railroad stock,
and probably never will have. If they have got
a French phrase for a railroad, it is as much as
you can expect of them. They are very far
from a revolution; have no quarrel with Church
or State, but their vice and their virtue is content. As for annexation, they have never
dreamed of it; indeed, they have not a clear
idea what or where the States are. The English government has been remarkably liberal to
its Catholic subjects in Canada, permitting them
to wear their own fetters, both political and religious, as far as was possible for subjects.
Their government is even too good for them.
Parliament passed "an act [in 1825] to provide
for the extinction of feudal and seigniorial rights
and burdens on lands in Lower Canada, and for
the gradual conversion of those tenures into the
tenure of free and common socage," etc. But
as late as 1831, at least, the design of the act was
likely to be frustrated, owing to the reluctance
of the seigniors and peasants. It has been observed by another that the French Canadians do
not extend nor perpetuate their influence. The
British, Irish, and other immigrants, who have

settled the townships, are found to have imitated the American settlers and not the French. They reminded me in this of the Indians, whom they were slow to displace, and to whose habits of life they themselves more readily conformed than the Indians to theirs. The Governor-General Denouville remarked, in 1685, that some had long thought that it was necessary to bring the Indians near them in order to Frenchify (*franciser*) them, but that they had every reason to think themselves in an error; for those who had come near them and were even collected in villages in the midst of the colony had not become French, but the French who had haunted them had become savages. Kalm said, "Though many nations imitate the French customs, yet I observed, on the contrary, that the French in Canada, in many respects, follow the customs of the Indians, with whom they converse every day. They make use of the tobacco-pipes, shoes, garters, and girdles of the Indians. They follow the Indian way of making war with exactness; they mix the same things with tobacco [he might have said that both French and English learned the use itself of this weed of the Indian]; they make use of the Indian bark-boats, and row them in the Indian way; they wrap square pieces of cloth round their feet instead of stockings; and have adopted many other Indian fashions." Thus, while the descendants of the Pilgrims are teaching the English to make pegged boots, the descendants of the French in Canada are wearing the Indian moccasin still. The French, to their credit be it said, to a certain extent respected the Indians as a separate and independent people, and spoke of them and contrasted themselves with them as the English have never done. They not only went to war with them as allies, but they lived at home with them as neighbors. In 1627 the French king declared "that the descendants of the French, settled in " New France, "and the savages who should be brought to the knowledge of the faith, and should make profession of it, should be counted and reputed French born (*Naturels François*); and as such could emigrate to France, when it seemed good to them, and there acquire, will, inherit, etc., etc., without obtaining letters of naturalization." When the English had possession of Quebec, in 1630, the Indians, attempting to practice the same familiarity with them that they had with the French, were driven out of their houses with blows; which accident taught them a difference between the two races, and attached them yet more to the French. The impression made on me was that the French Canadians were even sharing the fate of the Indians, or at least gradually disappearing in what is called the Saxon current.

The English did not come to America from a mere love of adventure, nor to truck with or convert the savages, nor to hold offices under the crown, as the French to a great extent did, but to live in earnest and with freedom. The latter overran a great extent of country, selling strong water, and collecting its furs, and converting its inhabitants, — or at least baptizing its dying infants (*enfans moribonds*), — without *improving* it. First, went the *coureur de bois* with the *eau de vie;* then followed, if he did not precede, the heroic missionary with the *eau d'immortalité.* It was freedom to hunt, and fish, and convert, not to work, that they sought. Hontan says that the *coureurs de bois* lived like sailors ashore. In no part of the seventeenth century could the French be said to have had a foothold in Canada; they held only by the fur of the wild animals which they were exterminating. To enable the poor seigneurs to get their living, it was permitted by a decree passed in the reign of Louis the Fourteenth, in 1685, "to all nobles and gentlemen settled in Canada, to engage in commerce, without being called to account or reputed to have done anything derogatory." The reader can infer to what extent they had engaged in agriculture, and how their farms must have shone by this time. The New England youth, on the other hand, were never *coureurs de bois* nor *voyageurs*, but backwoodsmen and sailors rather. Of all nations the English undoubtedly have proved hitherto that they had the most business here.

Yet I am not sure but I have most sympathy with that spirit of adventure which distinguished the French and Spaniards of those days, and made them especially the explorers of the American Continent, — which so early carried the former to the Great Lakes and the Mississippi on the north, and the latter to the same river on the south. It was long before our frontiers reached their settlements in the West. So far as inland discovery was concerned, the adventurous spirit of the English was that of sailors who land but for a day, and their enterprise the enterprise of traders.

There was apparently a greater equality of condition among the habitans of Montmorenci County than in New England. They are an almost exclusively agricultural, and so far independent population, each family producing nearly all the necessaries of life for itself. If the Canadian wants energy, perchance he possesses those virtues, social and others, which the Yankee lacks, in which case he cannot be regarded as a poor man.

CHAPTER IV

THE WALLS OF QUEBEC

AFTER spending the night at a farm-house in Chateau Richer, about a dozen miles northeast of Quebec, we set out on our return to the city. We stopped at the next house, a picturesque old stone mill, over the *Chipré*, — for so the name sounded, — such as you will nowhere see in the States, and asked the millers the age of the mill. They went upstairs to call the master; but the crabbed old miser asked why we wanted to know, and would tell us only for some compensation. I wanted French to give him a piece of my mind. I had got enough to talk on a pinch, but not to quarrel, so I had to come away, looking all I would have said. This was the utmost incivility we met with in Canada. In Beauport, within a few miles of Quebec, we turned aside to look at a church which was just being completed, — a very large and handsome edifice of stone, with a green bough stuck in its gable, of some significance to Catholics. The comparative wealth of the Church in this country was apparent; for in this village we did not

see one good house besides. They were all
humble cottages; and yet this appeared to me a
more imposing structure than any church in
Boston. But I am no judge of these things.

Reëntering Quebec through St. John's Gate,
we took a caleche in Market Square for the
Falls of the Chaudière, about nine miles southwest of the city, for which we were to pay so
much, beside forty sous for tolls. The driver,
as usual, spoke French only. The number of
these vehicles is very great for so small a town.
They are like one of our chaises that has lost its
top, only stouter and longer in the body, with a
seat for the driver where the dasher is with us,
and broad leather ears on each side to protect
the riders from the wheel and keep children
from falling out. They had an easy jaunting
look, which, as our hours were numbered, per-
suaded us to be riders. We met with them on
every road near Quebec these days, each with
its complement of two inquisitive-looking for-
eigners and a Canadian driver, the former evidently enjoying their novel experience, for commonly it is only the horse whose language you
do not understand; but they were one remove
further from him by the intervention of an
equally unintelligible driver. We crossed the
St. Lawrence to Point Levi in a French Canadian ferry-boat, which was inconvenient and

dirty, and managed with great noise and bustle. The current was very strong and tumultuous, and the boat tossed enough to make some sick, though it was only a mile across; yet the wind was not to be compared with that of the day before, and we saw that the Canadians had a good excuse for not taking us over to the Isle of Orleans in a pirogue, however shiftless they may be for not having provided any other conveyance. The route which we took to the Chaudière did not afford us those views of Quebec which we had expected, and the country and inhabitants appeared less interesting to a traveler than those we had seen. The Falls of the Chaudière are three miles from its mouth on the south side of the St. Lawrence. Though they were the largest which I saw in Canada, I was not proportionately interested by them, probably from satiety. I did not see any peculiar propriety in the name *Chaudière*, or caldron. I saw here the most brilliant rainbow that I ever imagined. It was just across the stream below the precipice, formed on the mist which this tremendous fall produced; and I stood on a level with the key-stone of its arch. It was not a few faint prismatic colors merely, but a full semicircle, only four or five rods in diameter, though as wide as usual, so intensely bright as to pain the eye, and apparently as substantial as an arch of stone. It changed its position and colors as we moved, and was the brighter because the sun shone so clearly and the mist was so thick. Evidently a picture painted on mist for the men and animals that came to the falls to look at; but for what special purpose beyond this, I know not. At the farthest point in this ride, and when most inland, unexpectedly at a turn in the road we descried the frowning citadel of Quebec in the horizon, like the beak of a bird of prey. We returned by the river road under the bank, which is very high, abrupt, and rocky. When we were opposite to Quebec, I was surprised to see that in the Lower Town, under the shadow of the rock, the lamps were lit, twinkling not unlike crystals in a cavern, while the citadel high above, and we, too, on the south shore, were in broad daylight. As we were too late for the ferry-boat that night, we put up at a *maison de pension* at Point Levi. The usual two-story stove was here placed against an opening in the partition shaped like a fireplace, and so warmed several rooms. We could not understand their French here very well, but the *potage* was just like what we had had before. There were many small chambers with doorways, but no doors. The walls of our chamber, all around and over-head, were neatly ceiled, and the timbers cased

with wood unpainted. The pillows were checkered and tasseled, and the usual long-pointed
red woolen or worsted night-cap was placed on
each. I pulled mine out to see how it was
made. It was in the form of a double cone, one
end tucked into the other; just such, it appeared, as I saw men wearing all day in the
streets. Probably I should have put it on if
the cold had been then, as it is sometimes there,
thirty or forty degrees below zero.

When we landed at Quebec the next morning
a man lay on his back on the wharf, apparently
dying, in the midst of a crowd and directly in
the path of the horses, groaning, " *O ma conscience!* " I thought that he pronounced his
French more distinctly than any I heard, as if
the dying had already acquired the accents of a
universal language. Having secured the only
unengaged berths in the Lord Sydenham
steamer, which was to leave Quebec before sundown, and being resolved, now that I had seen
somewhat of the country, to get an idea of the
city, I proceeded to walk round the Upper
Town, or fortified portion, which is two miles
and three quarters in circuit, alone, as near as
I could get to the cliff and the walls, like a rat
looking for a hole; going round by the southwest, where there is but a single street between
the cliff and the water, and up the long wooden

stairs, through the suburbs northward to the King's Woodyard, which I thought must have been a long way from his fireplace, and under the cliffs of the St. Charles, where the drains issue under the walls, and the walls are loopholed for musketry; so returning by Mountain Street and Prescott Gate to the Upper Town. Having found my way by an obscure passage near the St. Louis Gate to the glacis on the north of the citadel proper, — I believe that I was the only visitor then in the city who got in there, — I enjoyed a prospect nearly as good as from within the citadel itself, which I had explored some days before. As I walked on the glacis I heard the sound of a bagpipe from the soldiers' dwellings in the rock, and was further soothed and affected by the sight of a soldier's cat walking up a cleeted plank into a high loophole, designed for *mus-catry*, as serene as Wisdom herself, and with a gracefully waving motion of her tail, as if her ways were ways of pleasantness and all her paths were peace. Scaling a slat fence, where a small force might have checked me, I got out of the esplanade into the Governor's Garden, and read the well-known inscription on Wolfe and Montcalm's monument, which for saying much in little, and that to the purpose, undoubtedly deserved the prize medal which it received: —

MORTEM . VIRTUS . COMMUNEM .
FAMAM . HISTORIA .
MONUMENTUM . POSTERITAS .
DEDIT.

Valor gave them one death, history one fame,
posterity one monument. The Government
Garden has for nosegays, amid kitchen vegetables, beside the common garden flowers, the
usual complement of cannon directed toward
some future and possible enemy. I then returned up St. Louis Street to the esplanade and
ramparts there, and went round the Upper
Town once more, though I was very tired, this
time on the *inside* of the wall; for I knew that
the wall was the main thing in Quebec, and had
cost a great deal of money, and therefore I must
make the most of it. In fact, these are the only
remarkable walls we have in North America,
though we have a good deal of Virginia fence,
it is true. Moreover, I cannot say but I yielded
in some measure to the soldier instinct, and,
having but a short time to spare, thought it best
to examine the wall thoroughly, that I might be
the better prepared if I should ever be called
that way again in the service of my country. I
committed all the gates to memory, in their order, which did not cost me so much trouble as
it would have done at the hundred-gated city,

there being only five; nor were they so hard to
remember as those seven of Bœotian Thebes;
and, moreover, I thought that, if seven champions were enough against the latter, one would
be enough against Quebec, though he bore for
all armor and device only an umbrella and a
bundle. I took the nunneries as I went, for I
had learned to distinguish them by the blinds;
and I observed also the foundling hospitals and
the convents, and whatever was attached to, or
in the vicinity of the walls. All the rest I
omitted, as naturally as one would the inside of
an inedible shell-fish. These were the only
pearls, and the wall the only mother-of-pearl
for me. Quebec is chiefly famous for the thickness of its parietal bones. The technical terms
of its conchology may stagger a beginner a little at first, such as *banlieue, esplanade, glacis,
ravelin, cavalier,* etc., etc., but with the aid of
a comprehensive dictionary you soon learn the
nature of your ground. I was surprised at the
extent of the artillery barracks, built so long
ago, — *Casernes Nouvelles,* they used to be
called, — nearly six hundred feet in length by
forty in depth, where the sentries, like peripa-
tetic philosophers, were so absorbed in thought
as not to notice me when I passed in and out at
the gates. Within are "small arms of every
description, sufficient for the equipment of

twenty thousand men," so arranged as to give a startling *coup d'œil* to strangers. I did not enter, not wishing to get a black eye; for they are said to be "in a state of complete repair and readiness for immediate use." Here, for a short time, I lost sight of the wall, but I recovered it again on emerging from the barrack yard. There I met with a Scotchman who appeared to have business with the wall, like myself; and, being thus mutually drawn together by a similarity of tastes, we had a little conversation *sub mœnibus*, that is, by an angle of the wall, which sheltered us. He lived about thirty miles northwest of Quebec; had been nineteen years in the country; said he was disappointed that he was not brought to America after all, but found himself still under British rule and where his own language was not spoken; that many Scotch, Irish, and English were disappointed in like manner, and either went to the States, or pushed up the river to Canada West, nearer to the States, and where their language was spoken. He talked of visiting the States sometime; and, as he seemed ignorant of geography, I warned him that it was one thing to visit the State of Massachusetts, and another to visit the State of California. He said it was colder there than usual at that season, and he was lucky to have brought his thick togue, or frock-coat, with him; thought it would snow, and then be pleasant and warm. That is the way we are always thinking. However, his words were music to me in my thin hat and sack.

At the ramparts on the cliff near the old Parliament House I counted twenty-four thirty-two-pounders in a row, pointed over the harbor, with their balls piled pyramid-wise between them, — there are said to be in all about one hundred and eighty guns mounted at Quebec, — all which were faithfully kept dusted by officials, in accordance with the motto, "In time of peace prepare for war;" but I saw no preparations for peace; she was plainly an uninvited guest.

Having thus completed the circuit of this fortress, both within and without, I went no farther by the wall for fear that I should become wall-eyed. However, I think that I deserve to be made a member of the Royal Sappers and Miners.

In short, I observed everywhere the most perfect arrangements for keeping a wall in order, not even permitting the lichens to grow on it, which some think an ornament; but then I saw no cultivation nor pasturing within it to pay for the outlay, and cattle were strictly forbidden to feed on the glacis under the severest penalties.

Where the dogs get their milk I don't know, and I fear it is bloody at best.

The citadel of Quebec says, "I *will* live here, and you shan't prevent me." To which you return, that you have not the slightest objection; live and let live. The Martello towers looked, for all the world, exactly like abandoned windmills, which had not had a grist to grind these hundred years. Indeed, the whole castle here was a "folly," — England's folly, — and, in more senses than one, a castle in the air. The inhabitants and the government are gradually waking up to a sense of this truth; for I heard something said about their abandoning the wall around the Upper Town, and confining the fortifications to the citadel of forty acres. Of course they will finally reduce their intrenchments to the circumference of their own brave hearts.

The most modern fortifications have an air of antiquity about them; they have the aspect of ruins in better or worse repair from the day they are built, because they are not really the work of this age. The very place where the soldier resides has a peculiar tendency to become old and dilapidated, as the word *barrack* implies. I couple all fortifications in my mind with the dismantled Spanish forts to be found in so many parts of the world; and if in any place they are not actually dismantled, it is because that there the intellect of the inhabitants is dismantled. The commanding officer of an old fort near Valdivia in South America, when a traveler remarked to him that, with one discharge, his gun-carriages would certainly fall to pieces, gravely replied, "No, I am sure, sir, they would stand two." Perhaps the guns of Quebec would stand three. Such structures carry us back to the Middle Ages, the siege of Jerusalem, and St. Jean d'Acre, and the days of the Bucaniers. In the armory of the citadel they showed me a clumsy implement, long since useless, which they called a Lombard gun. I thought that their whole citadel was such a Lombard gun, fit object for the museums of the curious. Such works do not consist with the development of the intellect. Huge stone structures of all kinds, both in their erection and by their influence when erected, rather oppress than liberate the mind. They are tombs for the souls of men, as frequently for their bodies also. The sentinel with his musket beside a man with his umbrella is spectral. There is not sufficient reason for his existence. Does my friend there, with a bullet resting on half an ounce of powder, think that he needs that argument in conversing with me? The fort was the first institution that was founded here, and it is amusing to read in Champlain how assiduously they worked at it almost from the first day of the settlement.   The founders of the colony thought this an excellent site for a wall, — and no doubt it was a better site, in some respects, for a wall than for a city, — but it chanced that a city got behind it.   It chanced, too, that a Lower Town got before it, and clung like an oyster to the outside of the crags, as you may see at low tide.   It is as if you were to come to a country village surrounded by palisades in the old Indian fashion, — interesting only as a relic of antiquity and barbarism.   A fortified town is like a man cased in the heavy armor of antiquity, with a horse-load of broadswords and small arms slung to him, endeavoring to go about his business.   Or is this an indispensable machinery for the good government of the country?   The inhabitants of California succeed pretty well, and are doing better and better every day, without any such institution.   What use has this fortress served, to look at it even from the soldiers' point of view?   At first the French took care of it; yet Wolfe sailed by it with impunity, and took the town of Quebec without experiencing any hindrance at last from its fortifications.   They were only the bone for which the parties fought.   Then the English began to take care of it.   So of any fort in the

world, — that in Boston Harbor, for instance.
We shall at length hear that an enemy sailed
by it in the night, for it cannot sail itself, and
both it and its inhabitants are always benighted.
How often we read that the enemy occupied a
position which commanded the old, and so the
fort was evacuated.   Have not the school-house
and the printing-press occupied a position which
commands such a fort as this?

However, this is a ruin kept in remarkably
good repair.   There are some eight hundred or
thousand men there to exhibit it.   One regiment goes bare-legged to increase the attraction.
If you wish to study the muscles of the leg
about the knee, repair to Quebec.   This universal exhibition in Canada of the tools and
sinews of war reminded me of the keeper of a
menagerie showing his animals' claws.   It was
the English leopard showing his claws.   Always
the royal something or other; as at the menagerie,
the Royal Bengal Tiger.   Silliman states that
"the cold is so intense in the winter nights, particularly on Cape Diamond, that the sentinels
cannot stand it more than one hour, and are relieved at the expiration of that time;" "and
even, as it is said, at much shorter intervals, in
case of the most extreme cold."   What a natural or unnatural fool must that soldier be, — to
say nothing of his government, — who, when

quicksilver is freezing and blood is ceasing to
be quick, will stand to have his face frozen,
watching the walls of Quebec, though, so far as
they are concerned, both honest and dishonest
men all the world over have been in their beds
nearly half a century, — or at least for that
space travelers have visited Quebec only as they
would read history. I shall never again wake
up in a colder night than usual, but I shall
think how rapidly the sentinels are relieving
one another on the walls of Quebec, their quicksilver being all frozen, as if apprehensive that
some hostile Wolfe may even then be scaling
the Heights of Abraham, or some persevering
Arnold about to issue from the wilderness;
some Malay or Japanese, perchance, coming
round by the northwest coast, have chosen that
moment to assault the citadel! Why, I should
as soon expect to find the sentinels still relieving
one another on the walls of Nineveh, which have
so long been buried to the world. What a
troublesome thing a wall is! I thought it was
to defend me, and not I it! Of course, if they
had no wall, they would not need to have any
sentinels.

You might venture to advertise this farm as
well fenced with substantial stone walls (saying
nothing about the eight hundred Highlanders
and Royal Irish who are required to keep them

from toppling down); stock and tools to go with the land if desired. But it would not be wise for the seller to exhibit his farm-book.

Why should Canada, wild and unsettled as it is, impress us as an older country than the States, unless because her institutions are old? All things appeared to contend there, as I have implied, with a certain rust of antiquity, such as forms on old armor and iron guns, — the rust of conventions and formalities. It is said that the metallic roofs of Montreal and Quebec keep sound and bright for forty years in some cases. But if the rust was not on the tinned roofs and spires, it was on the inhabitants and their institutions. Yet the work of burnishing goes briskly forward. I imagined that the government vessels at the wharves were laden with rotten-stone and oxalic acid, — that is what the first ship from England in the spring comes freighted with, — and the hands of the colonial legislature are cased in wash-leather. The principal exports must be *gun*ny bags, verdigris, and iron rust. Those who first built this fort, coming from Old France with the memory and tradition of feudal days and customs weighing on them, were unquestionably behind their age; and those who now inhabit and repair it are behind their ancestors or predecessors. Those old chevaliers thought that

they could transplant the feudal system to
America. It has been set out, but it has not
thriven. Notwithstanding that Canada was settled first, and, unlike New England, for a long
series of years enjoyed the fostering care of
the mother country; notwithstanding that, as
Charlevoix tells us, it had more of the ancient
noblesse among its early settlers than any other
of the French colonies, and perhaps than all
the others together, — there are in both the
Canadas but 600,000 of French descent to-day,
— about half so many as the population of
Massachusetts. The whole population of both
Canadas is but about 1,700,000 Canadians,
English, Irish, Scotch, Indians, and all, put together! Samuel Laing, in his essay on the
Northmen, to whom especially, rather than the
Saxons, he refers the energy and indeed the excellence of the English character, observes that,
when they occupied Scandinavia, "each man
possessed his lot of land without reference to,
or acknowledgment of, any other man, — without any local chief to whom his military service
or other quit-rent for his land was due, — without tenure from, or duty or obligation to, any
superior, real or fictitious, except the general
sovereign. The individual settler held his land,
as his descendants in Norway still express it, by
the same right as the King held his crown,

by udal right, or adel, — that is, noble right."
The French have occupied Canada, not *udally*,
or by noble right, but *feudally*, or by ignoble
right.   They are a nation of peasants.

It was evident that, both on account of the
feudal system and the aristocratic government,
a private man was not worth so much in Canada
as in the United States; and, if your wealth in
any measure consists in manliness, in originality, and independence, you had better stay here.
How could a peaceable, freethinking man live
neighbor to the Forty-ninth Regiment?   A New
Englander would naturally be a bad citizen,
probably a rebel, there, — certainly if he were
already a rebel at home.   I suspect that a poor
man who is not servile is a much rarer phenomenon there and in England than in the Northern
United States.   An Englishman, methinks, —
not to speak of other European nations, — habit-
ually regards himself merely as a constituent
part of the English nation; he is a member of
the royal regiment of Englishmen, and is proud
of his company, as he has reason to be proud of
it.   But an American — one who has made a
tolerable use of his opportunities — cares, comparatively, little about such things, and is ad-
vantageously nearer to the primitive and the
ultimate condition of man in these respects.   It
is a government, that English one, — like most

other European ones, — that cannot afford to
be forgotten, as you would naturally forget it;
under which one cannot be wholesomely neglected, and grow up a man and not an Englishman merely, — cannot be a poet even without
danger of being made poet-laureate! Give me
a country where it is the most natural thing in
the world for a government that does not understand you to let you alone. One would say that
a true Englishman could speculate only within
bounds. (It is true the Americans have proved
that they, in more than one sense, can *speculate* without bounds.) He has to pay his respects to so many things, that, before he knows it,
he *may* have paid away all he is worth. What
makes the United States government, on the
whole, more tolerable, — I mean for us lucky
white men, — is the fact that there is so much
less of government with us. Here it is only once
in a month or a year that a man *needs* remember that institution; and those who go to Con-
gress can play the game of the Kilkenny cats
there without fatal consequences to those who
stay at home, — their term is so short; but in
Canada you are reminded of the government
every day. It parades itself before you. It is
not content to be the servant, but will be the
master; and every day it goes out to the Plains
of Abraham or to the Champ de Mars and ex-

hibits itself and its tools. Everywhere there
appeared an attempt to make and to preserve
trivial and otherwise transient distinctions. In
the streets of Montreal and Quebec you met not
only with soldiers in red, and shuffling priests
in unmistakable black and white, with Sisters
of Charity gone into mourning for their de-
ceased relative, — not to mention the nuns of
various orders depending on the fashion of a
tear, of whom you heard, — but youths belonging to some seminary or other, wearing coats
edged with white, who looked as if their expanding hearts were already repressed with a
piece of tape. In short, the inhabitants of
Canada appeared to be suffering between two
fires, — the soldiery and the priesthood.

CHAPTER V

ABOUT twelve o'clock this day, being in the
Lower Town, I looked up at the signal-gun by
the flag-staff on Cape Diamond, and saw a soldier up in the heavens there making preparations to fire it, — both he and the gun in bold
relief against the sky. Soon after, being
warned by the boom of the gun to look up
again, there was only the cannon in the sky,
the smoke just blowing away from it, as if the
soldier, having touched it off, had concealed
himself for effect, leaving the sound to echo
grandly from shore to shore, and far up and
down the river. This answered the purpose of
a dinner-horn.

There are no such restaurateurs in Quebec
or Montreal as there are in Boston. I hunted
an hour or two in vain in this town to find one,
till I lost my appetite. In one house, called a
restaurateur, where lunches were advertised, I
found only tables covered with bottles and
glasses innumerable, containing apparently a

sample of every liquid that has been known since the earth dried up after the flood, but no scent of solid food did I perceive gross enough to excite a hungry mouse. In short, I saw nothing to tempt me there, but a large map of Canada against the wall. In another place I once more got as far as the bottles, and then asked for a bill of fare; was told to walk up stairs; had no bill of fare, nothing but fare. "Have you any pies or puddings?" I inquired, for I am obliged to keep my savageness in check by a low diet. "No, sir; we 've nice mutton-chop, roast beef, beef-steak, cutlets," and so on. A burly Englishman, who was in the midst of the siege of a piece of roast beef, and of whom I have never had a front view to this day, turned half round, with his mouth half full, and remarked, "You 'll find no pies nor puddings in Quebec, sir; they don't make any here." I found that it was even so, and therefore bought some musty cake and some fruit in the open market-place. This market-place by the water-side, where the old women sat by their tables in the open air, amid a dense crowd jabbering all languages, was the best place in Quebec to observe the people; and the ferry-boats, continually coming and going with their motley crews and cargoes, added much to the entertainment. I also saw them getting

water from the river, for Quebec is supplied
with water by cart and barrel. This city impressed me as wholly foreign and French, for
I scarcely heard the sound of the English language in the streets. More than three fifths of
the inhabitants are of French origin; and if
the traveler did not visit the fortifications particularly, he might not be reminded that the
English have any foothold here; and, in any
case, if he looked no farther than Quebec, they
would appear to have planted themselves in
Canada only as they have in Spain at Gibraltar; and he who plants upon a rock cannot
expect much increase. The novel sights and
sounds by the water-side made me think of such
ports as Boulogne, Dieppe, Rouen, and Havre
de Grace, which I have never seen; but I have
no doubt that they present similar scenes. I
was much amused from first to last with the
sounds made by the charette and caleche drivers. It was that part of their foreign language
that you heard the most of, — the French they
talked to their horses, — and which they talked
the loudest. It was a more novel sound to me
than the French of conversation. The streets
resounded with the cries, *" Qui donc ! "*
" Marche tôt ! " I suspect that many of our
horses which came from Canada would prick
up their ears at these sounds. Of the shops, I

was most attracted by those where furs and Indian works were sold, as containing articles of
genuine Canadian manufacture. I have been
told that two townsmen of mine, who were interested in horticulture, traveling once in Canada, and being in Quebec, thought it would be
a good opportunity to obtain seeds of the real
Canada crook-neck squash. So they went into
a shop where such things were advertised, and
inquired for the same. The shopkeeper had
the very thing they wanted. "But are you
sure," they asked, "that these are the genuine
Canada crook-neck?" "Oh, yes, gentlemen,"
answered he, "they are a lot which I have received directly from Boston." I resolved that
my Canada crook-neck seeds should be such as
had grown in Canada.

Too much has not been said about the scenery
of Quebec. The fortifications of Cape Diamond
are omnipresent. They preside, they frown
over the river and surrounding country. You
travel ten, twenty, thirty miles up or down the
river's banks, you ramble fifteen miles amid the
hills on either side, and then, when you have
long since forgotten them, perchance slept on
them by the way, at a turn of the road or of
your body, there they are still, with their geo-
metry against the sky. The child that is born
and brought up thirty miles distant, and has

never traveled to the city, reads his country's
history, sees the level lines of the citadel amid
the cloud-built citadels in the western horizon,
and is told that that is Quebec. No wonder if
Jacques Cartier's pilot exclaimed in Norman
French, *Que bec!* — "What a beak!" — when
he saw this cape, as some suppose. Every
modern traveler involuntarily uses a similar expression. Particularly it is said that its sudden apparition on turning Point Levi makes a
memorable impression on him who arrives by
water. The view from Cape Diamond has been
compared by European travelers with the most
remarkable views of a similar kind in Europe,
such as from Edinburgh Castle, Gibraltar,
Cintra, and others, and preferred by many. A
main peculiarity in this, compared with other
views which I have beheld, is that it is from the
ramparts of a fortified city, and not from a solitary and majestic river cape alone that this view
is obtained. I associate the beauty of Quebec
with the steel-like and flashing air, which may
be peculiar to that season of the year, in which
the blue flowers of the succory and some late
golden-rods and buttercups on the summit of
Cape Diamond were almost my only companions, — the former bluer than the heavens they
faced. Yet even I yielded in some degree to
the influence of historical associations, and

found it hard to attend to the geology of Cape Diamond or the botany of the Plains of Abraham. I still remember the harbor far beneath me, sparkling like silver in the sun, — the answering highlands of Point Levi on the southeast, — the frowning Cap Tourmente abruptly bounding the seaward view far in the northeast, — the villages of Lorette and Charlesbourg on the north, — and further west the distant Val Cartier, sparkling with white cottages, hardly removed by distance through the clear air, — not to mention a few blue mountains along the horizon in that direction. You look out from the ramparts of the citadel beyond the frontiers of civilization. Yonder small group of hills, according to the guide-book, forms "the portal of the wilds which are trodden only by the feet of the Indian hunters as far as Hudson's Bay." It is but a few years since Bouchette declared that the country ten leagues north of the British capital of North America was as little known as the middle of Africa. Thus the citadel under my feet, and all historical associations, were swept away again by an influence from the wilds and from nature, as if the beholder had read her history, — an influence which, like the Great River itself, flowed from the Arctic fastnesses and Western forests with irresistible tide over all.

The most interesting object in Canada to me was the River St. Lawrence, known far and wide, and for centuries, as the Great River. Cartier, its discoverer, sailed up it as far as Montreal in 1535, — nearly a century before the coming of the Pilgrims; and I have seen a pretty accurate map of it so far, containing the city of "Hochelaga" and the river "Saguenay," in Ortelius's *Theatrum Orbis Terrarum*, printed at Antwerp in 1575, — the first edition having appeared in 1570, — in which the famous cities of "Norumbega" and "Orsinora" stand on the rough-blocked continent where New England is to-day, and the fabulous but unfortunate Isle of Demons, and Frislant, and others, lie off and on in the unfrequented sea, some of them prowling near what is now the course of the Cunard steamers. In this ponderous folio of the "Ptolemy of his age," said to be the first general atlas published after the revival of the sciences in Europe, only one page of which is devoted to the topography of the *Novus Orbis*, the St. Lawrence is the only large river, whether drawn from fancy or from observation, on the east side of North America. It was famous in Europe before the other rivers of North America were heard of, notwithstanding that the mouth of the Mississippi is said to have been discovered first, and its stream

was reached by Soto not long after; but the
St. Lawrence had attracted settlers to its cold
shores long before the Mississippi, or even the
Hudson, was known to the world.   Schoolcraft
was misled by Gallatin into saying that Nar-
vaez discovered the Mississippi.   De Vega does
not say so.   The first explorers declared that
the summer in that country was as warm as
France, and they named one of the bays in the
Gulf of St. Lawrence the Bay of Chaleur, or of
warmth; but they said nothing about the winter
being as cold as Greenland.   In the manuscript
account of Cartier's second voyage, attributed
by some to that navigator himself, it is called
"the greatest river, without comparison, that is
known to have ever been seen."   The savages
told him that it was the "*chemin du Canada*,"
— the highway to Canada, — "which goes so
far that no man had ever been to the end that
they had heard."   The Saguenay, one of its
tributaries, which the panorama has made
known to New England within three years, is
described by Cartier, in 1535, and still more
particularly by Jean Alphonse, in 1542, who
adds, "I think that this river comes from the
sea of Cathay, for in this place there issues a
strong current, and there runs there a terrible
tide."   The early explorers saw many whales
and other sea-monsters far up the St. Law-

rence. Champlain, in his map, represents a whale spouting in the harbor of Quebec, three hundred and sixty miles from what is called the mouth of the river; and Charlevoix takes his reader to the summit of Cape Diamond to see the "porpoises, white as snow," sporting on the surface of the harbor of Quebec. And Boucher says in 1664, "from there (Tadoussac) to Montreal is found a great quantity of *Marsouins blancs*." Several whales have been taken pretty high up the river since I was there. P. A. Gosse, in his "Canadian Naturalist," p. 171 (London, 1840), speaks of "the white dolphin of the St. Lawrence (*Delphinus Canadensis*)," as considered different from those of the sea. "The Natural History Society of Montreal offered a prize, a few years ago, for an essay on the *Cetacea* of the St. Lawrence, which was, I believe, handed in." In Champlain's day it was commonly called "the Great River of Canada." More than one nation has claimed it. In Ogilby's "America of 1670," in the map *Novi Belgii*, it is called "De Groote Rivier van Niew Nederlandt." It bears different names in different parts of its course, as it flows through what were formerly the territories of different nations. From the Gulf to Lake Ontario it is called at present the St. Lawrence; from Montreal to the same place it is frequently called

the Cateraqui; and higher up it is known suc-
cessively as the Niagara, Detroit, St. Clair, St.
Mary's, and St. Louis rivers. Humboldt,
speaking of the Orinoco, says that this name is
unknown in the interior of the country; so likewise the tribes that dwell about the sources of
the St. Lawrence have never heard the name
which it bears in the lower part of its course.
It rises near another father of waters, — the
Mississippi, — issuing from a remarkable spring
far up in the woods, called Lake Superior, fifteen hundred miles in circumference; and several other springs there are thereabouts which
feed it. It makes such a noise in its tumbling
down at one place as is heard all round the
world. Bouchette, the Surveyor-General of
the Canadas, calls it "the most splendid river on
the globe;" says that it is two thousand statute
miles long (more recent geographers make it
four or five hundred miles longer); that at the
Rivière du Sud it is eleven miles wide; at the
Traverse, thirteen; at the Paps of Matane,
twenty-five; at the Seven Islands, seventy-
three; and at its mouth, from Cape Rosier to
the Mingan Settlements in Labrador, near one
hundred and five (?) miles wide. According to
Captain Bayfield's recent chart it is about
ninety-six geographical miles wide at the latter
place, measuring at right angles with the stream.

It has much the largest estuary, regarding both length and breadth, of any river on the globe. Humboldt says that the river Plate, which has the broadest estuary of the South American rivers, is ninety-two geographical miles wide at its mouth; also he found the Orinoco to be more than three miles wide at five hundred and sixty miles from its mouth; but he does not tell us that ships of six hundred tons can sail up it so far, as they can up the St. Lawrence to Montreal, — an equal distance. If he had described a fleet of such ships at anchor in a city's port so far inland, we should have got a very different idea of the Orinoco. Perhaps Charlevoix describes the St. Lawrence truly as the most *navigable* river in the world. Between Montreal and Quebec it averages about two miles wide. The tide is felt as far up as Three Rivers, four hundred and thirty-two miles, which is as far as from Boston to Washington. As far up as Cap aux Oyes, sixty or seventy miles below Quebec, Kalm found a great part of the plants near the shore to be marine, as glasswort (*Salicornia*), seaside pease (*Pisum maritimum*), sea-milkwort (*Glaux*), beach-grass (*Psamma arenarium*), seaside plantain (*Plantago maritima*), the sea-rocket (*Bunias cakile*), etc.

The geographer Guyot observes that the

Marañon is three thousand miles long, and gathers its waters from a surface of a million and a half square miles; that the Mississippi is also three thousand miles long, but its basin covers only from eight to nine hundred thousand square miles; that the St. Lawrence is eighteen hundred miles long, and its basin covers more than a million square miles (Darby says five hundred thousand); and speaking of the lakes, he adds, "These vast fresh-water seas, together with the St. Lawrence, cover a surface of nearly one hundred thousand square miles, and it has been calculated that they contain about one half of all the fresh water on the surface of our planet." But all these calculations are necessarily very rude and inaccurate. Its tributaries, the Ottawa, St. Maurice, and Saguenay, are great rivers themselves. The latter is said to be more than one thousand (?) feet deep at its mouth, while its cliffs rise perpendicularly an equal distance above its surface. Pilots say there are no soundings till one hundred and fifty miles up the St. Lawrence. The greatest sounding in the river, given on Bayfield's chart of the gulf and river, is two hundred and twenty-eight fathoms. McTaggart, an engineer, observes that "the Ottawa is larger than all the rivers in Great Britain, were they running in one." The traveler Grey writes: "A dozen Dan-

ubes, Rhines, Taguses, and Thameses would be
nothing to twenty miles of fresh water in
breadth [as where he happened to be], from ten
to forty fathoms in depth." And again:
"There is not perhaps in the whole extent of
this immense continent so fine an approach to
it as by the river St. Lawrence. In the Southern States you have, in general, a level country
for many miles inland; here you are introduced
at once into a majestic scenery, where everything is on a grand scale, — mountains, woods,
lakes, rivers, precipices, waterfalls."

We have not yet the data for a minute comparison of the St. Lawrence with the South
American rivers; but it is obvious that, taking
it in connection with its lakes, its estuary, and
its falls, it easily bears off the palm from all
the rivers on the globe; for though, as Bouchette observes, it may not carry to the ocean a
greater volume of water than the Amazon and
Mississippi, its surface and cubic mass are far
greater than theirs. But, unfortunately, this
noble river is closed by ice from the beginning
of December to the middle of April. The arrival of the first vessel from England when the
ice breaks up is, therefore, a great event, as
when the salmon, shad, and alewives come up a
river in the spring to relieve the famishing inhabitants on its banks. Who can say what

would have been the history of this continent if, as has been suggested, this river had emptied into the sea where New York stands!

After visiting the Museum and taking one more look at the wall, I made haste to the Lord Sydenham steamer, which at five o'clock was to leave for Montreal. I had already taken a seat on deck, but finding that I had still an hour and a half to spare, and remembering that large map of Canada which I had seen in the parlor of the restaurateur in my search after pudding, and realizing that I might never see the like out of the country, I returned thither, asked liberty to look at the map, rolled up the mahogany table, put my handkerchief on it, stood on it, and copied all I wanted before the maid came in and said to me standing on the table, "Some gentlemen want the room, sir;" and I retreated without having broken the neck of a single bottle, or my own, very thankful and willing to pay for all the solid food I had got. We were soon abreast of Cap Rouge, eight miles above Quebec, after we got underway. It was in this place, then called "*Fort du France Roy*," that the Sieur de Roberval with his company, having sent home two of his three ships, spent the winter of 1542–43. It appears that they fared in the following manner (I translate from the original): "Each mess had only two loaves,

weighing each a pound, and half a pound of
beef. They ate pork for dinner, with half a
pound of butter, and beef for supper, with
about two handfuls of beans without butter.
Wednesdays, Fridays, and Saturdays they ate
salted cod, and sometimes green, for dinner,
with butter; and porpoise and beans for supper.
Monsieur Roberval administered good justice,
and punished each according to his offense.
One, named Michel Gaillon, was hung for
theft; John of Nantes was put in irons and im-
prisoned for his fault; and others were likewise
put in irons; and many were whipped, both
men and women; by which means they lived in
peace and tranquillity." In an account of a
voyage up this river, printed in the Jesuit Relations in the year 1664, it is said: "It was an
interesting navigation for us in ascending the
river from Cap Tourmente to Quebec, to see on
this side and on that, for the space of eight
leagues, the farms and the houses of the company, built by our French, all along these
shores. On the right, the seigniories of Beauport, of Notre Dame des Anges; and on the
left, this beautiful Isle of Orleans." The same
traveler names among the fruits of the country
observed at the Isles of Richelieu, at the head
of Lake St. Peter, "kinds (*des espèces*) of little
apples or haws (*semelles*), and of pears, which
only ripen with the frost."

Night came on before we had passed the high banks. We had come from Montreal to Quebec in one night. The return voyage, against the stream, takes but an hour longer. Jacques Cartier, the first white man who is known to have ascended this river, thus speaks of his voyage from what is now Quebec to the foot of Lake St. Peter, or about halfway to Montreal: "From the said day, the 19th, even to the 28th of the said month [September, 1535], we had been navigating up the said river without losing hour or day, during which time we had seen and found as much country and lands as level as we could desire, full of the most beautiful trees in the world," which he goes on to describe. But we merely slept and woke again to find that we had passed through all that country which he was eight days in sailing through. He must have had a troubled sleep. We were not long enough on the river to realize that it had length; we got only the impression of its breadth, as if we had passed over a lake a mile or two in breadth and several miles long, though we might thus have slept through a European kingdom. Being at the head of Lake St. Peter, on the above-mentioned 28th of September, dealing with the natives, Cartier says: "We inquired of them by signs if this was the route to Hochelaga [Montreal]; and they answered that it was, and that there were yet three days' journeys to go there." He finally arrived at Hochelaga on the 2d of October.

When I went on deck at dawn we had already passed through Lake St. Peter, and saw islands ahead of us. Our boat advancing with a strong and steady pulse over the calm surface, we felt as if we were permitted to be awake in the scenery of a dream. Many vivacious Lombardy poplars along the distant shores gave them a novel and lively, though artificial, look, and contrasted strangely with the slender and graceful elms on both shores and islands. The church of Varennes, fifteen miles from Montreal, was conspicuous at a great distance before us, appearing to belong to, and rise out of, the river; and now, and before, Mount Royal indicated where the city was. We arrived about seven o'clock, and set forth immediately to ascend the mountain, two miles distant, going across lots in spite of numerous signs threatening the severest penalties to trespassers, past an old building known as the Mac Tavish property, — Simon Mac Tavish, I suppose, whom Silliman refers to as "in a sense the founder of the Northwestern Company." His tomb was behind in the woods, with a remarkably high wall and higher monument. The family returned to Europe. He could not have imagined how dead

he would be in a few years, and all the more
dead and forgotten for being buried under such
a mass of gloomy stone, where not even memory
could get at him without a crowbar. Ah! poor
man, with that last end of his! However, he
may have been the worthiest of mortals for
aught that I know. From the mountain-top
we got a view of the whole city; the flat, fertile, extensive island; the noble sea of the St.
Lawrence swelling into lakes; the mountains
about St. Hyacinthe, and in Vermont and New
York; and the mouth of the Ottawa in the west,
overlooking that St. Anne's where the voyageur
sings his "parting hymn," and bids adieu to
civilization, — a name, thanks to Moore's
verses, the most suggestive of poetic associations
of any in Canada. We, too, climbed the hill
which Cartier, first of white men, ascended, and
named Mont - real (the 3d of October, O. S.,
1535), and, like him, "we saw the said river as
far as we could see, *grand, large, et spacieux,*
going to the southwest," toward that land
whither Donnacona had told the discoverer that
he had been a month's journey from Canada,
where there grew "*force Canelle et Girofle,*"
much cinnamon and cloves, and where also, as
the natives told him, were three great lakes and
afterward *une mer douce,* — a sweet sea, — *de
laquelle n'est mention avoir vu le bout,* of which

there is no mention to have seen the end. But instead of an Indian town far in the interior of a new world, with guides to show us where the river came from, we found a splendid and bustling stone-built city of white men, and only a few squalid Indians offered to sell us baskets at the Lachine Railroad Depot, and Hochelaga is, perchance, but the fancy name of an engine company or an eating-house.

We left Montreal Wednesday, the 2d of October, late in the afternoon. In the La Prairie cars the Yankees made themselves merry, imitating the cries of the charette drivers to perfection, greatly to the amusement of some French Canadian travelers, and they kept it up all the way to Boston. I saw one person on board the boat at St. John's, and one or two more elsewhere in Canada, wearing homespun gray great-coats, or capotes, with conical and comical hoods, which fell back between their shoulders like small bags, ready to be turned up over the head when occasion required, though a hat usurped that place now. They looked as if they would be convenient and proper enough as long as the coats were new and tidy, but would soon come to have a beggarly and unsightly look, akin to rags and dust-holes. We reached Burlington early in the morning, where the Yankees tried to pass off their Canada coppers, but the news-boys knew better. Returning through the Green Mountains, I was reminded that I had not seen in Canada such brilliant autumnal tints as I had previously seen in Vermont. Perhaps there was not yet so great and sudden a contrast with the summer heats in the former country as in these mountain valleys. As we were passing through Ashburnham, by a new white house which stood at some distance in a field, one passenger exclaimed, so that all in the car could hear him, "There, there's not so good a house as that in all Canada!" I did not much wonder at his remark, for there is a neatness, as well as evident prosperity, a certain elastic easiness of circumstances, so to speak, when not rich, about a New England house, as if the proprietor could at least afford to make repairs in the spring, which the Canadian houses do not suggest. Though of stone, they are no better constructed than a stone barn would be with us; the only building, except the chateau, on which money and taste are expended, being the church. In Canada an ordinary New England house would be mistaken for the chateau, and while every village here contains at least several gentlemen or "squires," *there* there is but one to a seigniory.

I got home this Thursday evening, having spent just one week in Canada and traveled

eleven hundred miles. The whole expense of
this journey, including two guide-books and a
map, which cost one dollar twelve and a half
cents, was twelve dollars seventy-five cents. I
do not suppose that I have seen all British
America; that could not be done by a cheap
excursion, unless it were a cheap excursion to
the Icy Sea, as seen by Hearne or Mackenzie,
and then, no doubt, some interesting features
would be omitted. I wished to go a little way
behind the word *Canadense*, of which natural-
ists make such frequent use; and I should like
still right well to make a longer excursion on
foot through the wilder parts of Canada, which
perhaps might be called *Iter Canadense*.

NATURAL HISTORY OF MASSACHUSETTS[1]

Books of natural history make the most cheerful winter reading. I read in Audubon with a thrill of delight, when the snow covers the ground, of the magnolia, and the Florida keys, and their warm sea-breezes; of the fence-rail, and the cotton-tree, and the migrations of the rice-bird; of the breaking up of winter in Labrador, and the melting of the snow on the forks of the Missouri; and owe an accession of health to these reminiscences of luxuriant nature.

> Within the circuit of this plodding life,
> There enter moments of an azure hue,
> Untarnished fair as is the violet
> Or anemone, when the spring strews them
> By some meandering rivulet, which make
> The best philosophy untrue that aims
> But to console man for his grievances.
> I have remembered when the winter came,
> High in my chamber in the frosty nights,
> When in the still light of the cheerful moon,

[1] *Reports — on the Fishes, Reptiles, and Birds; the Herbaceous Plants and Quadrupeds; the Insects Injurious to Vegetation; and the Invertebrate Animals of Massachusetts.* Published agreeably to an Order of the Legislature, by the Commissioners on the Zoölogical and Botanical Survey of the State.

On every twig and rail and jutting spout,
The icy spears were adding to their length
Against the arrows of the coming sun,
How in the shimmering noon of summer past
Some unrecorded beam slanted across
The upland pastures where the Johnswort grew ;
Or heard, amid the verdure of my mind,
The bee's long smothered hum, on the blue flag
Loitering amidst the mead ; or busy rill,
Which now through all its course stands still and dumb,
Its own memorial, — purling at its play
Along the slopes, and through the meadows next,
Until its youthful sound was hushed at last
In the staid current of the lowland stream ;
Or seen the furrows shine but late upturned,
And where the fieldfare followed in the rear,
When all the fields around lay bound and hoar
Beneath a thick integument of snow.
So by God's cheap economy made rich
To go upon my winter's task again.

I am singularly refreshed in winter when I
hear of service-berries, poke-weed, juniper. Is
not heaven made up of these cheap summer glories? There is a singular health in those words,
Labrador and East Main, which no desponding
creed recognizes. How much more than Fed-
eral are these States. If there were no other
vicissitudes than the seasons, our interest would
never tire. Much more is adoing than Con-
gress wots of. What journal do the persim-
mon and the buckeye keep, and the sharp-
shinned hawk? What is transpiring from
summer to winter in the Carolinas, and the

Great Pine Forest, and the Valley of the Mo-
hawk? The merely political aspect of the land
is never very cheering; men are degraded when
considered as the members of a political organi-
zation. On this side all lands present only the
symptoms of decay. I see but Bunker Hill and
Sing-Sing, the District of Columbia and Sulli-
van's Island, with a few avenues connecting
them. But paltry are they all beside one blast
of the east or the south wind which blows over
them.

In society you will not find health, but in
nature. Unless our feet at least stood in the
midst of nature, all our faces would be pale and
livid. Society is always diseased, and the best
is the most so. There is no scent in it so wholesome as that of the pines, nor any fragrance so
penetrating and restorative as the life-everlast-
ing in high pastures. I would keep some book
of natural history always by me as a sort of
elixir, the reading of which should restore the
tone of the system. To the sick, indeed, nature
is sick, but to the well, a fountain of health.
To him who contemplates a trait of natural
beauty no harm nor disappointment can come.
The doctrines of despair, of spiritual or political
tyranny or servitude, were never taught by such
as shared the serenity of nature. Surely good
courage will not flag here on the Atlantic bor-

der, as long as we are flanked by the Fur Countries. There is enough in that sound to cheer
one under any circumstances. The spruce, the
hemlock, and the pine will not countenance despair. Methinks some creeds in vestries and
churches do forget the hunter wrapped in furs
by the Great Slave Lake, and that the Esquimaux sledges are drawn by dogs, and in the
twilight of the northern night the hunter does
not give over to follow the seal and walrus on
the ice. They are of sick and diseased imagi-
nations who would toll the world's knell so soon.
Cannot these sedentary sects do better than prepare the shrouds and write the epitaphs of those
other busy living men? The practical faith of
all men belies the preacher's consolation. What
is any man's discourse to me, if I am not sensible of something in it as steady and cheery as
the creak of crickets? In it the woods must be
relieved against the sky. Men tire me when I
am not constantly greeted and refreshed as by
the flux of sparkling streams. Surely joy is
the condition of life. Think of the young fry
that leap in ponds, the myriads of insects ushered into being on a summer evening, the incessant note of the hyla with which the woods ring
in the spring, the nonchalance of the butterfly
carrying accident and change painted in a thousand hues upon its wings, or the brook minnow

stoutly stemming the current, the lustre of
whose scales, worn bright by the attrition, is reflected upon the bank.

We fancy that this din of religion, literature,
and philosophy, which is heard in pulpits, lyce-
ums, and parlors, vibrates through the universe,
and is as catholic a sound as the creaking of the
earth's axle; but if a man sleep soundly, he will
forget it all between sunset and dawn. It is
the three-inch swing of a pendulum in a cup-
board, which the great pulse of nature vibrates
by and through each instant. When we lift
our eyelids and open our ears, it disappears
with smoke and rattle like the cars on a railroad. When I detect a beauty in any of the
recesses of nature, I am reminded, by the serene
and retired spirit in which it requires to be contemplated, of the inexpressible privacy of a life,
— how silent and unambitious it is. The
beauty there is in mosses must be considered
from the holiest, quietest nook. What an admirable training is science for the more active
warfare of life. Indeed, the unchallenged bravery, which these studies imply, is far more impressive than the trumpeted valor of the war-
rior. I am pleased to learn that Thales was up
and stirring by night not unfrequently, as his
astronomical discoveries prove. Linnæus, setting out for Lapland, surveys his "comb" and

"spare shirt," "leathern breeches" and "gauze cap to keep off gnats," with as much complacency as Bonaparte a park of artillery for the Russian campaign. The quiet bravery of the man is admirable. His eye is to take in fish, flower, and bird, quadruped and biped. Science is always brave; for to know is to know good; doubt and danger quail before her eye. What the coward overlooks in his hurry, she calmly scrutinizes, breaking ground like a pioneer for the array of arts that follow in her train. But cowardice is unscientific; for there cannot be a science of ignorance. There may be a science of bravery, for that advances; but a retreat is rarely well conducted; if it is, then is it an orderly advance in the face of circumstances.

But to draw a little nearer to our promised topics. Entomology extends the limits of being in a new direction, so that I walk in nature with a sense of greater space and freedom. It suggests besides, that the universe is not rough-hewn, but perfect in its details. Nature will bear the closest inspection; she invites us to lay our eye level with the smallest leaf, and take an insect view of its plain. She has no interstices; every part is full of life. I explore, too, with pleasure, the sources of the myriad sounds which crowd the summer noon, and which seem the very grain and stuff of which eternity is made. Who does not remember the shrill roll-call of the harvest fly? There were ears for these sounds in Greece long ago, as Anacreon's ode will show.

> " We pronounce thee happy, Cicada,
> For on the tops of the trees,
> Drinking a little dew,
> Like any king thou singest,
> For thine are they all,
> Whatever thou seest in the fields,
> And whatever the woods bear.
> Thou art the friend of the husbandmen,
> In no respect injuring any one ;
> And thou art honored among men,
> Sweet prophet of summer.
> The Muses love thee,
> And Phœbus himself loves thee,
> And has given thee a shrill song ;
> Age does not wrack thee,
> Thou skillful, earthborn, song-loving,
> Unsuffering, bloodless one ;
> Almost thou art like the gods."

In the autumn days, the creaking of crickets is heard at noon over all the land, and as in summer they are heard chiefly at nightfall, so then by their incessant chirp they usher in the evening of the year. Nor can all the vanities that vex the world alter one whit the measure that night has chosen. Every pulse-beat is in exact time with the cricket's chant and the tick-ings of the death-watch in the wall. Alternate with these if you can.

About two hundred and eighty birds either reside permanently in the State, or spend the summer only, or make us a passing visit. Those which spend the winter with us have obtained our warmest sympathy. The nut-hatch and chickadee flitting in company through the dells of the wood, the one harshly scolding at the intruder, the other with a faint lisping note enticing him on; the jay screaming in the orchard; the crow cawing in unison with the storm; the partridge, like a russet link extended over from autumn to spring, preserving unbroken the chain of summers; the hawk with warrior-like firmness abiding the blasts of winter; the robin [1] and lark lurking by warm springs in the woods; the familiar snow-bird culling a few seeds in the garden, or a few crumbs in the yard; and occasionally the shrike, with heedless and unfrozen melody bringing back summer again: —

> His steady sails he never furls
> At any time o' year,
> And perching now on Winter's curls,
> He whistles in his ear.

[1] A white robin and a white quail have occasionally been seen. It is mentioned in Audubon as remarkable that the nest of a robin should be found on the ground; but this bird seems to be less particular than most in the choice of a building spot. I have seen its nest placed under the thatched roof of a deserted barn, and in one instance, where the adjacent country was nearly destitute of trees, together with two of the phœbe, upon the end of a board in the loft of a saw-mill, but a few feet

As the spring advances, and the ice is melting in the river, our earliest and straggling visitors make their appearance. Again does the old Teian poet sing as well for New England as for Greece, in the

RETURN OF SPRING

Behold, how Spring appearing,
The Graces send forth roses;
Behold, how the wave of the sea
Is made smooth by the calm;
Behold, how the duck dives;
Behold, how the crane travels;
And Titan shines constantly bright.
The shadows of the clouds are moving;
The works of man shine;
The earth puts forth fruits;
The fruit of the olive puts forth.
The cup of Bacchus is crowned,
Along the leaves, along the branches,
The fruit, bending them down, flourishes.

The ducks alight at this season in the still water, in company with the gulls, which do not fail to improve an east wind to visit our meadows, and swim about by twos and threes, pluming themselves, and diving to peck at the root of the lily, and the cranberries which the frost has not loosened. The first flock of geese is seen beating to north, in long harrows and waving lines; the jingle of the song-sparrow salutes us

from the saw, which vibrated several inches with the motion of the machinery.

from the shrubs and fences; the plaintive note
of the lark comes clear and sweet from the
meadow; and the bluebird, like an azure ray,
glances past us in our walk. The fish-hawk,
too, is occasionally seen at this season sailing
majestically over the water, and he who has once
observed it will not soon forget the majesty of
its flight. It sails the air like a ship of the line,
worthy to struggle with the elements, falling
back from time to time like a ship on its beam
ends, and holding its talons up as if ready for
the arrows, in the attitude of the national bird.
It is a great presence, as of the master of river
and forest. Its eye would not quail before the
owner of the soil, but make him feel like an intruder on its domains. And then its retreat,
sailing so steadily away, is a kind of advance. I
have by me one of a pair of ospreys, which have
for some years fished in this vicinity, shot by a
neighboring pond, measuring more than two feet
in length, and six in the stretch of its wings.
Nuttall mentions that "The ancients, particularly Aristotle, pretended that the ospreys taught
their young to gaze at the sun, and those who
were unable to do so were destroyed. Linnæus
even believed, on ancient authority, that one of
the feet of this bird had all the toes divided, while
the other was partly webbed, so that it could
swim with one foot, and grasp a fish with the

other." But that educated eye is now dim, and
those talons are nerveless. Its shrill scream
seems yet to linger in its throat, and the roar of
the sea in its wings. There is the tyranny of Jove
in its claws, and his wrath in the erectile feathers
of the head and neck. It reminds me of the
Argonautic expedition, and would inspire the
dullest to take flight over Parnassus.

The booming of the bittern, described by
Goldsmith and Nuttall, is frequently heard in
our fens, in the morning and evening, sounding
like a pump, or the chopping of wood in a frosty
morning in some distant farm-yard. The manner
in which this sound is produced I have not seen
anywhere described. On one occasion, the bird
has been seen by one of my neighbors to thrust
its bill into the water, and suck up as much as it
could hold, then, raising its head, it pumped it
out again with four or five heaves of the neck,
throwing it two or three feet, and making the
sound each time.

At length the summer's eternity is ushered in
by the cackle of the flicker among the oaks on
the hillside, and a new dynasty begins with calm
security.

In May and June the woodland quire is in full
tune, and given the immense spaces of hollow air,
and this curious human ear, one does not see how
the void could be better filled.

> Each summer sound
> Is a summer round.

As the season advances, and those birds which make us but a passing visit depart, the woods become silent again, and but few feathers ruffle the drowsy air. But the solitary rambler may still find a response and expression for every mood in the depths of the wood.

> Sometimes I hear the veery's [1] clarion,
> Or brazen trump of the impatient jay,
> And in secluded woods the chickadee
> Doles out her scanty notes, which sing the praise
> Of heroes, and set forth the loveliness
> Of virtue evermore.

The phœbe still sings in harmony with the sultry weather by the brink of the pond, nor are the desultory hours of noon in the midst of the village without their minstrel.

> Upon the lofty elm-tree sprays
> The vireo rings the changes sweet,
> During the trivial summer days,
> Striving to lift our thoughts above the street.

With the autumn begins in some measure a new spring. The plover is heard whistling high

[1] This bird, which is so well described by Nuttall, but is apparently unknown by the author of the Report, is one of the most common in the woods in this vicinity, and in Cambridge I have heard the college yard ring with its trill. The boys call it " *yorrick*," from the sound of its querulous and chiding note, as it flits near the traveler through the underwood. The cowbird's egg is occasionally found in its nest, as mentioned by Audubon.

in the air over the dry pastures, the finches flit from tree to tree, the bobolinks and flickers fly in flocks, and the goldfinch rides on the earliest blast, like a winged hyla peeping amid the rustle of the leaves. The crows, too, begin now to congregate; you may stand and count them as they fly low and straggling over the landscape, singly or by twos and threes, at intervals of half a mile, until a hundred have passed.

I have seen it suggested somewhere that the crow was brought to this country by the white man; but I shall as soon believe that the white man planted these pines and hemlocks. He is no spaniel to follow our steps; but rather flits about the clearings like the dusky spirit of the Indian, reminding me oftener of Philip and Powhatan, than of Winthrop and Smith. He is a relic of the dark ages. By just so slight, by just so lasting a tenure does superstition hold the world ever; there is the rook in England, and the crow in New England.

> Thou dusky spirit of the wood,
> Bird of an ancient brood,
> Flitting thy lonely way,
> A meteor in the summer's day,
> From wood to wood, from hill to hill,
> Low over forest, field, and rill,
> What wouldst thou say?
> Why shouldst thou haunt the day?
> What makes thy melancholy float?
> What bravery inspires thy throat,

And bears thee up above the clouds,
Over desponding human crowds,
Which far below
Lay thy haunts low ?

. The late walker or sailor, in the October
evenings, may hear the murmurings of the snipe,
circling over the meadows, the most spirit-like
sound in nature; and still later in the autumn,
when the frosts have tinged the leaves, a solitary
loon pays a visit to our retired ponds, where he
may lurk undisturbed till the season of moult-
ing is passed, making the woods ring with his
wild laughter.   This bird, the Great Northern
Diver, well deserves its name; for when pursued with a boat, it will dive, and swim like
a fish under water, for sixty rods or more, as
fast as a boat can be paddled, and its pursuer,
if he would discover his game again, must put
his ear to the surface to hear where it comes
up.   When it comes to the surface, it throws
the water off with one shake of its wings, and
calmly swims about until again disturbed.

These are the sights and sounds which reach
our senses oftenest during the year.   But sometimes one hears a quite new note, which has for
background other Carolinas and Mexicos than
the books describe, and learns that his ornithology has done him no service.

It appears from the Report that there are

about forty quadrupeds belonging to the State, and among these one is glad to hear of a few bears, wolves, lynxes, and wildcats.

When our river overflows its banks in the spring, the wind from the meadows is laden with a strong scent of musk, and by its freshness advertises me of an unexplored wildness. Those backwoods are not far off then. I am affected by the sight of the cabins of the muskrat, made of mud and grass, and raised three or four feet along the river, as when I read of the barrows of Asia. The musk-rat is the beaver of the settled States. Their number has even increased within a few years in this vicinity. Among the rivers which empty into the Merrimack, the Concord is known to the boatmen as a dead stream. The Indians are said to have called it Musketaquid, or Prairie River. Its current being much more sluggish and its water more muddy than the rest, it abounds more in fish and game of every kind. According to the History of the town, "The fur-trade was here once very important. As early as 1641, a company was formed in the colony, of which Major Willard of Concord was superintendent, and had the exclusive right to trade with the Indians in furs and other articles; and for this right they were obliged to pay into the public treasury one twentieth of all the furs they obtained." There are trappers in our midst still, as well as on the streams of the far West, who night and morning go the round of their traps, without fear of the Indian. One of these takes from one hundred and fifty to two hundred musk-rats in a year, and even thirty-six have been shot by one man in a day. Their fur, which is not nearly as valuable as formerly, is in good condition in the winter and spring only; and upon the breaking up of the ice, when they are driven out of their holes by the water, the greatest number is shot from boats, either swimming or resting on their stools, or slight supports of grass and reeds, by the side of the stream. Though they exhibit considerable cunning at other times, they are easily taken in a trap, which has only to be placed in their holes, or wherever they frequent, without any bait being used, though it is sometimes rubbed with their musk. In the winter the hunter cuts holes in the ice, and shoots them when they come to the surface. Their burrows are usually in the high banks of the river, with the entrance under water, and rising within to above the level of high water. Sometimes their nests, composed of dried meadow-grass and flags, may be discovered where the bank is low and spongy, by the yielding of the ground under the feet. They have from three to seven or eight young in the spring.

Frequently, in the morning or evening, a long ripple is seen in the still water, where a musk-rat is crossing the stream, with only its nose above the surface, and sometimes a green bough in its mouth to build its house with. When it finds itself observed, it will dive and swim five or six rods under water, and at length conceal itself in its hole, or the weeds. It will remain under water for ten minutes at a time, and on one occasion has been seen, when undisturbed, to form an air-bubble under the ice, which contracted and expanded as it breathed at leisure. When it suspects danger on shore, it will stand erect like a squirrel, and survey its neighborhood for several minutes, without moving.

In the fall, if a meadow intervene between their burrows and the stream, they erect cabins of mud and grass, three or four feet high, near its edge. These are not their breeding-places, though young are sometimes found in them in late freshets, but rather their hunting-lodges, to which they resort in the winter with their food, and for shelter. Their food consists chiefly of flags and fresh-water mussels, the shells of the latter being left in large quantities around their lodges in the spring.

The Penobscot Indian wears the entire skin of a musk-rat, with the legs and tail dangling,

and the head caught under his girdle, for a
pouch, into which he puts his fishing tackle, and
essences to scent his traps with.

The bear, wolf, lynx, wildcat, deer, beaver,
and marten have disappeared; the otter is
rarely if ever seen here at present; and the
mink is less common than formerly.

Perhaps of all our untamed quadrupeds, the
fox has obtained the widest and most familiar
reputation, from the time of Pilpay and Æsop
to the present day. His recent tracks still give
variety to a winter's walk. I tread in the steps
of the fox that has gone before me by some
hours, or which perhaps I have started, with
such a tiptoe of expectation as if I were on the
trail of the Spirit itself which resides in the
wood, and expected soon to catch it in its lair.
I am curious to know what has determined its
graceful curvatures, and how surely they were
coincident with the fluctuations of some mind.
I know which way a mind wended, what horizon
it faced, by the setting of these tracks, and
whether it moved slowly or rapidly, by their
greater or less intervals and distinctness; for
the swiftest step leaves yet a lasting trace.
Sometimes you will see the trails of many together, and where they have gamboled and gone
through a hundred evolutions, which testify to
a singular listlessness and leisure in nature.

When I see a fox run across the pond on the snow, with the carelessness of freedom, or at intervals trace his course in the sunshine along the ridge of a hill, I give up to him sun and earth as to their true proprietor. He does not go in the sun, but it seems to follow him, and there is a visible sympathy between him and it. Sometimes, when the snow lies light, and but five or six inches deep, you may give chase and come up with one on foot. In such a case he will show a remarkable presence of mind, choosing only the safest direction, though he may lose ground by it. Notwithstanding his fright, he will take no step which is not beautiful. His pace is a sort of leopard canter, as if he were in no wise impeded by the snow, but were husbanding his strength all the while. When the ground is uneven, the course is a series of graceful curves, conforming to the shape of the surface. He runs as though there were not a bone in his back. Occasionally dropping his muzzle to the ground for a rod or two, and then tossing his head aloft, when satisfied of his course. When he comes to a declivity, he will put his forefeet together, and slide swiftly down it, shoving the snow before him. He treads so softly that you would hardly hear it from any nearness, and yet with such expression that it would not be quite inaudible at any distance.

Of fishes, seventy-five genera and one hundred and seven species are described in the Report. The fisherman will be startled to learn that there are but about a dozen kinds in the ponds and streams of any inland town; and almost nothing is known of their habits. Only their names and residence make one love fishes. I would know even the number of their fin-rays, and how many scales compose the lateral line. I am the wiser in respect to all knowledges, and the better qualified for all fortunes, for knowing that there is a minnow in the brook. Methinks I have need even of his sympathy, and to be his fellow in a degree.

I have experienced such simple delight in the trivial matters of fishing and sporting, formerly, as might have inspired the muse of Homer or Shakespeare; and now, when I turn the pages and ponder the plates of the Angler's Souvenir, I am fain to exclaim, —

> " Can these things be,
> And overcome us like a summer's cloud ? "

Next to nature, it seems as if man's actions were the most natural, they so gently accord with her. The small seines of flax stretched across the shallow and transparent parts of our river are no more intrusion than the cobweb in the sun. I stay my boat in mid-current, and look down in the sunny water to see the civil

meshes of his nets, and wonder how the bluster-
ing people of the town could have done this
elvish work. The twine looks like a new river
weed, and is to the river as a beautiful memento
of man's presence in nature, discovered as silently and delicately as a footprint in the sand.

When the ice is covered with snow, I do not
suspect the wealth under my feet; that there
is as good as a mine under me wherever I go.
How many pickerel are poised on easy fin fathoms below the loaded wain. The revolution of
the seasons must be a curious phenomenon to
them. At length the sun and wind brush aside
their curtain, and they see the heavens again.

Early in the spring, after the ice has melted,
is the time for spearing fish. Suddenly the
wind shifts from northeast and east to west and
south, and every icicle, which has tinkled on
the meadow grass so long, trickles down its
stem, and seeks its level unerringly with a million
comrades. The steam curls up from every roof
and fence.

> I see the civil sun drying earth's tears,
> Her tears of joy, which only faster flow.

In the brooks is heard the slight grating
sound of small cakes of ice, floating with various speed, full of content and promise, and
where the water gurgles under a natural bridge,
you may hear these hasty rafts hold conversa-

tion in an undertone.   Every rill is a channel
for the juices of the meadow.   In the ponds the
ice cracks with a merry and inspiriting din, and
down the larger streams is whirled grating
hoarsely, and crashing its way along, which
was so lately a highway for the woodman's team
and the fox, sometimes with the tracks of the
skaters still fresh upon it, and the holes cut for
pickerel.   Town committees anxiously inspect
the bridges and causeways, as if by mere eye-
force to intercede with the ice and save the
treasury.

> The river swelleth more and more,
> Like some sweet influence stealing o'er
> The passive town ; and for a while
> Each tussock makes a tiny isle,
> Where, on some friendly Ararat,
> Resteth the weary water-rat.
>
> No ripple shows Musketaquid,
> Her very current e'en is hid,
> As deepest souls do calmest rest,
> When thoughts are swelling in the breast,
> And she that in the summer's drought
> Doth make a rippling and a rout,
> Sleeps from Nahshawtuck to the Cliff,
> Unruffled by a single skiff.
> But by a thousand distant hills
> The louder roar a thousand rills,
> And many a spring which now is dumb,
> And many a stream with smothered hum,
> Doth swifter well and faster glide,
> Though buried deep beneath the tide.

Our village shows a rural Venice,
Its broad lagoons where yonder fen is;
As lovely as the Bay of Naples
Yon placid cove amid the maples;
And in my neighbor's field of corn
I recognize the Golden Horn.

Here Nature taught from year to year,
When only red men came to hear, —
Methinks 'twas in this school of art
Venice and Naples learned their part;
But still their mistress, to my mind,
Her young disciples leaves behind.

The fisherman now repairs and launches his boat. The best time for spearing is at this season, before the weeds have begun to grow, and while the fishes lie in the shallow water, for in summer they prefer the cool depths, and in the autumn they are still more or less concealed by the grass. The first requisite is fuel for your crate; and for this purpose the roots of the pitch-pine are commonly used, found under decayed stumps, where the trees have been felled eight or ten years.

With a crate, or jack, made of iron hoops, to contain your fire, and attached to the bow of your boat about three feet from the water, a fish-spear with seven tines and fourteen feet long, a large basket or barrow to carry your fuel and bring back your fish, and a thick outer garment, you are equipped for a cruise. It should be a warm and still evening; and then, with a fire crackling merrily at the prow, you may launch forth like a cucullo into the night. The dullest soul cannot go upon such an expedition without some of the spirit of adventure; as if he had stolen the boat of Charon and gone down the Styx on a midnight expedition into the realms of Pluto. And much speculation does this wandering star afford to the musing night-walker, leading him on and on, jack-o'-lantern-like, over the meadows; or, if he is wiser, he amuses himself with imagining what of human life, far in the silent night, is flitting moth-like round its candle. The silent navigator shoves his craft gently over the water, with a smothered pride and sense of benefaction, as if he were the phosphor, or light-bringer, to these dusky realms, or some sister moon, blessing the spaces with her light. The waters, for a rod or two on either hand and several feet in depth, are lit up with more than noonday distinctness, and he enjoys the opportunity which so many have desired, for the roofs of a city are indeed raised, and he surveys the midnight economy of the fishes. There they lie in every variety of posture; some on their backs, with their white bellies uppermost, some suspended in mid-water, some sculling gently along with a dreamy motion of the fins, and others quite active and wide awake, — a scene not unlike what the human city would present. Occasionally he will encounter a turtle selecting the choicest morsels, or a musk-rat resting on a tussock. He may exercise his dexterity, if he sees fit, on the more distant and active fish, or fork the nearer into his boat, as potatoes out of a pot, or even take the sound sleepers with his hands. But these last accomplishments he will soon learn to dispense with, distinguishing the real object of his pursuit, and find compensation in the beauty and never-ending novelty of his position. The pines growing down to the water's edge will show newly as in the glare of a conflagration; and as he floats under the willows with his light, the song-sparrow will often wake on her perch, and sing that strain at midnight, which she had meditated for the morning. And when he has done, he may have to steer his way home through the dark by the north star, and he will feel himself some degrees nearer to it for having lost his way on the earth.

The fishes commonly taken in this way are pickerel, suckers, perch, eels, pouts, breams, and shiners, — from thirty to sixty weight in a night. Some are hard to be recognized in the unnatural light, especially the perch, which, his dark bands being exaggerated, acquires a ferocious aspect. The number of these transverse bands, which the Report states to be seven, is, however, very variable, for in some of our ponds they have nine and ten even.

It appears that we have eight kinds of tortoises, twelve snakes, — but one of which is venomous, — nine frogs and toads, nine salamanders, and one lizard, for our neighbors.

I am particularly attracted by the motions of the serpent tribe. They make our hands and feet, the wings of the bird, and the fins of the fish seem very superfluous, as if nature had only indulged her fancy in making them. The black snake will dart into a bush when pursued, and circle round and round with an easy and graceful motion, amid the thin and bare twigs, five or six feet from the ground, as a bird flits from bough to bough, or hang in festoons between the forks. Elasticity and flexibleness in the simpler forms of animal life are equivalent to a complex system of limbs in the higher; and we have only to be as wise and wily as the serpent, to perform as difficult feats without the vulgar assistance of hands and feet.

In May, the snapping turtle, *Emysaurus serpentina*, is frequently taken on the meadows and in the river. The fisherman, taking sight over the calm surface, discovers its snout projecting above the water, at the distance of many rods, and easily secures his prey through its unwill-

ingness to disturb the water by swimming hastily away, for, gradually drawing its head under, it remains resting on some limb or clump
of grass. Its eggs, which are buried at a distance from the water, in some soft place, as
a pigeon-bed, are frequently devoured by the
skunk. It will catch fish by daylight, as a
toad catches flies, and is said to emit a transparent fluid from its mouth to attract them.

Nature has taken more care than the fondest
parent for the education and refinement of her
children. Consider the silent influence which
flowers exert, no less upon the ditcher in the
meadow than the lady in the bower. When I
walk in the woods, I am reminded that a wise
purveyor has been there before me; my most
delicate experience is typified there. I am
struck with the pleasing friendships and unani-
mities of nature, as when the lichen on the trees
takes the form of their leaves. In the most
stupendous scenes you will see delicate and
fragile features, as slight wreaths of vapor, dew-
lines, feathery sprays, which suggest a high
refinement, a noble blood and breeding, as it
were. It is not hard to account for elves and
fairies; they represent this light grace, this
ethereal gentility. Bring a spray from the
wood, or a crystal from the brook, and place it
on your mantel, and your household ornaments

will seem plebeian beside its nobler fashion and bearing. It will wave superior there, as if used to a more refined and polished circle. It has a salute and a response to all your enthusiasm and heroism.

In the winter, I stop short in the path to admire how the trees grow up without forethought, regardless of the time and circumstances. They do not wait as man does, but now is the golden age of the sapling. Earth, air, sun, and rain are occasion enough; they were no better in primeval centuries. The "winter of *their* discontent" never comes. Witness the buds of the native poplar standing gayly out to the frost on the sides of its bare switches. They express a naked confidence. With cheerful heart one could be a sojourner in the wilderness, if he were sure to find there the catkins of the willow or the alder. When I read of them in the accounts of northern adventurers, by Baffin's Bay or Mackenzie's River, I see how even there, too, I could dwell. They are our little vegetable redeemers. Methinks our virtue will hold out till they come again. They are worthy to have had a greater than Minerva or Ceres for their inventor. Who was the benignant goddess that bestowed them on mankind?

Nature is mythical and mystical always, and works with the license and extravagance of genius. She has her luxurious and florid style as well as art. Having a pilgrim's cup to make, she gives to the whole, stem, bowl, handle, and nose, some fantastic shape, as if it were to be the car of some fabulous marine deity, a Nereus or Triton.

In the winter, the botanist need not confine himself to his books and herbarium, and give over his out-door pursuits, but may study a new department of vegetable physiology, what may be called crystalline botany, then. The winter of 1837 was unusually favorable for this. In December of that year, the Genius of vegetation seemed to hover by night over its summer haunts with unusual persistency. Such a hoarfrost as is very uncommon here or anywhere, and whose full effects can never be witnessed after sunrise, occurred several times. As I went forth early on a still and frosty morning, the trees looked like airy creatures of darkness caught napping; on this side huddled together, with their gray hairs streaming, in a secluded valley which the sun had not penetrated; on that, hurrying off in Indian file along some water-course, while the shrubs and grasses, like elves and fairies of the night, sought to hide their diminished heads in the snow. The river, viewed from the high bank, appeared of a yellowish green color, though all the landscape was white. Every tree, shrub, and spire of grass, that could raise its head above the snow, was covered with a dense ice-foliage, answering, as it were, leaf for leaf to its summer dress. Even the fences had put forth leaves in the night. The centre, diverging, and more minute fibres were perfectly distinct, and the edges regularly indented. These leaves were on the side of the twig or stubble opposite to the sun, meeting it for the most part at right angles, and there were others standing out at all possible angles upon these and upon one another, with no twig or stubble supporting them. When the first rays of the sun slanted over the scene, the grasses seemed hung with innumerable jewels, which jingled merrily as they were brushed by the foot of the traveler, and reflected all the hues of the rainbow, as he moved from side to side. It struck me that these ghost leaves, and the green ones whose forms they assume, were the creatures of but one law; that in obedience to the same law the vegetable juices swell gradually into the perfect leaf, on the one hand, and the crystalline particles troop to their standard in the same order, on the other. As if the material were indifferent, but the law one and invariable, and every plant in the spring but pushed up into and filled a permanent and eternal mould, which, summer and winter forever, is waiting to be filled.

This foliate structure is common to the coral and the plumage of birds, and to how large a part of animate and inanimate nature. The same independence of law on matter is observable in many other instances, as in the natural rhymes, when some animal form, color, or odor has its counterpart in some vegetable. As, indeed, all rhymes imply an eternal melody, independent of any particular sense.

As confirmation of the fact, that vegetation is but a kind of crystallization, every one may observe how, upon the edge of the melting frost on the window, the needle-shaped particles are bundled together so as to resemble fields waving with grain, or shocks rising here and there from the stubble; on one side the vegetation of the torrid zone, high-towering palms and wide-spread banyans, such as are seen in pictures of oriental scenery; on the other, arctic pines stiff frozen, with downcast branches.

Vegetation has been made the type of all growth; but as in crystals the law is more obvious, their material being more simple, and for the most part more transient and fleeting, would it not be as philosophical as convenient to consider all growth, all filling up within the limits of nature, but a crystallization more or less rapid?

On this occasion, in the side of the high bank

of the river, wherever the water or other cause had formed a cavity, its throat and outer edge, like the entrance to a citadel, bristled with a glistening ice-armor. In one place you might see minute ostrich-feathers, which seemed the waving plumes of the warriors filing into the fortress; in another, the glancing, fan-shaped banners of the Lilliputian host; and in another, the needle-shaped particles collected into bundles, resembling the plumes of the pine, might pass for a phalanx of spears. From the under side of the ice in the brooks, where there was a thicker ice below, depended a mass of crystallization, four or five inches deep, in the form of prisms, with their lower ends open, which, when the ice was laid on its smooth side, resembled the roofs and steeples of a Gothic city, or the vessels of a crowded haven under a press of canvas. The very mud in the road, where the ice had melted, was crystallized with deep rectilinear fissures, and the crystalline masses in the sides of the ruts resembled exactly asbestos in the disposition of their needles. Around the roots of the stubble and flower-stalks, the frost was gathered into the form of irregular conical shells, or fairy rings. In some places the ice crystals were lying upon granite rocks, directly over crystals of quartz, the frost-work of a longer night, crystals of a longer period; but, to some eye unprejudiced by

the short term of human life, melting as fast as
the former.

In the Report on the Invertebrate Animals,
this singular fact is recorded, which teaches us
to put a new value on time and space: "The
distribution of the marine shells is well worthy
of notice as a geological fact. Cape Cod, the
right arm of the Commonwealth, reaches out into
the ocean, some fifty or sixty miles. It is nowhere many miles wide; but this narrow point
of land has hitherto proved a barrier to the migrations of many species of Mollusca. Several
genera and numerous species, which are separated by the intervention of only a few miles of
land, are effectually prevented from mingling
by the Cape, and do not pass from one side to
the other. . . . Of the one hundred and ninety-
seven marine species, eighty-three do not pass
to the south shore, and fifty are not found on the
north shore of the Cape."

That common mussel, the *Unio complanatus*,
or more properly *fluviatilis*, left in the spring by
the musk-rat upon rocks and stumps, appears
to have been an important article of food with
the Indians. In one place, where they are said
to have feasted, they are found in large quantities, at an elevation of thirty feet above the
river, filling the soil to the depth of a foot, and
mingled with ashes and Indian remains.

The works we have placed at the head of our chapter, with as much license as the preacher selects his text, are such as imply more labor than enthusiasm. The State wanted complete catalogues of its natural riches, with such additional facts merely as would be directly useful.

The reports on Fishes, Reptiles, Insects, and Invertebrate Animals, however, indicate labor and research, and have a value independent of the object of the legislature.

Those on Herbaceous Plants and Birds cannot be of much value, as long as Bigelow and Nuttall are accessible. They serve but to indicate, with more or less exactness, what species are found in the State. We detect several errors ourselves, and a more practiced eye would no doubt expand the list.

The Quadrupeds deserved a more final and instructive report than they have obtained.

These volumes deal much in measurements and minute descriptions, not interesting to the general reader, with only here and there a colored sentence to allure him, like those plants growing in dark forests, which bear only leaves without blossoms. But the ground was comparatively unbroken, and we will not complain of the pioneer, if he raises no flowers with his first crop. Let us not underrate the value of a fact; it will one day flower in a truth. It is aston-

ishing how few facts of importance are added in
a century to the natural history of any animal.
The natural history of man himself is still being
gradually written. Men are knowing enough
after their fashion. Every countryman and
dairy-maid knows that the coats of the fourth
stomach of the calf will curdle milk, and what
particular mushroom is a safe and nutritious
diet. You cannot go into any field or wood, but
it will seem as if every stone had been turned,
and the bark on every tree ripped up. But,
after all, it is much easier to discover than to
see when the cover is off. It has been well said
that "the attitude of inspection is prone." Wisdom does not inspect, but behold. We must look
a long time before we can see. Slow are the
beginnings of philosophy. He has something
demoniacal in him, who can discern a law or
couple two facts. We can imagine a time
when "Water runs down hill" may have been
taught in the schools. The true man of science
will know nature better by his finer organiza-
tion; he will smell, taste, see, hear, feel, better
than other men. His will be a deeper and finer
experience. We do not learn by inference and
deduction and the application of mathematics to
philosophy, but by direct intercourse and sympathy. It is with science as with ethics, — we
cannot know truth by contrivance and method;

the Baconian is as false as any other, and with all the helps of machinery and the arts, the most scientific will still be the healthiest and friendliest man, and possess a more perfect Indian wisdom.

A WALK TO WACHUSETT

The needles of the pine
All to the west incline.

CONCORD, *July* 19, 1842.

SUMMER and winter our eyes had rested on
the dim outline of the mountains in our horizon, to which distance and indistinctness lent a
grandeur not their own, so that they served
equally to interpret all the allusions of poets
and travelers; whether with Homer, on a spring
morning, we sat down on the many-peaked
Olympus, or with Virgil and his compeers
roamed the Etrurian and Thessalian hills, or
with Humboldt measured the more modern
Andes and Teneriffe. Thus we spoke our mind
to them, standing on the Concord cliffs: —

With frontier strength ye stand your ground,
With grand content ye circle round,
Tumultuous silence for all sound,
Ye distant nursery of rills,
Monadnock, and the Peterboro' hills;
Like some vast fleet,
Sailing through rain and sleet,
Through winter's cold and summer's heat;
Still holding on, upon your high emprise,
Until ye find a shore amid the skies;

Not skulking close to land,
With cargo contraband,
For they who sent a venture out by ye
Have set the sun to see
Their honesty.
Ships of the line, each one,
Ye to the westward run,
Always before the gale,
Under a press of sail,
With weight of metal all untold.
I seem to feel ye, in my firm seat here,
Immeasurable depth of hold,
And breadth of beam, and length of running gear.

Methinks ye take luxurious pleasure
In your novel western leisure;
So cool your brows, and freshly blue,
As Time had nought for ye to do;
For ye lie at your length,
An unappropriated strength,
Unhewn primeval timber,
For knees so stiff, for masts so limber;
The stock of which new earths are made,
One day to be our western trade,
Fit for the stanchions of a world
Which through the seas of space is hurled.

While we enjoy a lingering ray,
Ye still o'ertop the western day,
Reposing yonder, on God's croft,
Like solid stacks of hay.
Edged with silver, and with gold,
The clouds hang o'er in damask fold,
And with such depth of amber light
The west is dight,
Where still a few rays slant,
That even heaven seems extravagant.

On the earth's edge mountains and trees
Stand as they were on air graven,
Or as the vessels in a haven
Await the morning breeze.
I fancy even
Through your defiles windeth the way to heaven;
And yonder still, in spite of history's page,
Linger the golden and the silver age;
Upon the laboring gale
The news of future centuries is brought,
And of new dynasties of thought,
From your remotest vale.

But special I remember thee,
Wachusett, who like me
Standest alone without society.
Thy far blue eye,
A remnant of the sky,
Seen through the clearing or the gorge
Or from the windows on the forge,
Doth leaven all it passes by.
Nothing is true,
But stands 'tween me and you,
Thou western pioneer,
Who know'st not shame nor fear,
By venturous spirit driven,
Under the eaves of heaven,
And can'st expand thee there,
And breathe enough of air?
Upholding heaven, holding down earth,
Thy pastime from thy birth,
Not steadied by the one, nor leaning on the other;
May I approve myself thy worthy brother!

At length, like Rasselas, and other inhabitants of happy valleys, we resolved to scale the
blue wall which bound the western horizon,

though not without misgivings that thereafter
no visible fairyland would exist for us. But
we will not leap at once to our journey's end,
though near, but imitate Homer, who conducts
his reader over the plain, and along the re-
sounding sea, though it be but to the tent of
Achilles. In the spaces of thought are the
reaches of land and water, where men go and
come. The landscape lies far and fair within,
and the deepest thinker is the farthest traveled.

At a cool and early hour on a pleasant morning in July, my companion and I passed rapidly
through Acton and Stow, stopping to rest and
refresh us on the bank of a small stream, a tributary of the Assabet, in the latter town. As
we traversed the cool woods of Acton, with
stout staves in our hands, we were cheered by
the song of the red-eye, the thrushes, the
phœbe, and the cuckoo; and as we passed
through the open country, we inhaled the fresh
scent of every field, and all nature lay passive,
to be viewed and traveled. Every rail, every
farm-house, seen dimly in the twilight, every
tinkling sound told of peace and purity, and we
moved happily along the dank roads, enjoying
not such privacy as the day leaves when it withdraws, but such as it has not profaned. It was
solitude with light; which is better than darkness. But anon, the sound of the mower's rifle

was heard in the fields, and this, too, mingled with the lowing of kine.

This part of our route lay through the country of hops, which plant perhaps supplies the want of the vine in American scenery, and may remind the traveler of Italy and the South of France, whether he traverses the country when the hop-fields, as then, present solid and regular masses of verdure, hanging in graceful festoons from pole to pole, the cool coverts where lurk the gales which refresh the wayfarer; or in September, when the women and children, and the neighbors from far and near, are gathered to pick the hops into long troughs; or later still, when the poles stand piled in vast pyramids in the yards, or lie in heaps by the roadside.

The culture of the hop, with the processes of picking, drying in the kiln, and packing for the market, as well as the uses to which it is applied, so analogous to the culture and uses of the grape, may afford a theme for future poets.

The mower in the adjacent meadow could not tell us the name of the brook on whose banks we had rested, or whether it had any, but his younger companion, perhaps his brother, knew that it was Great Brook. Though they stood very near together in the field, the things they knew were very far apart; nor did they suspect each other's reserved knowledge, till the

stranger came by. In Bolton, while we rested
on the rails of a cottage fence, the strains of
music which issued from within, probably in
compliment to us, sojourners, reminded us that
thus far men were fed by the accustomed pleasures. So soon did we, wayfarers, begin to
learn that man's life is rounded with the same
few facts, the same simple relations everywhere,
and it is vain to travel to find it new. The
flowers grow more various ways than he. But
coming soon to higher land, which afforded a
prospect of the mountains, we thought we had
not traveled in vain, if it were only to hear a
truer and wilder pronunciation of their names
from the lips of the inhabitants; not *Way*-tatic,
Way-chusett, but *Wor*-tatic, *Wor*-chusett. It
made us ashamed of our tame and civil pronunciation, and we looked upon them as born and
bred farther west than we. Their tongues had
a more generous accent than ours, as if breath
was cheaper where they wagged. A countryman, who speaks but seldom, talks copiously,
as it were, as his wife sets cream and cheese
before you without stint. Before noon we had
reached the highlands overlooking the valley of
Lancaster (affording the first fair and open
prospect into the west), and there, on the top of
a hill, in the shade of some oaks, near to where
a spring bubbled out from a leaden pipe, we

rested during the heat of the day, reading Virgil and enjoying the scenery. It was such a place as one feels to be on the outside of the earth; for from it we could, in some measure, see the form and structure of the globe. There lay Wachusett, the object of our journey, lowering upon us with unchanged proportions, though with a less ethereal aspect than had greeted our morning gaze, while further north, in successive order, slumbered its sister mountains along the horizon.

We could get no further into the Æneid than

> — atque altæ mœnia Romæ,
> — and the wall of high Rome,

before we were constrained to reflect by what myriad tests a work of genius has to be tried; that Virgil, away in Rome, two thousand years off, should have to unfold his meaning, the inspiration of Italian vales, to the pilgrim on New England hills. This life so raw and modern, that so civil and ancient; and yet we read Virgil, mainly to be reminded of the identity of human nature in all ages, and, by the poet's own account, we are both the children of a late age, and live equally under the reign of Jupiter.

> "He shook honey from the leaves, and removed fire,
> And stayed the wine, everywhere flowing in rivers;
> That experience, by meditating, might invent various arts
> By degrees, and seek the blade of corn in furrows,
> And strike out hidden fire from the veins of the flint."

The old world stands serenely behind the new, as one mountain yonder towers behind another, more dim and distant. Rome imposes her story still upon this late generation. The very children in the school we had that morning passed had gone through her wars, and recited her alarms, ere they had heard of the wars of neighboring Lancaster. The roving eye still rests inevitably on her hills, and she still holds up the skirts of the sky on that side, and makes the past remote.

The lay of the land hereabouts is well worthy the attention of the traveler. The hill on which we were resting made part of an extensive range, running from southwest to northeast, across the country, and separating the waters of the Nashua from those of the Concord, whose banks we had left in the morning, and by bearing in mind this fact, we could easily determine whither each brook was bound that crossed our path. Parallel to this, and fifteen miles further west, beyond the deep and broad valley in which lie Groton, Shirley, Lancaster, and Boylston, runs the Wachusett range, in the same general direction. The descent into the valley on the Nashua side is by far the most sudden; and a couple of miles brought us to the southern branch of the Nashua, a shallow but rapid stream, flowing between high and gravelly banks. But we soon learned that there were no *gelidæ valles* into which we had descended, and, missing the coolness of the morning air, feared it had become the sun's turn to try his power upon us.

> " The sultry sun had gained the middle sky,
>   And not a tree, and not an herb was nigh,"

and with melancholy pleasure we echoed the melodious plaint of our fellow-traveler, Hassan, in the desert, —

> " Sad was the hour, and luckless was the day,
>   When first from Schiraz' walls I bent my way."

The air lay lifeless between the hills, as in a seething caldron, with no leaf stirring, and instead of the fresh odor of grass and clover, with which we had before been regaled, the dry scent of every herb seemed merely medicinal. Yielding, therefore, to the heat, we strolled into the woods, and along the course of a rivulet, on whose banks we loitered, observing at our leisure the products of these new fields. He who traverses the woodland paths, at this season, will have occasion to remember the small, drooping, bell-like flowers and slender red stem of the dogsbane, and the coarser stem and berry of the poke, which are both common in remoter and wilder scenes; and if "the sun casts such a reflecting heat from the sweet-fern" as makes him faint, when he is climbing the bare hills, as they complained who first penetrated into these parts, the cool fragrance of the swamp pink restores him again, when traversing the valleys between.

As we went on our way late in the afternoon, we refreshed ourselves by bathing our feet in every rill that crossed the road, and anon, as we were able to walk in the shadows of the hills, recovered our morning elasticity. Passing through Sterling, we reached the banks of the Stillwater, in the western part of the town, at evening, where is a small village collected. We fancied that there was already a certain western look about this place, a smell of pines and roar of water, recently confined by dams, belying its name, which were exceedingly grateful. When the first inroad has been made, a few acres leveled, and a few houses erected, the forest looks wilder than ever. Left to herself, nature is always more or less civilized, and delights in a certain refinement; but where the axe has encroached upon the edge of the forest, the dead and unsightly limbs of the pine, which she had concealed with green banks of verdure, are exposed to sight. This village had, as yet, no post-office, nor any settled name. In the small villages which we entered, the villagers gazed after us, with a complacent, almost compassionate look, as if we were just making our *début* in the world at a late hour. "Nevertheless," did they seem to say, "come and study us, and learn men and manners." So is each one's world but a clearing in the forest, so much open and inclosed ground. The landlord had not yet returned from the field with his men, and the cows had yet to be milked. But we remembered the inscription on the wall of the Swedish inn, "You will find at Trolhate excellent bread, meat, and wine, provided you bring them with you," and were contented. But I must confess it did somewhat disturb our pleasure, in this withdrawn spot, to have our own village newspaper handed us by our host, as if the greatest charm the country offered to the traveler was the facility of communication with the town. Let it recline on its own everlasting hills, and not be looking out from their summits for some petty Boston or New York in the horizon.

At intervals we heard the murmuring of water, and the slumberous breathing of crickets, throughout the night; and left the inn the next morning in the gray twilight, after it had been hallowed by the night air, and when only the innocent cows were stirring, with a kind of regret. It was only four miles to the base of the mountain, and the scenery was already more

picturesque.   Our road lay along the course of
the Stillwater, which was brawling at the bottom of a deep ravine, filled with pines and
rocks, tumbling fresh from the mountains, so
soon, alas! to commence its career of useful-
ness.   At first, a cloud hung between us and
the summit, but it was soon blown away.   As
we gathered the raspberries, which grew abundantly by the roadside, we fancied that that
action was consistent with a lofty prudence; as
if the traveler who ascends into a mountainous
region should fortify himself by eating of such
light ambrosial fruits as grow there, and drinking of the springs which gush out from the
mountain sides, as he gradually inhales the
subtler and purer atmosphere of those elevated
places, thus propitiating the mountain gods by
a sacrifice of their own fruits.   The gross products of the plains and valleys are for such as
dwell therein; but it seemed to us that the juices
of this berry had relation to the thin air of the
mountain-tops.

In due time we began to ascend the mountain, passing, first, through a grand sugar-maple wood, which bore the marks of the auger,
then a denser forest, which gradually became
dwarfed, till there were no trees whatever.   We
at length pitched our tent on the summit.   It is
but nineteen hundred feet above the village of

Princeton, and three thousand above the level
of the sea; but by this slight elevation it is infinitely removed from the plain, and when we
reached it we felt a sense of remoteness, as if
we had traveled into distant regions, to Arabia
Petræa, or the farthest east. A robin upon a
staff was the highest object in sight. Swallows
were flying about us, and the chewink and
cuckoo were heard near at hand. The summit
consists of a few acres, destitute of trees, covered with bare rocks, interspersed with blueberry bushes, raspberries, gooseberries, straw-
berries, moss, and a fine wiry grass. The
common yellow lily and dwarf - cornel grow
abundantly in the crevices of the rocks. This
clear space, which is gently rounded, is bounded
a few feet lower by a thick shrubbery of oaks,
with maples, aspens, beeches, cherries, and occasionally a mountain-ash intermingled, among
which we found the bright blue berries of the
Solomon's seal, and the fruit of the pyrola.
From the foundation of a wooden observatory,
which was formerly erected on the highest
point, forming a rude, hollow structure of stone,
a dozen feet in diameter, and five or six in
height, we could see Monadnock, in simple
grandeur, in the northwest, rising nearly a thousand feet higher, still the "far blue mountain,"
though with an altered profile. The first day

the weather was so hazy that it was in vain we endeavored to unravel the obscurity. It was like looking into the sky again, and the patches of forest here and there seemed to flit like clouds over a lower heaven. As to voyagers of an aërial Polynesia, the earth seemed like a larger island in the ether; on every side, even as low as we, the sky shutting down, like an unfathomable deep, around it, a blue Pacific island, where who knows what islanders inhabit? and as we sail near its shores we see the waving of trees and hear the lowing of kine.

We read Virgil and Wordsworth in our tent, with new pleasure there, while waiting for a clearer atmosphere, nor did the weather prevent our appreciating the simple truth and beauty of Peter Bell : —

> " And he had lain beside his asses,
>   On lofty Cheviot hills ;

> " And he had trudged through Yorkshire dales,
>   Among the rocks and winding *scars*,
>   Where deep and low the hamlets lie
>   Beneath their little patch of sky,
>   And little lot of stars."

Who knows but this hill may one day be a Helvellyn, or even a Parnassus, and the Muses haunt here, and other Homers frequent the neighboring plains ?

> Not unconcerned Wachusett rears his head
>   Above the field, so late from nature won,
> With patient brow reserved, as one who read
>   New annals in the history of man.

The blueberries which the mountain afforded, added to the milk we had brought, made our frugal supper, while for entertainment the even-song of the wood-thrush rang along the ridge. Our eyes rested on no painted ceiling nor car-peted hall, but on skies of nature's painting, and hills and forests of her embroidery. Before sunset, we rambled along the ridge to the north, while a hawk soared still above us. It was a place where gods might wander, so solemn and solitary, and removed from all contagion with the plain. As the evening came on, the haze was condensed in vapor, and the landscape be-came more distinctly visible, and numerous sheets of water were brought to light.

> Et jam summa procul villarum culmina fumant,
> Majoresque cadunt altis de montibus umbræ.

> And now the tops of the villas smoke afar off,
> And the shadows fall longer from the high mountains.

As we stood on the stone tower while the sun was setting, we saw the shades of night creep gradually over the valleys of the east, and the inhabitants went into their houses, and shut their doors, while the moon silently rose up, and took possession of that part. And then the same scene was repeated on the west side, as far as the Connecticut and the Green Mountains, and the sun's rays fell on us two alone, of all New England men.

It was the night but one before the full of the moon, so bright that we could see to read distinctly by moonlight, and in the evening strolled over the summit without danger. There was, by chance, a fire blazing on Monadnock that night, which lighted up the whole western horizon, and, by making us aware of a community of mountains, made our position seem less solitary. But at length the wind drove us to the shelter of our tent, and we closed its door for the night, and fell asleep.

It was thrilling to hear the wind roar over the rocks, at intervals when we waked, for it had grown quite cold and windy. The night was in its elements, simple even to majesty in that bleak place, — a bright moonlight and a piercing wind. It was at no time darker than twilight within the tent, and we could easily see the moon through its transparent roof as we lay; for there was the moon still above us, with Jupiter and Saturn on either hand, looking down on Wachusett, and it was a satisfaction to know that they were our fellow-travelers still, as high and out of our reach as our own destiny. Truly the stars were given for a consolation to man. We should not know but our life were fated to be always groveling, but it is permitted to behold them, and surely they are deserving of a fair destiny. We see laws which never fail, of whose failure we never conceived; and their lamps burn all the night, too, as well as all day, — so rich and lavish is that nature which can afford this superfluity of light.

The morning twilight began as soon as the moon had set, and we arose and kindled our fire, whose blaze might have been seen for thirty miles around. As the daylight increased, it was remarkable how rapidly the wind went down. There was no dew on the summit, but coldness supplied its place. When the dawn had reached its prime, we enjoyed the view of a distinct horizon line, and could fancy ourselves at sea, and the distant hills the waves in the horizon, as seen from the deck of a vessel. The cherry-birds flitted around us, the nuthatch and flicker were heard among the bushes, the titmouse perched within a few feet, and the song of the wood-thrush again rang along the ridge. At length we saw the sun rise up out of the sea, and shine on Massachusetts; and from this moment the atmosphere grew more and more transparent till the time of our departure, and we began to realize the extent of the view, and how the earth, in some degree, answered to the heavens in breadth, the white villages to the constellations in the sky. There was little of the sublimity and grandeur which belong to mountain scenery, but an immense landscape to pon-

der on a summer's day. We could see how
ample and roomy is nature. As far as the eye
could reach there was little life in the landscape;
the few birds that flitted past did not crowd.
The travelers on the remote highways, which in-
tersect the country on every side, had no fellow-
travelers for miles, before or behind. On
every side, the eye ranged over successive circles
of towns, rising one above another, like the terraces of a vineyard, till they were lost in the
horizon. Wachusett is, in fact, the observatory
of the State. There lay Massachusetts, spread
out before us in its length and breadth, like a
map. There was the level horizon, which told
of the sea on the east and south, the well-known
hills of New Hampshire on the north, and the
misty summits of the Hoosac and Green Mountains, first made visible to us the evening before, blue and unsubstantial, like some bank of
clouds which the morning wind would dissipate,
on the northwest and west. These last distant
ranges on which the eye rests unwearied, commence with an abrupt bowlder in the north,
beyond the Connecticut, and travel southward,
with three or four peaks dimly seen. But Monadnock, rearing its masculine front in the northwest, is the grandest feature. As we beheld it,
we knew that it was the height of land between
the two rivers, on this side the valley of the

Merrimack, on that of the Connecticut, fluctuating with their blue seas of air, — these rival vales, already teeming with Yankee men along their respective streams, born to what destiny who shall tell? Watatic and the neighboring hills, in this State and in New Hampshire, are a continuation of the same elevated range on which we were standing. But that New Hampshire bluff, — that promontory of a State, — lowering day and night on this our State of Massachusetts, will longest haunt our dreams.

We could at length realize the place mountains occupy on the land, and how they come into the general scheme of the universe. When first we climb their summits and observe their lesser irregularities, we do not give credit to the comprehensive intelligence which shaped them; but when afterward we behold their outlines in the horizon, we confess that the hand which moulded their opposite slopes, making one to balance the other, worked round a deep centre, and was privy to the plan of the universe. So is the least part of nature in its bearings referred to all space. These lesser mountain ranges, as well as the Alleghanies, run from northeast to southwest, and parallel with these mountain streams are the more fluent rivers, answering to the general direction of the coast, the bank of the great ocean stream itself. Even the clouds, with their thin bars, fall into the same direction by preference, and such even is the course of the prevailing winds, and the migration of men and birds. A mountain-chain determines many things for the statesman and philosopher. The improvements of civilization rather creep along its sides than cross its summit. How often is it a barrier to prejudice and fanaticism? In passing over these heights of land, through their thin atmosphere, the follies of the plain are refined and purified; and as many species of plants do not scale their summits, so many species of folly no doubt do not cross the Alleghanies; it is only the hardy mountain-plant that creeps quite over the ridge, and descends into the valley beyond.

We get a dim notion of the flight of birds, especially of such as fly high in the air, by having ascended a mountain. We can now see what landmarks mountains are to their migrations; how the Catskills and Highlands have hardly sunk to them, when Wachusett and Monadnock open a passage to the northeast; how they are guided, too, in their course by the rivers and valleys; and who knows but by the stars, as well as the mountain ranges, and not by the petty landmarks which we use. The bird whose eye takes in the Green Mountains on the one side, and the ocean on the other, need not be at a loss to find its way.

At noon we descended the mountain, and, having returned to the abodes of men, turned our faces to the east again; measuring our progress, from time to time, by the more ethereal hues which the mountain assumed. Passing swiftly through Stillwater and Sterling, as with a downward impetus, we found ourselves almost at home again in the green meadows of Lancaster, so like our own Concord, for both are watered by two streams which unite near their centres, and have many other features in common. There is an unexpected refinement about this scenery; level prairies of great extent, interspersed with elms and hop-fields and groves of trees, give it almost a classic appearance. This, it will be remembered, was the scene of Mrs. Rowlandson's capture, and of other events in the Indian wars, but from this July afternoon, and under that mild exterior, those times seemed as remote as the irruption of the Goths. They were the dark age of New England. On beholding a picture of a New England village as it then appeared, with a fair open prospect, and a light on trees and river, as if it were broad noon, we find we had not thought the sun shone in those days, or that men lived in broad daylight then. We do not imagine the sun shining on hill and valley during Philip's war, nor on the war-path of Paugus, or Standish, or Church, or Lovell, with serene summer weather, but a dim twilight or night did those events transpire in.   They must have fought in the shade of their own dusky deeds.

At length, as we plodded along the dusty roads, our thoughts became as dusty as they; all thought indeed stopped, thinking broke down, or proceeded only passively in a sort of rhythmical cadence of the confused material of thought, and we found ourselves mechanically repeating some familiar measure which timed with our tread; some verse of the Robin Hood ballads, for instance, which one can recommend to travel by: —

> " Sweavens are swift, sayd lyttle John,
>   As the wind blows over the hill;
> For if it be never so loud this night,
>   To-morrow it may be still."

And so it went up hill and down till a stone interrupted the line, when a new verse was chosen: —

> " His shoote it was but loosely shot,
>   Yet flewe not the arrowe in vaine,
> For it met one of the sheriffe's men,
>   And William-a-Trent was slaine."

There is, however, this consolation to the most wayworn traveler, upon the dustiest road, that the path his feet describe is so perfectly symbolical of human life, — now climbing the hills, now descending into the vales. From the summits he beholds the heavens and the horizon, from the vales he looks up to the heights again. He is treading his old lessons still, and though he may be very weary and travel-worn, it is yet sincere experience.

Leaving the Nashua, we changed our route a little, and arrived at Stillriver Village, in the western part of Harvard, just as the sun was setting. From this place, which lies to the northward, upon the western slope of the same range of hills on which we had spent the noon before, in the adjacent town, the prospect is beautiful, and the grandeur of the mountain outlines unsurpassed. There was such a repose and quiet here at this hour, as if the very hill-sides were enjoying the scene, and as we passed slowly along, looking back over the country we had traversed, and listening to the evening song of the robin, we could not help contrasting the equanimity of nature with the bustle and impatience of man. His words and actions presume always a crisis near at hand, but she is forever silent and unpretending.

And now that we have returned to the desultory life of the plain, let us endeavor to import a little of that mountain grandeur into it. We will remember within what walls we lie, and understand that this level life too has its sum-

mit, and why from the mountain-top the deepest
valleys have a tinge of blue; that there is elevation in every hour, as no part of the earth is
so low that the heavens may not be seen from,
and we have only to stand on the summit of our
hour to command an uninterrupted horizon.

We rested that night at Harvard, and the
next morning, while one bent his steps to the
nearer village of Groton, the other took his separate and solitary way to the peaceful meadows
of Concord; but let him not forget to record
the brave hospitality of a farmer and his wife,
who generously entertained him at their board,
though the poor wayfarer could only congratu-
late the one on the continuance of hay weather,
and silently accept the kindness of the other.
Refreshed by this instance of generosity, no
less than by the substantial viands set before
him, he pushed forward with new vigor, and
reached the banks of the Concord before the sun
had climbed many degrees into the heavens.

THE LANDLORD

UNDER the one word "house" are included the school-house, the alms-house, the jail, the tavern, the dwelling-house; and the meanest shed or cave in which men live contains the elements of all these. But nowhere on the earth stands the entire and perfect house. The Parthenon, St. Peter's, the Gothic minster, the palace, the hovel, are but imperfect executions of an imperfect idea. Who would dwell in them? Perhaps to the eye of the gods the cottage is more holy than the Parthenon, for they look down with no especial favor upon the shrines formally dedicated to them, and that should be the most sacred roof which shelters most of humanity. Surely, then, the gods who are most interested in the human race preside over the Tavern, where especially men congregate. Methinks I see the thousand shrines erected to Hospitality shining afar in all countries, as well Mahometan and Jewish, as Christian, khans and caravansaries and inns, whither all pilgrims without distinction resort.

Likewise we look in vain, east or west over

the earth, to find the perfect man; but each
represents only some particular excellence.
The Landlord is a man of more open and general sympathies, who possesses a spirit of hospitality which is its own reward, and feeds and
shelters men from pure love of the creatures.
To be sure, this profession is as often filled by
imperfect characters, and such as have sought
it from unworthy motives, as any other, but so
much the more should we prize the true and
honest Landlord when we meet with him.

Who has not imagined to himself a country
inn, where the traveler shall really feel *in*, and
at home, and at his public-house, who was before at his private house; whose host is indeed
a *host*, and a *lord* of the *land*, a self-appointed
brother of his race; called to his place, beside,
by all the winds of heaven and his good genius,
as truly as the preacher is called to preach; a
man of such universal sympathies, and so broad
and genial a human nature, that he would fain
sacrifice the tender but narrow ties of private
friendship, to a broad, sunshiny, fair-weather-
and-foul friendship for his race; who loves men,
not as a philosopher, with philanthropy, nor as
an overseer of the poor, with charity, but by a
necessity of his nature, as he loves dogs and
horses; and standing at his open door from
morning till night would fain see more and more

of them come along the highway, and is never
satiated. To him the sun and moon are but
travelers, the one by day and the other by night;
and they too patronize his house. To his imagination all things travel save his sign-post
and himself; and though you may be his neighbor for years, he will show you only the civilities of the road. But on the other hand, while
nations and individuals are alike selfish and
exclusive, he loves all men equally; and if he
treats his nearest neighbor as a stranger, since
he has invited all nations to share his hospitality, the farthest traveled is in some measure
kindred to him who takes him into the bosom of
his family.

He keeps a house of entertainment at the sign
of the Black Horse or the Spread Eagle, and is
known far and wide, and his fame travels with
increasing radius every year. All the neighborhood is in his interest, and if the traveler
ask how far to a tavern, he receives some such
answer as this: "Well, sir, there's a house
about three miles from here, where they haven't
taken down their sign yet; but it's only ten
miles to Slocum's, and that's a capital house,
both for man and beast." At three miles he
passes a cheerless barrack, standing desolate
behind its sign-post, neither public nor private,
and has glimpses of a discontented couple who

have mistaken their calling. At ten miles see where the Tavern stands, — really an *entertaining* prospect, — so public and inviting that only the rain and snow do not enter. It is no gay pavilion, made of bright stuffs, and furnished with nuts and gingerbread, but as plain and sincere as a caravansary; located in no Tarrytown, where you receive only the civilities of commerce, but far in the fields it exercises a primitive hospitality, amid the fresh scent of new hay and raspberries, if it be summer time, and the tinkling of cow-bells from invisible pastures; for it is a land flowing with milk and honey, and the newest milk courses in a broad, deep stream across the premises.

In these retired places the tavern is first of all a house, — elsewhere, last of all, or never, — and warms and shelters its inhabitants. It is as simple and sincere in its essentials as the caves in which the first men dwelt, but it is also as open and public. The traveler steps across the threshold, and lo! he too is master, for he only can be called proprietor of the house here who behaves with most propriety in it. The Landlord stands clear back in nature, to my imagination, with his axe and spade felling trees and raising potatoes with the vigor of a pioneer; with Promethean energy making nature yield her increase to supply the wants of

so many; and he is not so exhausted, nor of so
short a stride, but that he comes forward even
to the highway to this wide hospitality and pub-
licity. Surely, he has solved some of the prob-
lems of life. He comes in at his back door,
holding a log fresh cut for the hearth upon his
shoulder with one hand, while he greets the
newly arrived traveler with the other.

Here at length we have free range, as not in
palaces, nor cottages, nor temples, and intrude
nowhere. All the secrets of housekeeping are
exhibited to the eyes of men, above and below,
before and behind. This is the necessary way
to live, men have confessed, in these days, and
shall he skulk and hide? And why should we
have any serious disgust at kitchens? Perhaps
they are the holiest recess of the house. There
is the hearth, after all, — and the settle, and
the fagots, and the kettle, and the crickets.
We have pleasant reminiscences of these. They
are the heart, the left ventricle, the very vital
part of the house. Here the real and sincere
life which we meet in the streets was actually
fed and sheltered. Here burns the taper that
cheers the lonely traveler by night, and from
this hearth ascend the smokes that populate the
valley to his eyes by day. On the whole, a
man may not be so little ashamed of any other
part of his house, for here is his sincerity and

earnest, at least. It may not be here that the
besoms are plied most, — it is not here that they
need to be, for dust will not settle on the kitchen
floor more than in nature.

Hence it will not do for the Landlord to possess too fine a nature. He must have health
above the common accidents of life, subject to
no modern fashionable diseases; but no taste,
rather a vast relish or appetite. His sentiments
on all subjects will be delivered as freely as the
wind blows; there is nothing private or individual in them, though still original, but they are
public, and of the hue of the heavens over his
house, — a certain out-of-door obviousness and
transparency not to be disputed. What he
does, his manners are not to be complained of,
though abstractly offensive, for it is what man
does, and in him the race is exhibited. When
he eats, he is liver and bowels and the whole
digestive apparatus to the company, and so all
admit the thing is done. He must have no
idiosyncrasies, no particular bents or tendencies
to this or that, but a general, uniform, and
healthy development, such as his portly person
indicates, offering himself equally on all sides
to men. He is not one of your peaked and in-
hospitable men of genius, with particular tastes,
but, as we said before, has one uniform relish,
and taste which never aspires higher than a

tavern-sign, or the cut of a weather-cock. The man of genius, like a dog with a bone, or the slave who has swallowed a diamond, or a patient with the gravel, sits afar and retired, off the road, hangs out no sign of refreshment for man and beast, but says, by all possible hints and signs, I wish to be alone, — good-by, — farewell. But the Landlord can afford to live without privacy. He entertains no private thought, he cherishes no solitary hour, no Sabbath-day, but thinks, — enough to assert the dignity of reason, — and talks, and reads the newspaper. What he does not tell to one traveler he tells to another. He never wants to be alone, but sleeps, wakes, eats, drinks, sociably, still remembering his race. He walks abroad through the thoughts of men, and the Iliad and Shakespeare are tame to him, who hears the rude but homely incidents of the road from every traveler. The mail might drive through his brain in the midst of his most lonely soliloquy, without disturbing his equanimity, provided it brought plenty of news and passengers. There can be no *pro*-fanity where there is no fane behind, and the whole world may see quite round him. Per-chance his lines have fallen to him in dustier places, and he has heroically sat down where two roads meet, or at the Four Corners or the Five Points, and his life is sublimely trivial for

the good of men. The dust of travel blows
ever in his eyes, and they preserve their clear,
complacent look. The hourlies and half-hour-
lies, the dailies and weeklies, whirl on well-worn
tracks, round and round his house, as if it were
the goal in the stadium, and still he sits within
in unruffled serenity, with no show of retreat.
His neighbor dwells timidly behind a screen of
poplars and willows, and a fence with sheaves
of spears at regular intervals, or defended
against the tender palms of visitors by sharp
spikes, — but the traveler's wheels rattle over
the door-step of the tavern, and he cracks his
whip in the entry. He is truly glad to see you,
and sincere as the bull's-eye over his door.
The traveler seeks to find, wherever he goes,
some one who will stand in this broad and catholic relation to him, who will be an inhabitant
of the land to him a stranger, and represent its
human nature, as the rock stands for its inanimate nature; and this is he. As his crib furnishes provender for the traveler's horse, and
his larder provisions for his appetite, so his conversation furnishes the necessary aliment to his
spirits. He knows very well what a man wants,
for he is a man himself, and as it were the farthest traveled, though he has never stirred from
his door. He understands his needs and destiny. He would be well fed and lodged, there

can be no doubt, and have the transient sympathy of a cheerful companion, and of a heart which always prophesies fair weather. And after all the greatest men, even, want much more the sympathy which every honest fellow can give, than that which the great only can impart. If he is not the most upright, let us allow him this praise, that he is the most downright of men. He has a hand to shake and to be shaken, and takes a sturdy and unquestionable interest in you, as if he had assumed the care of you, but if you will break your neck, he will even give you the best advice as to the method.

The great poets have not been ungrateful to their landlords. Mine host of the Tabard Inn, in the Prologue to the Canterbury Tales, was an honor to his profession : —

> " A semely man our Hoste was, with alle,
> For to han been a marshal in an halle.
> A large man he was, with eyen stepe ;
> A fairer burgeis was ther non in Chepe :
> Bold of his speche, and wise, and well ytaught,
> And of manhood him lacked righte naught.
> Eke thereto was he right a mery man,
> And after souper plaien he began,
> And spake of mirthe amonges other thinges,
> Whan that we hadden made our reckoninges."

He is the true house-band, and centre of the company, — of greater fellowship and practical

social talent than any. He it is that proposes
that each shall tell a tale to while away the time
to Canterbury, and leads them himself, and
concludes with his own tale, —

> "Now, by my fader's soule that is ded,
>   But ye be mery, smiteth of my hed:
>   Hold up your hondes withouten more speche."

If we do not look up to the Landlord, we look
round for him on all emergencies, for he is a
man of infinite experience, who unites hands
with wit. He is a more public character than
a statesman, — a publican, and not consequently
a sinner; and surely, he, if any, should be ex-
empted from taxation and military duty.

Talking with our host is next best and instructive to talking with one's self. It is a
more conscious soliloquy; as it were, to speak
generally, and try what we would say provided
we had an audience. He has indulgent and
open ears, and does not require petty and particular statements. "Heigh-ho!" exclaims the
traveler. Them's my sentiments, thinks mine
host, and stands ready for what may come next,
expressing the purest sympathy by his demeanor. "Hot as blazes!" says the other.
"Hard weather, sir, — not much stirring nowadays," says he. He is wiser than to contradict
his guest in any case; he lets him go on; he
lets him travel.

The latest sitter leaves him standing far in the night, prepared to live right on, while suns rise and set, and his "good-night" has as brisk a sound as his "good-morning;" and the earliest riser finds him tasting his liquors in the bar ere flies begin to buzz, with a countenance fresh as the morning star over the sanded floor, — and not as one who had watched all night for travelers. And yet, if beds be the subject of conversation, it will appear that no man has been a sounder sleeper in his time.

Finally, as for his moral character, we do not hesitate to say that he has no grain of vice or meanness in him, but represents just that degree of virtue which all men relish without being obliged to respect. He is a good man, as his bitters are good, — an unquestionable goodness. Not what is called a good man, — good to be considered, as a work of art in galleries and museums, — but a good fellow, that is, good to be associated with. Who ever thought of the religion of an inn-keeper, — whether he was joined to the Church, partook of the sacrament, said his prayers, feared God, or the like? No doubt he has had his experiences, has felt a change, and is a firm believer in the perseverance of the saints. In this last, we suspect, does the peculiarity of his religion consist. But he keeps an inn, and not a conscience. How

many fragrant charities and sincere social virtues are implied in this daily offering of himself
to the public! He cherishes good-will to all,
and gives the wayfarer as good and honest advice to direct him on his road as the priest.

To conclude, the tavern will compare favorably with the church. The church is the place
where prayers and sermons are delivered, but
the tavern is where they are to take effect, and
if the former are good, the latter cannot be
bad.

A WINTER WALK

THE wind has gently murmured through the blinds, or puffed with feathery softness against the windows, and occasionally sighed like a summer zephyr lifting the leaves along, the livelong night. The meadow-mouse has slept in his snug gallery in the sod, the owl has sat in a hollow tree in the depth of the swamp, the rabbit, the squirrel, and the fox have all been housed. The watch-dog has lain quiet on the hearth, and the cattle have stood silent in their stalls. The earth itself has slept, as it were its first, not its last sleep, save when some street-sign or wood-house door has faintly creaked upon its hinge, cheering forlorn nature at her midnight work, — the only sound awake 'twixt Venus and Mars, — advertising us of a remote inward warmth, a divine cheer and fellowship, where gods are met together, but where it is very bleak for men to stand. But while the earth has slumbered, all the air has been alive with feathery flakes descending, as if some northern Ceres reigned, showering her silvery grain over all the fields.

We sleep, and at length awake to the still reality of a winter morning. The snow lies warm as cotton or down upon the window-sill; the broadened sash and frosted panes admit a dim and private light, which enhances the snug cheer within. The stillness of the morning is impressive. The floor creaks under our feet as we move toward the window to look abroad through some clear space over the fields. We see the roofs stand under their snow burden. From the eaves and fences hang stalactites of snow, and in the yard stand stalagmites covering some concealed core. The trees and shrubs rear white arms to the sky on every side; and where were walls and fences, we see fantastic forms stretching in frolic gambols across the dusky landscape, as if nature had strewn her fresh designs over the fields by night as models for man's art.

Silently we unlatch the door, letting the drift fall in, and step abroad to face the cutting air. Already the stars have lost some of their sparkle, and a dull, leaden mist skirts the horizon. A lurid brazen light in the east proclaims the approach of day, while the western landscape is dim and spectral still, and clothed in a sombre Tartarian light, like the shadowy realms. They are Infernal sounds only that you hear; the crowing of cocks, the barking of dogs, the

chopping of wood, the lowing of kine, all seem
to come from Pluto's barn-yard and beyond the
Styx, — not for any melancholy they suggest,
but their twilight bustle is too solemn and mysterious for earth.   The recent tracks of the fox
or otter, in the yard, remind us that each hour
of the night is crowded with events, and the
primeval nature is still working and making
tracks in the snow.   Opening the gate, we tread
briskly along the lone country road, crunching
the dry and crisped snow under our feet, or
aroused by the sharp clear creak of the wood
sled, just starting for the distant market, from
the early farmer's door, where it has lain the
summer long, dreaming amid the chips and stubble; while far through the drifts and powdered
windows we see the farmer's early candle, like
a paled star, emitting a lonely beam, as if some
severe virtue were at its matins there.   And one
by one the smokes begin to ascend from the
chimneys amid the trees and snows.

> The sluggish smoke curls up from some deep dell,
> The stiffened air exploring in the dawn,
> And making slow acquaintance with the day
> Delaying now upon its heavenward course,
> In wreathed loiterings dallying with itself,
> With as uncertain purpose and slow deed
> As its half-wakened master by the hearth,
> Whose mind still slumbering and sluggish thoughts
> Have not yet swept into the onward current
> Of the new day ; — and now it streams afar,

The while the chopper goes with step direct,
And mind intent to swing the early axe.
     First in the dusky dawn he sends abroad
His early scout, his emissary, smoke,
The earliest, latest pilgrim from the roof,
To feel the frosty air, inform the day;
And while he crouches still beside the hearth,
Nor musters courage to unbar the door,
It has gone down the glen with the light wind,
And o'er the plain unfurled its venturous wreath,
Draped the tree-tops, loitered upon the hill,
And warmed the pinions of the early bird;
And now, perchance, high in the crispy air,
Has caught sight of the day o'er the earth's edge,
And greets its master's eye at his low door,
As some refulgent cloud in the upper sky.

We hear the sound of wood-chopping at the farmers' doors, far over the frozen earth, the baying of the house-dog, and the distant clarion of the cock, — though the thin and frosty air conveys only the finer particles of sound to our ears, with short and sweet vibrations, as the waves subside soonest on the purest and lightest liquids, in which gross substances sink to the bottom. They come clear and bell-like, and from a greater distance in the horizon, as if there were fewer impediments than in summer to make them faint and ragged. The ground is sonorous, like seasoned wood, and even the ordinary rural sounds are melodious, and the jingling of the ice on the trees is sweet and liquid. There is the least possible moisture in the atmosphere, all being dried up, or congealed, and it is of such extreme tenuity and elasticity that it becomes a source of delight. The withdrawn and tense sky seems groined like the aisles of a cathedral, and the polished air sparkles as if there were crystals of ice floating in it. As they who have resided in Greenland tell us that when it freezes "the sea smokes like burning turf-land, and a fog or mist arises, called frost-smoke," which "cutting smoke frequently raises blisters on the face and hands, and is very pernicious to the health." But this pure stinging cold is an elixir to the lungs, and not so much a frozen mist as a crystallized midsummer haze, refined and purified by cold.

The sun at length rises through the distant woods, as if with the faint clashing swinging sound of cymbals, melting the air with his beams, and with such rapid steps the morning travels, that already his rays are gilding the distant western mountains. Meanwhile we step hastily along through the powdery snow, warmed by an inward heat, enjoying an Indian summer still, in the increased glow of thought and feeling. Probably if our lives were more conformed to nature, we should not need to defend ourselves against her heats and colds, but find her our constant nurse and friend, as do plants and quadrupeds. If our bodies were fed with pure

and simple elements, and not with a stimulating
and heating diet, they would afford no more
pasture for cold than a leafless twig, but thrive
like the trees, which find even winter genial to
their expansion.

The wonderful purity of nature at this season
is a most pleasing fact. Every decayed stump
and moss-grown stone and rail, and the dead
leaves of autumn, are concealed by a clean nap-
kin of snow. In the bare fields and tinkling
woods, see what virtue survives. In the coldest
and bleakest places, the warmest charities still
maintain a foothold. A cold and searching
wind drives away all contagion, and nothing can
withstand it but what has a virtue in it, and accordingly, whatever we meet with in cold and
bleak places, as the tops of mountains, we respect for a sort of sturdy innocence, a Puritan
toughness. All things beside seem to be called
in for shelter, and what stays out must be part
of the original frame of the universe, and of
such valor as God himself. It is invigorating
to breathe the cleansed air. Its greater fineness
and purity are visible to the eye, and we would
fain stay out long and late, that the gales may
sigh through us, too, as through the leafless
trees, and fit us for the winter, — as if we hoped
so to borrow some pure and steadfast virtue,
which will stead us in all seasons.

There is a slumbering subterranean fire in nature which never goes out, and which no cold can chill. It finally melts the great snow, and in January or July is only buried under a thicker or thinner covering. In the coldest day it flows somewhere, and the snow melts around every tree. This field of winter rye, which sprouted late in the fall, and now speedily dissolves the snow, is where the fire is very thinly covered. We feel warmed by it. In the winter, warmth stands for all virtue, and we resort in thought to a trickling rill, with its bare stones shining in the sun, and to warm springs in the woods, with as much eagerness as rabbits and robins. The steam which rises from swamps and pools is as dear and domestic as that of our own kettle. What fire could ever equal the sunshine of a winter's day, when the meadow mice come out by the wall-sides, and the chickadee lisps in the defiles of the wood? The warmth comes directly from the sun, and is not radiated from the earth, as in summer; and when we feel his beams on our backs as we are treading some snowy dell, we are grateful as for a special kindness, and bless the sun which has followed us into that by-place.

This subterranean fire has its altar in each man's breast; for in the coldest day, and on the bleakest hill, the traveler cherishes a warmer

fire within the folds of his cloak than is kindled
on any hearth. A healthy man, indeed, is the
complement of the seasons, and in winter, summer is in his heart. There is the south. Thither
have all birds and insects migrated, and around
the warm springs in his breast are gathered the
robin and the lark.

At length, having reached the edge of the
woods, and shut out the gadding town, we enter
within their covert as we go under the roof of a
cottage, and cross its threshold, all ceiled and
banked up with snow. They are glad and warm
still, and as genial and cheery in winter as in
summer. As we stand in the midst of the pines
in the flickering and checkered light which
straggles but little way into their maze, we wonder if the towns have ever heard their simple
story. It seems to us that no traveler has ever
explored them, and notwithstanding the wonders
which science is elsewhere revealing every day,
who would not like to hear their annals? Our
humble villages in the plain are their contribution. We borrow from the forest the boards
which shelter and the sticks which warm us.
How important is their evergreen to the winter,
that portion of the summer which does not fade,
the permanent year, the unwithered grass. Thus
simply, and with little expense of altitude, is the
surface of the earth diversified. What would

human life be without forests, those natural cities? From the tops of mountains they appear like smooth-shaven lawns, yet whither shall we walk but in this taller grass?

In this glade covered with bushes of a year's growth, see how the silvery dust lies on every seared leaf and twig, deposited in such infinite and luxurious forms as by their very variety atone for the absence of color. Observe the tiny tracks of mice around every stem, and the triangular tracks of the rabbit. A pure elastic heaven hangs over all, as if the impurities of the summer sky, refined and shrunk by the chaste winter's cold, had been winnowed from the heavens upon the earth.

Nature confounds her summer distinctions at this season. The heavens seem to be nearer the earth. The elements are less reserved and distinct. Water turns to ice, rain to snow. The day is but a Scandinavian night. The winter is an arctic summer.

How much more living is the life that is in nature, the furred life which still survives the stinging nights, and, from amidst fields and woods covered with frost and snow, sees the sun rise.

" The foodless wilds
Pour forth their brown inhabitants."

The gray squirrel and rabbit are brisk and play-

ful in the remote glens, even on the morning of
the cold Friday. Here is our Lapland and
Labrador, and for our Esquimaux and Knisten-
aux, Dog-ribbed Indians, Novazemblaites, and
Spitzbergeners, are there not the ice-cutter and
wood-chopper, the fox, musk-rat, and mink?

Still, in the midst of the arctic day, we may
trace the summer to its retreats, and sympathize
with some contemporary life. Stretched over
the brooks, in the midst of the frost - bound
meadows, we may observe the submarine cottages of the caddice-worms, the larvæ of the
Plicipennes; their small cylindrical cases built
around themselves, composed of flags, sticks,
grass, and withered leaves, shells, and pebbles,
in form and color like the wrecks which strew
the bottom, — now drifting along over the pebbly
bottom, now whirling in tiny eddies and dashing
down steep falls, or sweeping rapidly along with
the current, or else swaying to and fro at the
end of some grass - blade or root. Anon they
will leave their sunken habitations, and, crawling
up the stems of plants, or to the surface, like
gnats, as perfect insects henceforth, flutter over
the surface of the water, or sacrifice their short
lives in the flame of our candles at evening.
Down yonder little glen the shrubs are drooping
under their burden, and the red alder-berries
contrast with the white ground. Here are the

marks of a myriad feet which have already been
abroad. The sun rises as proudly over such
a glen as over the valley of the Seine or the
Tiber, and it seems the residence of a pure and
self-subsistent valor, such as they never witnessed; which never knew defeat nor fear. Here
reign the simplicity and purity of a primitive
age, and a health and hope far remote from
towns and cities. Standing quite alone, far in
the forest, while the wind is shaking down snow
from the trees, and leaving the only human
tracks behind us, we find our reflections of a
richer variety than the life of cities. The chickadee and nuthatch are more inspiring society
than statesmen and philosophers, and we shall
return to these last as to more vulgar companions. In this lonely glen, with its brook drain-
ing the slopes, its creased ice and crystals of all
hues, where the spruces and hemlocks stand up
on either side, and the rush and sere wild oats
in the rivulet itself, our lives are more serene
and worthy to contemplate.

As the day advances, the heat of the sun is
reflected by the hillsides, and we hear a faint
but sweet music, where flows the rill released
from its fetters, and the icicles are melting on
the trees; and the nuthatch and partridge are
heard and seen. The south wind melts the snow
at noon, and the bare ground appears with its

withered grass and leaves, and we are invigorated by the perfume which exhales from it, as by the scent of strong meats.

Let us go into this deserted woodman's hut, and see how he has passed the long winter nights and the short and stormy days. For here man has lived under this south hillside, and it seems a civilized and public spot. We have such associations as when the traveler stands by the ruins of Palmyra or Hecatompolis. Singing birds and flowers perchance have begun to appear here, for flowers as well as weeds follow in the footsteps of man. These hemlocks whispered over his head, these hickory logs were his fuel, and these pitch-pine roots kindled his fire; yonder fuming rill in the hollow, whose thin and airy vapor still ascends as busily as ever, though he is far off now, was his well. These hemlock boughs, and the straw upon this raised platform, were his bed, and this broken dish held his drink. But he has not been here this season, for the phœbes built their nest upon this shelf last summer. I find some embers left as if he had but just gone out, where he baked his pot of beans; and while at evening he smoked his pipe, whose stemless bowl lies in the ashes, chatted with his only companion, if perchance he had any, about the depth of the snow on the morrow, already falling fast and thick without,

or disputed whether the last sound was the
screech of an owl, or the creak of a bough, or
imagination only; and through his broad chimney throat, in the late winter evening, ere he
stretched himself upon the straw, he looked up
to learn the progress of the storm, and, seeing
the bright stars of Cassiopeia's chair shining
brightly down upon him, fell contentedly asleep.

See how many traces from which we may
learn the chopper's history. From this stump
we may guess the sharpness of his ax, and from
the slope of the stroke, on which side he stood,
and whether he cut down the tree without going
round it or changing hands; and, from the flex-
ure of the splinters, we may know which way it
fell. This one chip contains inscribed on it the
whole history of the wood-chopper and of the
world. On this scrap of paper, which held his
sugar or salt, perchance, or was the wadding of
his gun, sitting on a log in the forest, with what
interest we read the tattle of cities, of those
larger huts, empty and to let, like this, in High
Streets and Broadways. The eaves are drip-
ping on the south side of this simple roof, while
the titmouse lisps in the pine and the genial
warmth of the sun around the door is somewhat kind and human.

After two seasons, this rude dwelling does not
deform the scene. Already the birds resort to

it, to build their nests, and you may track to its door the feet of many quadrupeds. Thus, for a long time, nature overlooks the encroachment and profanity of man. The wood still cheerfully and unsuspiciously echoes the strokes of the axe that fells it, and while they are few and seldom, they enhance its wildness, and all the elements strive to naturalize the sound.

Now our path begins to ascend gradually to the top of this high hill, from whose precipitous south side we can look over the broad country of forest and field and river, to the distant snowy mountains. See yonder thin column of smoke curling up through the woods from some invisible farmhouse; the standard raised over some rural homestead. There must be a warmer and more genial spot there below, as where we detect the vapor from a spring forming a cloud above the trees. What fine relations are established between the traveler who discovers this airy column from some eminence in the forest and him who sits below. Up goes the smoke as silently and naturally as the vapor exhales from the leaves, and as busy disposing itself in wreaths as the housewife on the hearth below. It is a hieroglyphic of man's life, and suggests more intimate and important things than the boiling of a pot. Where its fine column rises above the forest, like an ensign, some human life has

planted itself, — and such is the beginning of
Rome, the establishment of the arts, and the
foundation of empires, whether on the prairies of
America or the steppes of Asia.

And now we descend again, to the brink of
this woodland lake, which lies in a hollow of the
hills, as if it were their expressed juice, and
that of the leaves which are annually steeped in
it. Without outlet or inlet to the eye, it has still
its history, in the lapse of its waves, in the
rounded pebbles on its shore, and in the pines
which grow down to its brink. It has not been
idle, though sedentary, but, like Abu Musa,
teaches that "sitting still at home is the heavenly
way; the going out is the way of the world."
Yet in its evaporation it travels as far as any.
In summer it is the earth's liquid eye; a mirror
in the breast of nature. The sins of the wood
are washed out in it. See how the woods form
an amphitheatre about it, and it is an arena for
all the genialness of nature. All trees direct the
traveler to its brink, all paths seek it out, birds
fly to it, quadrupeds flee to it, and the very
ground inclines toward it. It is nature's saloon,
where she has sat down to her toilet. Consider
her silent economy and tidiness; how the sun
comes with his evaporation to sweep the dust
from its surface each morning, and a fresh surface is constantly welling up; and annually,

after whatever impurities have accumulated herein, its liquid transparency appears again in the spring. In summer a hushed music seems to sweep across its surface. But now a plain sheet of snow conceals it from our eyes, except where the wind has swept the ice bare, and the sere leaves are gliding from side to side, tacking and veering on their tiny voyages. Here is one just keeled up against a pebble on shore, a dry beech - leaf, rocking still, as if it would start again. A skillful engineer, methinks, might project its course since it fell from the parent stem. Here are all the elements for such a calculation. Its present position, the direction of the wind, the level of the pond, and how much more is given. In its scarred edges and veins is its log rolled up.

We fancy ourselves in the interior of a larger house. The surface of the pond is our deal table or sanded floor, and the woods rise abruptly from its edge, like the walls of a cottage. The lines set to catch pickerel through the ice look like a larger culinary preparation, and the men stand about on the white ground like pieces of forest furniture. The actions of these men, at the distance of half a mile over the ice and snow, impress us as when we read the exploits of Alexander in history. They seem not unworthy of the scenery, and as momentous as the conquest of kingdoms.

Again we have wandered through the arches of the wood, until from its skirts we hear the distant booming of ice from yonder bay of the river, as if it were moved by some other and subtler tide than oceans know. To me it has a strange sound of home, thrilling as the voice of one's distant and noble kindred. A mild summer sun shines over forest and lake, and though there is but one green leaf for many rods, yet nature enjoys a serene health. Every sound is fraught with the same mysterious assurance of health, as well now the creaking of the boughs in January, as the soft sough of the wind in July.

> When Winter fringes every bough
>   With his fantastic wreath,
> And puts the seal of silence now
>   Upon the leaves beneath;
>
> When every stream in its penthouse
>   Goes gurgling on its way,
> And in his gallery the mouse
>   Nibbleth the meadow hay;
>
> Methinks the summer still is nigh,
>   And lurketh underneath,
> As that same meadow-mouse doth lie
>   Snug in that last year's heath.
>
> And if perchance the chickadee
>   Lisp a faint note anon,
> The snow is summer's canopy,
>   Which she herself put on.

Fair blossoms deck the cheerful trees,
　And dazzling fruits depend,
The north wind sighs a summer breeze,
　The nipping frosts to fend,

Bringing glad tidings unto me,
　The while I stand all ear,
Of a serene eternity,
　Which need not winter fear.

Out on the silent pond straightway
　The restless ice doth crack,
And pond sprites merry gambols play
　Amid the deafening rack.

Eager I hasten to the vale,
　As if I heard brave news,
How nature held high festival,
　Which it were hard to lose.

I gambol with my neighbor ice,
　And sympathizing quake,
As each new crack darts in a trice
　Across the gladsome lake.

One with the cricket in the ground,
　And fagot on the hearth,
Resounds the rare domestic sound
　Along the forest path.

Before night we will take a journey on skates
along the course of this meandering river, as
full of novelty to one who sits by the cottage
fire all the winter's day, as if it were over the
polar ice, with Captain Parry or Franklin; following the winding of the stream, now flowing

amid hills, now spreading out into fair meadows, and forming a myriad coves and bays where the pine and hemlock overarch. The river flows in the rear of the towns, and we see all things from a new and wilder side. The fields and gardens come down to it with a frankness, and freedom from pretension, which they do not wear on the highway. It is the outside and edge of the earth. Our eyes are not offended by violent contrasts. The last rail of the farmer's fence is some swaying willow bough, which still preserves its freshness, and here at length all fences stop, and we no longer cross any road. We may go far up within the country now by the most retired and level road, never climbing a hill, but by broad levels ascending to the upland meadows. It is a beautiful illustration of the law of obedience, the flow of a river; the path for a sick man, a highway down which an acorn cup may float secure with its freight. Its slight occasional falls, whose precipices would not diversify the landscape, are celebrated by mist and spray, and attract the traveler from far and near. From the remote interior, its current conducts him by broad and easy steps, or by one gentler inclined plane, to the sea. Thus by an early and constant yielding to the inequalities of the ground it secures itself the easiest passage.

No domain of nature is quite closed to man at

all times, and now we draw near to the empire of
the fishes. Our feet glide swiftly over unfathomed
depths, where in summer our line tempted the
pout and perch, and where the stately pickerel
lurked in the long corridors formed by the bul-
rushes. The deep, impenetrable marsh, where
the heron waded, and bittern squatted, is made
pervious to our swift shoes, as if a thousand railroads had been made into it. With one impulse
we are carried to the cabin of the musk - rat,
that earliest settler, and see him dart away under
the transparent ice, like a furred fish, to his hole
in the bank; and we glide rapidly over meadows
where lately " the mower whet his scythe,"
through beds of frozen cranberries mixed with
meadow grass. We skate near to where the
blackbird, the pewee, and the kingbird hung
their nests over the water, and the hornets
builded from the maple in the swamp. How
many gay warblers, following the sun, have radiated from this nest of silver-birch and thistle-
down. On the swamp's outer edge was hung
the supermarine village, where no foot penetrated. In this hollow tree the wood-duck reared
her brood, and slid away each day to forage in
yonder fen.

In winter, nature is a cabinet of curiosities,
full of dried specimens, in their natural order
and position. The meadows and forests are a

hortus siccus. The leaves and grasses stand
perfectly pressed by the air without screw or
gum, and the birds' nests are not hung on an
artificial twig, but where they builded them.
We go about dryshod to inspect the summer's
work in the rank swamp, and see what a growth
have got the alders, the willows, and the maples;
testifying to how many warm suns, and fertilizing dews and showers. See what strides their
boughs took in the luxuriant summer, — and
anon these dormant buds will carry them on-
ward and upward another span into the heavens.

Occasionally we wade through fields of snow,
under whose depths the river is lost for many
rods, to appear again to the right or left, where
we least expected; still holding on its way underneath, with a faint, stertorous, rumbling
sound, as if, like the bear and marmot, it too
had hibernated, and we had followed its faint
summer-trail to where it earthed itself in snow
and ice. At first we should have thought that
rivers would be empty and dry in midwinter,
or else frozen solid till the spring thawed them;
but their volume is not diminished even, for
only a superficial cold bridges their surfaces.
The thousand springs which feed the lakes and
streams are flowing still. The issues of a few
surface springs only are closed, and they go to
swell the deep reservoirs. Nature's wells are

below the frost. The summer brooks are not
filled with snow-water, nor does the mower
quench his thirst with that alone. The streams
are swollen when the snow melts in the spring,
because nature's work has been delayed, the
water being turned into ice and snow, whose
particles are less smooth and round, and do not
find their level so soon.

Far over the ice, between the hemlock woods
and snow-clad hills, stands the pickerel fisher,
his lines set in some retired cove, like a Finlan-
der, with his arms thrust into the pouches of his
dreadnought; with dull, snowy, fishy thoughts,
himself a finless fish, separated a few inches
from his race; dumb, erect, and made to be enveloped in clouds and snows, like the pines on
shore. In these wild scenes, men stand about
in the scenery, or move deliberately and heavily, having sacrificed the sprightliness and vi-
vacity of towns to the dumb sobriety of nature.
He does not make the scenery less wild, more
than the jays and musk-rats, but stands there as
a part of it, as the natives are represented in the
voyages of early navigators, at Nootka Sound,
and on the Northwest coast, with their furs about
them, before they were tempted to loquacity by
a scrap of iron. He belongs to the natural
family of man, and is planted deeper in nature
and has more root than the inhabitants of towns.

Go to him, ask what luck, and you will learn that he too is a worshiper of the unseen. Hear with what sincere deference and waving gesture in his tone he speaks of the lake pickerel, which he has never seen, his primitive and ideal race of pickerel. He is connected with the shore still, as by a fish-line, and yet remembers the season when he took fish through the ice on the pond, while the peas were up in his garden at home.

But now, while we have loitered, the clouds have gathered again, and a few straggling snow-flakes are beginning to descend. Faster and faster they fall, shutting out the distant objects from sight. The snow falls on every wood and field, and no crevice is forgotten; by the river and the pond, on the hill and in the valley. Quadrupeds are confined to their coverts and the birds sit upon their perches this peaceful hour. There is not so much sound as in fair weather, but silently and gradually every slope, and the gray walls and fences, and the polished ice, and the sere leaves, which were not buried before, are concealed, and the tracks of men and beasts are lost. With so little effort does nature reassert her rule and blot out the traces of men. Hear how Homer has described the same: "The snow-flakes fall thick and fast on a winter's day. The winds are lulled, and the snow falls incessant, covering the tops of the mountains, and the hills, and the plains where the lotus-tree grows, and the cultivated fields, and they are falling by the inlets and shores of the foaming sea, but are silently dissolved by the waves." The snow levels all things, and infolds them deeper in the bosom of nature, as, in the slow summer, vegetation creeps up to the entablature of the temple, and the turrets of the castle, and helps her to prevail over art.

The surly night - wind rustles through the wood, and warns us to retrace our steps, while the sun goes down behind the thickening storm, and birds seek their roosts, and cattle their stalls.

> " Drooping the lab'rer ox
> Stands covered o'er with snow, and *now* demands
> The fruit of all his toil."

Though winter is represented in the almanac as an old man, facing the wind and sleet, and drawing his cloak about him, we rather think of him as a merry wood-chopper, and warm-blooded youth, as blithe as summer. The unexplored grandeur of the storm keeps up the spirits of the traveler. It does not trifle with us, but has a sweet earnestness. In winter we lead a more inward life. Our hearts are warm and cheery, like cottages under drifts, whose windows and doors are half concealed, but from whose chimneys the smoke cheerfully ascends. The imprisoning drifts increase the sense of comfort which the house affords, and in the coldest days we are content to sit over the hearth and see the sky through the chimney top, enjoying the quiet and serene life that may be had in a warm corner by the chimney side, or feeling our pulse by listening to the low of cattle in the street, or the sound of the flail in distant barns all the long afternoon. No doubt a skillful physician could determine our health by observing how these simple and natural sounds affected us. We enjoy now, not an oriental, but a boreal leisure, around warm stoves and fireplaces, and watch the shadow of motes in the sunbeams.

Sometimes our fate grows too homely and familiarly serious ever to be cruel. Consider how for three months the human destiny is wrapped in furs. The good Hebrew Revelation takes no cognizance of all this cheerful snow. Is there no religion for the temperate and frigid zones? We know of no scripture which records the pure benignity of the gods on a New England winter night. Their praises have never been sung, only their wrath deprecated. The best scripture, after all, records but a meagre faith. Its saints live reserved and austere. Let a brave, devout man spend the year in the woods of Maine or Labrador, and see if the Hebrew

Scriptures speak adequately to his condition and experience, from the setting in of winter to the breaking up of the ice.

Now commences the long winter evening around the farmer's hearth, when the thoughts of the indwellers travel far abroad, and men are by nature and necessity charitable and liberal to all creatures. Now is the happy resistance to cold, when the farmer reaps his reward, and thinks of his preparedness for winter, and, through the glittering panes, sees with equanimity "the mansion of the northern bear," for now the storm is over, —

> "The full ethereal round,
> Infinite worlds disclosing to the view,
> Shines out intensely keen ; and all one cope
> Of starry glitter glows from pole to pole."

THE SUCCESSION OF FOREST TREES [1]

EVERY man is entitled to come to Cattleshow, even a transcendentalist; and for my part I am more interested in the men than in the cattle. I wish to see once more those old familiar faces, whose names I do not know, which for me represent the Middlesex country, and come as near being indigenous to the soil as a white man can; the men who are not above their business, whose coats are not too black, whose shoes do not shine very much, who never wear gloves to conceal their hands. It is true, there are some queer specimens of humanity attracted to our festival, but all are welcome. I am pretty sure to meet once more that weak-minded and whimsical fellow, generally weak-bodied too, who prefers a crooked stick for a cane; perfectly useless, you would say, only *bizarre*, fit for a cabinet, like a petrified snake. A ram's horn would be as convenient, and is yet more curiously twisted. He brings that much indulged bit of the country with him, from some town's end or other, and

[1] An Address read to the Middlesex Agricultural Society in Concord, September, 1860.

introduces it to Concord groves, as if he had promised it so much sometime. So some, it seems to me, elect their rulers for their crookedness. But I think that a straight stick makes the best cane, and an upright man the best ruler. Or why choose a man to do plain work who is distinguished for his oddity? However, I do not know but you will think that they have committed this mistake who invited me to speak to you to-day.

In my capacity of surveyor, I have often talked with some of you, my employers, at your dinner - tables, after having gone round and round and behind your farming, and ascertained exactly what its limits were. Moreover, taking a surveyor's and a naturalist's liberty, I have been in the habit of going across your lots much oftener than is usual, as many of you, perhaps to your sorrow, are aware. Yet many of you, to my relief, have seemed not to be aware of it; and, when I came across you in some out-of-the-way nook of your farms, have inquired, with an air of surprise, if I were not lost, since you had never seen me in that part of the town or county before; when, if the truth were known, and it had not been for betraying my secret, I might with more propriety have inquired if *you* were not lost, since I had never seen *you* there before. I have several times shown the proprietor the shortest way out of his wood-lot.

the pines have sprung up from nothing, and I am aware that I am not at all peculiar in asserting that they come from seeds, though the mode of their propagation *by nature* has been but little attended to. They are very extensively raised from the seed in Europe, and are beginning to be here.

When you cut down an oak wood, a pine wood will not *at once* spring up there unless there are, or have been quite recently, seed-bearing pines near enough for the seeds to be blown from them. But, adjacent to a forest of pines, if you prevent other crops from growing there, you will surely have an extension of your pine forest, provided the soil is suitable.

As for the heavy seeds and nuts which are not furnished with wings, the notion is still a very common one that, when the trees which bear these spring up where none of their kind were noticed before, they have come from seeds or other principles spontaneously generated there in an unusual manner, or which have lain dormant in the soil for centuries, or perhaps been called into activity by the heat of a burning. I do not believe these assertions, and I will state some of the ways in which, according to my observation, such forests are planted and raised.

Every one of these seeds, too, will be found to be winged or legged in another fashion. Surely it is not wonderful that cherry-trees of all kinds are widely dispersed, since their fruit is well known to be the favorite food of various birds. Many kinds are called bird-cherries, and they appropriate many more kinds, which are not so called.   Eating cherries is a bird-like employment, and unless we disperse the seeds occasionally, as they do, I shall think that the birds have the best right to them.   See how artfully the seed of a cherry is placed in order that a bird may be compelled to transport it — in the very midst of a tempting pericarp, so that the creature that would devour this must commonly take the stone also into its mouth or bill.   If you ever ate a cherry, and did not make two bites of it, you must have perceived it — right in the centre of the luscious morsel, a large earthy residuum left on the tongue.   We thus take into our mouths cherry stones as big as peas, a dozen at once, for Nature can persuade us to do almost anything when she would compass her ends.   Some wild men and children instinctively swallow these, as the birds do when in a hurry, it being the shortest way to get rid of them.   Thus, though these seeds are not provided with vegetable wings, Nature has impelled the thrush tribe to take them into their bills and fly away with them; and they are winged in another sense, and more effectually than the seeds of pines, for these are carried even against the wind. The consequence is, that cherry-trees grow not only here but there. The same is true of a great many other seeds.

But to come to the observation which suggested these remarks. As I have said, I suspect that I can throw some light on the fact, that when hereabouts a dense pine wood is cut down, oaks and other hard woods may at once take its place. I have got only to show that the acorns and nuts, provided they are grown in the neighborhood, are regularly planted in such woods; for I assert that if an oak-tree has not grown within ten miles, and man has not carried acorns thither, then an oak wood will not spring up *at once*, when a pine wood is cut down.

Apparently, there were only pines there before. They are cut off, and after a year or two you see oaks and other hard woods springing up there, with scarcely a pine amid them, and the wonder commonly is, how the seed could have lain in the ground so long without decaying. But the truth is, that it has not lain in the ground so long, but is regularly planted each year by various quadrupeds and birds.

In this neighborhood, where oak and pines are about equally dispersed, if you look through the thickest pine wood, even the seemingly unmixed pitch-pine ones, you will commonly detect many little oaks, birches, and other hard woods, sprung from seeds carried into the thicket by squirrels and other animals, and also blown thither, but which are overshadowed and choked by the pines. The denser the evergreen wood, the more likely it is to be well planted with these seeds, because the planters incline to resort with their forage to the closest covert. They also carry it into birch and other woods. This planting is carried on annually, and the oldest seedlings annually die; but when the pines are cleared off, the oaks, having got just the start they want, and now secured favorable conditions, immediately spring up to trees.

The shade of a dense pine wood is more unfavorable to the springing up of pines of the same species than of oaks within it, though the former may come up abundantly when the pines are cut, if there chance to be sound seed in the ground.

But when you cut off a lot of hard wood, very often the little pines mixed with it have a similar start, for the squirrels have carried off the nuts to the pines, and not to the more open wood, and they commonly make pretty clean work of it; and moreover, if the wood was old, the sprouts will be feeble or entirely fail; to say nothing about the soil being, in a measure, exhausted for this kind of crop.

If a pine wood is surrounded by a white oak one chiefly, white oaks may be expected to succeed when the pines are cut. If it is surrounded instead by an edging of shrub-oaks, then you will probably have a dense shrub-oak thicket.

I have no time to go into details, but will say, in a word, that while the wind is conveying the seeds of pines into hard woods and open lands, the squirrels and other animals are conveying the seeds of oaks and walnuts into the pine woods, and thus a rotation of crops is kept up.

I affirmed this confidently many years ago, and an occasional examination of dense pine woods confirmed me in my opinion. It has long been known to observers that squirrels bury nuts in the ground, but I am not aware that any one has thus accounted for the regular succession of forests.

On the 24th of September, in 1857, as I was paddling down the Assabet, in this town, I saw a red squirrel run along the bank under some herbage, with something large in its mouth. It stopped near the foot of a hemlock, within a couple of rods of me, and, hastily pawing a hole with its forefeet, dropped its booty into it, covered it up, and retreated part way up the trunk of the tree. As I approached the shore to examine the deposit, the squirrel, descending part way, betrayed no little anxiety about its treasure, and made two or three motions to recover it before it finally retreated. Digging there, I found two green pig-nuts joined together, with the thick husks on, buried about an inch and a half under the reddish soil of decayed hemlock leaves, — just the right depth to plant it. In short, this squirrel was then engaged in accomplishing two objects, to wit, laying up a store of winter food for itself, and planting a hickory wood for all creation. If the squirrel was killed, or neglected its deposit, a hickory would spring up. The nearest hickory-tree was twenty rods distant. These nuts were there still just fourteen days later, but were gone when I looked again, November 21st, or six weeks later still.

I have since examined more carefully several dense woods, which are said to be, and are apparently, exclusively pine, and always with the same result. For instance, I walked the same day to a small, but very dense and handsome white-pine grove, about fifteen rods square, in the east part of this town. The trees are large for Concord, being from ten to twenty inches in diameter, and as exclusively pine as any wood that I know. Indeed, I selected this wood because I thought it the least likely to contain anything else. It stands on an open plain or pasture, except that it adjoins another small pine wood, which has a few little oaks in it, on the southeast side. On every other side, it was at least thirty rods from the nearest woods. Standing on the edge of this grove and looking through it, for it is quite level and free from underwood, for the most part bare, red-carpeted ground, you would have said that there was not a hard-wood tree in it, young or old. But on looking carefully along over its floor I discovered, though it was not till my eye had got used to the search, that, alternating with thin ferns, and small blueberry bushes, there was, not merely here and there, but as often as every five feet and with a degree of regularity, a little oak, from three to twelve inches high, and in one place I found a green acorn dropped by the base of a pine.

I confess I was surprised to find my theory so perfectly proved in this case. One of the principal agents in this planting, the red squirrels, were all the while curiously inspecting me, while I was inspecting their plantation. Some of the little oaks had been browsed by cows, which resorted to this wood for shade.

After seven or eight years, the hard woods evidently find such a locality unfavorable to their growth, the pines being allowed to stand. As an evidence of this, I observed a diseased red-maple twenty-five feet long, which had been recently prostrated, though it was still covered with green leaves, the only maple in any position in the wood.

But although these oaks almost invariably die if the pines are not cut down, it is probable that they do better for a few years under their shelter than they would anywhere else.

The very extensive and thorough experiments of the English have at length led them to adopt a method of raising oaks almost precisely like this, which somewhat earlier had been adopted by nature and her squirrels here; they have simply rediscovered the value of pines as nurses for oaks. The English experimenters seem, early and generally, to have found out the importance of using trees of some kind as nurse-plants for the young oaks. I quote from Loudon what he describes as "the ultimatum on the subject of planting and sheltering oaks," — "an abstract of the practice adopted by the government officers in the national forests" of England, prepared by Alexander Milne.

At first some oaks had been planted by themselves, and others mixed with Scotch pines; "but in all cases," says Mr. Milne, "where oaks were planted actually among the pines and surrounded by them [though the soil might be inferior], the oaks were found to be much the best." " For several years past, the plan pursued has been to plant the inclosures with Scotch pines only [a tree very similar to our pitch-pine], and when the pines have got to the height of five or six feet, then to put in good strong oak plants of about four or five years' growth among the pines, — not cutting away any pines at first, unless they happen to be so strong and thick as to overshadow the oaks. In about two years it becomes necessary to shred the branches of the pines, to give light and air to the oaks, and in about two or three more years to begin gradually to remove the pines altogether, taking out a certain number each year, so that, at the end of twenty or twenty-five years, not a single Scotch pine shall be left; although, for the first ten or twelve years, the plantation may have appeared to contain nothing else but pine. The advantage of this mode of planting has been found to be that the pines dry and ameliorate the soil, destroying the coarse grass and brambles which frequently choke and injure oaks; and that no mending over is necessary, as scarcely an oak so planted is found to fail."

Thus much the English planters have discovered by patient experiment, and, for aught I know, they have taken out a patent for it; but they appear not to have discovered that it was discovered before, and that they are merely adopting the method of Nature, which she long ago made patent to all. She is all the while planting the oaks amid the pines without our knowledge, and at last, instead of government officers, we send a party of wood-choppers to cut down the pines, and so rescue an oak forest, at which we wonder as if it had dropped from the skies.

As I walk amid hickories, even in August, I hear the sound of green pig-nuts falling from time to time, cut off by the chickaree over my head. In the fall, I notice on the ground, either within or in the neighborhood of oak woods, on all sides of the town, stout oak twigs three or four inches long, bearing half a dozen empty acorn-cups, which twigs have been gnawed off by squirrels, on both sides of the nuts, in order to make them more portable. The jays scream and the red squirrels scold while you are clubbing and shaking the chestnut-trees, for they are there on the same errand, and two of a trade never agree. I frequently see a red or gray squirrel cast down a green chestnut-bur, as I am going through the woods, and I used to think, sometimes, that they were cast at me. In fact, they are so busy about it, in the midst of the chestnut season, that you cannot stand long in the woods without hearing one fall. A sportsman told me that he had, the day before, — that was in the middle of October, — seen a green chestnut-bur dropped on our great river meadow, fifty rods from the nearest wood, and much further from the nearest chestnut-tree, and he could not tell how it came there. Occasionally, when chestnutting in midwinter, I find thirty or forty nuts in a pile, left in its gallery, just under the leaves, by the common wood-mouse (*mus leucopus*).

But especially, in the winter, the extent to which this transportation and planting of nuts is carried on is made apparent by the snow. In almost every wood, you will see where the red or gray squirrels have pawed down through the snow in a hundred places, sometimes two feet deep, and almost always directly to a nut or a pine-cone, as directly as if they had started from it and bored upward, — which you and I could not have done. It would be difficult for us to find one before the snow falls. Commonly, no doubt, they had deposited them there in the fall. You wonder if they remember the localities, or discover them by the scent. The red squirrel commonly has its winter abode in the earth under a thicket of evergreens, frequently under a small clump of evergreens in the midst of a deciduous wood. If there are any nut-trees, which still retain their nuts, standing at a distance without the wood, their paths often lead directly to and from them. We therefore need not suppose

an oak standing here and there *in* the wood in
order to seed it, but if a few stand within
twenty or thirty rods of it, it is sufficient.

I think that I may venture to say that every
white-pine cone that falls to the earth naturally
in this town, before opening and losing its seeds,
and almost every pitch-pine one that falls at all,
is cut off by a squirrel, and they begin to pluck
them long before they are ripe, so that when the
crop of white-pine cones is a small one, as it
commonly is, they cut off thus almost every one
of these before it fairly ripens. I think, moreover, that their design, if I may so speak, in
cutting them off green, is, partly, to prevent
their opening and losing their seeds, for these
are the ones for which they dig through the snow,
and the only white-pine cones which contain anything then. I have counted in one heap, within
a diameter of four feet, the cores of 239 pitch-
pine cones which had been cut off and stripped
by the red squirrel the previous winter.

The nuts thus left on the surface, or buried
just beneath it, are placed in the most favorable
circumstances for germinating. I have sometimes wondered how those which merely fell on
the surface of the earth got planted; but, by the
end of December, I find the chestnut of the same
year partially mixed with the mould, as it were,
under the decaying and mouldy leaves, where

there is all the moisture and manure they want, for the nuts fall fast. In a plentiful year, a large proportion of the nuts are thus covered loosely an inch deep, and are, of course, somewhat concealed from squirrels. One winter, when the crop had been abundant, I got, with the aid of a rake, many quarts of these nuts as late as the tenth of January, and though some bought at the store the same day were more than half of them mouldy, I did not find a single mouldy one among these which I picked from under the wet and mouldy leaves, where they had been snowed on once or twice. Nature knows how to pack them best. They were still plump and tender. Apparently, they do not heat there, though wet. In the spring they were all sprouting.

Loudon says that "when the nut [of the common walnut of Europe] is to be preserved through the winter for the purpose of planting in the following spring, it should be laid in a rotheap, as soon as gathered, with the husk on, and the heap should be turned over frequently in the course of the winter."

Here, again, he is stealing Nature's "thunder." How can a poor mortal do otherwise? for it is she that finds fingers to steal with, and the treasure to be stolen. In the planting of the seeds of most trees, the best gardeners do no

more than follow Nature, though they may not
know it. Generally, both large and small ones
are most sure to germinate, and succeed best,
when only beaten into the earth with the back
of a spade, and then covered with leaves or
straw. These results to which planters have
arrived remind us of the experience of Kane and
his companions at the North, who, when learning
to live in that climate, were surprised to find
themselves steadily adopting the customs of the
natives, simply becoming Esquimaux. So, when
we experiment in planting forests, we find ourselves at last doing as Nature does. Would it
not be well to consult with Nature in the outset?
for she is the most extensive and experienced
planter of us all, not excepting the Dukes of
Athol.

In short, they who have not attended particularly to this subject are but little aware to what
an extent quadrupeds and birds are employed,
especially in the fall, in collecting, and so disseminating and planting the seeds of trees. It is
the almost constant employment of the squirrels
at that season, and you rarely meet with one that
has not a nut in its mouth, or is not just going
to get one. One squirrel-hunter of this town
told me that he knew of a walnut-tree which
bore particularly good nuts, but that on going to
gather them one fall, he found that he had been

anticipated by a family of a dozen red squirrels.
He took out of the tree, which was hollow, one
bushel and three pecks by measurement, without the husks, and they supplied him and his
family for the winter. It would be easy to mul-
tiply instances of this kind. How commonly in
the fall you see the cheek-pouches of the striped
squirrel distended by a quantity of nuts! This
species gets its scientific name, *Tamias*, or the
steward, from its habit of storing up nuts and
other seeds. Look under a nut-tree a month
after the nuts have fallen, and see what proportion of sound nuts to the abortive ones and
shells you will find ordinarily. They have been
already eaten, or dispersed far and wide. The
ground looks like a platform before a grocery,
where the gossips of the village sit to crack nuts
and less savory jokes. You have come, you
would say, after the feast was over, and are presented with the shells only.

Occasionally, when threading the woods in the
fall, you will hear a sound as if some one had
broken a twig, and, looking up, see a jay pecking
at an acorn, or you will see a flock of them at
once about it, in the top of an oak, and hear
them break them off. They then fly to a suitable limb, and placing the acorn under one foot,
hammer away at it busily, making a sound like
a woodpecker's tapping, looking round from time

to time to see if any foe is approaching, and soon
reach the meat, and nibble at it, holding up their
heads to swallow, while they hold the remainder
very firmly with their claws. Nevertheless it
often drops to the ground before the bird has
done with it. I can confirm what William Bartram wrote to Wilson, the ornithologist, that
"The jay is one of the most useful agents in the
economy of nature, for disseminating forest trees
and other nuciferous and hard-seeded vegetables
on which they feed. Their chief employment
during the autumnal season is foraging to supply
their winter stores. In performing this necessary duty they drop abundance of seed in their
flight over fields, hedges, and by fences, where
they alight to deposit them in the post-holes,
etc. It is remarkable what numbers of young
trees rise up in fields and pastures after a wet
winter and spring. These birds alone are
capable, in a few years' time, to replant all
the cleared lands."

I have noticed that squirrels also frequently
drop their nuts in open land, which will still
further account for the oaks and walnuts which
spring up in pastures, for, depend on it, every
new tree comes from a seed. When I examine
the little oaks, one or two years old, in such
places, I invariably find the empty acorn from
which they sprung.

So far from the seed having lain dormant in the soil since oaks grew there before, as many believe, it is well known that it is difficult to preserve the vitality of acorns long enough to transport them to Europe; and it is recommended in Loudon's "Arboretum," as the safest course, to sprout them in pots on the voyage. The same authority states that "very few acorns of any species will germinate after having been kept a year," that beechmast "only retains its vital properties one year," and the black-walnut "seldom more than six months after it has ripened." I have frequently found that in November, almost every acorn left on the ground had sprouted or decayed. What with frost, drouth, moisture, and worms, the greater part are soon destroyed. Yet it is stated by one botanical writer that "acorns that have lain for centuries, on being ploughed up, have soon vegetated."

Mr. George B. Emerson, in his valuable Report on the Trees and Shrubs of this State, says of the pines: "The tenacity of life of the seeds is remarkable. They will remain for many years unchanged in the ground, protected by the coolness and deep shade of the forest above them. But when the forest is removed, and the warmth of the sun admitted, they immediately vegetate." Since he does not tell us on what observation his remark is founded, I must doubt its truth. Besides, the experience of nurserymen makes it the more questionable.

The stories of wheat raised from seed buried with an ancient Egyptian, and of raspberries raised from seed found in the stomach of a man in England, who is supposed to have died sixteen or seventeen hundred years ago, are generally discredited, simply because the evidence is not conclusive.

Several men of science, Dr. Carpenter among them, have used the statement that beach-plums sprang up in sand which was dug up forty miles inland in Maine, to prove that the seed had lain there a very long time, and some have inferred that the coast has receded so far. But it seems to me necessary to their argument to show, first, that beach-plums grow only on a beach. They are not uncommon here, which is about half that distance from the shore; and I remember a dense patch a few miles north of us, twenty-five miles inland, from which the fruit was annually carried to market. How much further inland they grow, I know not. Dr. Charles T. Jackson speaks of finding "beach-plums" (perhaps they were this kind) more than one hundred miles inland in Maine.

It chances that similar objections lie against all the more notorious instances of the kind on record.

Yet I am prepared to believe that some seeds, especially small ones, may retain their vitality for centuries under favorable circumstances. In the spring of 1859, the old Hunt House, so called, in this town, whose chimney bore the date 1703, was taken down. This stood on land which belonged to John Winthrop, the first Governor of Massachusetts, and a part of the house was evidently much older than the above date, and belonged to the Winthrop family. For many years I have ransacked this neighborhood for plants, and I consider myself familiar with its productions. Thinking of the seeds which are said to be sometimes dug up at an unusual depth in the earth, and thus to reproduce long extinct plants, it occurred to me last fall that some new or rare plants might have sprung up in the cellar of this house, which had been covered from the light so long. Searching there on the 22d of September, I found, among other rank weeds, a species of nettle (*Urtica urens*) which I had not found before; dill, which I had not seen growing spontaneously; the Jerusalem oak (*Chenopodium botrys*), which I had seen wild in but one place; black nightshade (*Solanum nigrum*), which is quite rare hereabouts, and common tobacco, which, though it was often cultivated here in the last century, has for fifty years been an unknown plant in this town, and a few months before this not even I had heard that one man, in the north part of the town, was cultivating a few plants for his own use. I have no doubt that some or all of these plants sprang from seeds which had long been buried under or about that house, and that that tobacco is an additional evidence that the plant was formerly cultivated here. The cellar has been filled up this year, and four of those plants, including the tobacco, are now again extinct in that locality.

It is true, I have shown that the animals consume a great part of the seeds of trees, and so, at least, effectually prevent their becoming trees; but in all these cases, as I have said, the consumer is compelled to be at the same time the disperser and planter, and this is the tax which he pays to nature. I think it is Linnæus who says that while the swine is rooting for acorns he is planting acorns.

Though I do not believe that a plant will spring up where no seed has been, I have great faith in a seed — a, to me, equally mysterious origin for it. Convince me that you have a seed there, and I am prepared to expect wonders. I shall even believe that the millennium is at hand, and that the reign of justice is about to commence, when the Patent Office, or Government, begins to distribute, and the people to plant, the seeds of these things.

In the spring of 1857 I planted six seeds
sent to me from the Patent Office, and labeled,
I think, "*Poitrine jaune grosse*," large yellow
squash. Two came up, and one bore a squash
which weighed 123½ pounds, the other bore four,
weighing together 186¼ pounds. Who would
have believed that there was 310 pounds of
poitrine jaune grosse in that corner of my garden? These seeds were the bait I used to catch
it, my ferrets which I sent into its burrow, my
brace of terriers which unearthed it. A little
mysterious hoeing and manuring was all the
abracadabra presto-change that I used, and lo!
true to the label, they found for me 310 pounds
of *poitrine jaune grosse* there, where it never
was known to be, nor was before. These talis-
mans had perchance sprung from America at
first, and returned to it with unabated force.
The big squash took a premium at your fair that
fall, and I understood that the man who bought
it, intended to sell the seeds for ten cents a
piece. (Were they not cheap at that?) But I
have more hounds of the same breed. I learn
that one which I despatched to a distant town,
true to its instincts, points to the large yellow
squash there, too, where no hound ever found it
before, as its ancestors did here and in France.

Other seeds I have which will find other things
in that corner of my garden, in like fashion,

almost any fruit you wish, every year for ages, until the crop more than fills the whole garden. You have but little more to do than throw up your cap for entertainment these American days. Perfect alchemists I keep who can transmute substances without end, and thus the corner of my garden is an inexhaustible treasure-chest. Here you can dig, not gold, but the value which gold merely represents; and there is no Signor Blitz about it. Yet farmers' sons will stare by the hour to see a juggler draw ribbons from his throat, though he tells them it is all deception. Surely, men love darkness rather than light.

WALKING

I WISH to speak a word for Nature, for absolute freedom and wildness, as contrasted with a freedom and culture merely civil, — to regard man as an inhabitant, or a part and parcel of Nature, rather than a member of society. I wish to make an extreme statement, if so I may make an emphatic one, for there are enough champions of civilization: the minister and the school-committee and every one of you will take care of that.

I have met with but one or two persons in the course of my life who understood the art of Walking, that is, of taking walks, — who had a genius, so to speak, for *sauntering :* which word is beautifully derived "from idle people who roved about the country, in the Middle Ages, and asked charity, under pretense of going *à la Sainte Terre*," to the Holy Land, till the children exclaimed, "There goes a *Sainte-Terrer*," a Saunterer, a Holy-Lander. They who never go to the Holy Land in their walks, as they pretend, are indeed mere idlers and vagabonds;

but they who do go there are saunterers in the good sense, such as I mean. Some, however, would derive the word from *sans terre*, without land or a home, which, therefore, in the good sense, will mean, having no particular home, but equally at home everywhere. For this is the secret of successful sauntering. He who sits still in a house all the time may be the greatest vagrant of all; but the saunterer, in the good sense, is no more vagrant than the meandering river, which is all the while sedulously seeking the shortest course to the sea. But I prefer the first, which, indeed, is the most probable derivation. For every walk is a sort of crusade, preached by some Peter the Hermit in us, to go forth and reconquer this Holy Land from the hands of the Infidels.

It is true, we are but faint-hearted crusaders, even the walkers, nowadays, who undertake no persevering, never-ending enterprises. Our expeditions are but tours, and come round again at evening to the old hearth-side from which we set out. Half the walk is but retracing our steps. We should go forth on the shortest walk, perchance, in the spirit of undying adventure, never to return, — prepared to send back our embalmed hearts only as relics to our desolate kingdoms. If you are ready to leave father and mother, and brother and sister, and wife and

child and friends, and never see them again, —
if you have paid your debts, and made your will,
and settled all your affairs, and are a free man,
then you are ready for a walk.

To come down to my own experience, my
companion and I, for I sometimes have a companion, take pleasure in fancying ourselves
knights of a new, or rather an old, order, — not
Equestrians or Chevaliers, not Ritters or Riders,
but Walkers, a still more ancient and honorable
class, I trust.   The chivalric and heroic spirit
which once belonged to the Rider seems now to
reside in, or perchance to have subsided into,
the Walker, — not the Knight, but Walker,
Errant.   He is a sort of fourth estate, outside
of Church and State and People.

We have felt that we almost alone hereabouts
practiced this noble art; though, to tell the truth,
at least, if their own assertions are to be received, most of my townsmen would fain walk
sometimes, as I do, but they cannot.   No wealth
can buy the requisite leisure, freedom, and independence which are the capital in this profession.   It comes only by the grace of God.   It
requires a direct dispensation from Heaven to
become a walker.   You must be born into the
family of the Walkers.   *Ambulator nascitur,
non fit.*   Some of my townsmen, it is true, can
remember and have described to me some walks

which they took ten years ago, in which they were so blessed as to lose themselves for half an hour in the woods; but I know very well that they have confined themselves to the highway ever since, whatever pretensions they may make to belong to this select class. No doubt they were elevated for a moment as by the reminiscence of a previous state of existence, when even they were foresters and outlaws.

> " When he came to grene wode,
>   In a mery mornynge,
>   There he herde the notes small
>   Of byrdes mery syngynge.

> " It is ferre gone, sayd Robyn,
>   That I was last here;
>   Me lyste a lytell for to shote
>   At the donne dere."

I think that I cannot preserve my health and spirits, unless I spend four hours a day at least, — and it is commonly more than that, — sauntering through the woods and over the hills and fields, absolutely free from all worldly engagements. You may safely say, A penny for your thoughts, or a thousand pounds. When sometimes I am reminded that the mechanics and shopkeepers stay in their shops not only all the forenoon, but all the afternoon too, sitting with crossed legs, so many of them, — as if the legs were made to sit upon, and not to stand or walk upon, — I think that they deserve some credit for not having all committed suicide long ago.

I, who cannot stay in my chamber for a single day without acquiring some rust, and when sometimes I have stolen forth for a walk at the eleventh hour or four o'clock in the afternoon, too late to redeem the day, when the shades of night were already beginning to be mingled with the daylight, have felt as if I had committed some sin to be atoned for, — I confess that I am astonished at the power of endurance, to say nothing of the moral insensibility, of my neighbors who confine themselves to shops and offices the whole day for weeks and months, aye, and years almost together. I know not what manner of stuff they are of, — sitting there now at three o'clock in the afternoon, as if it were three o'clock in the morning. Bonaparte may talk of the three-o'clock-in-the-morning courage, but it is nothing to the courage which can sit down cheerfully at this hour in the afternoon over against one's self whom you have known all the morning, to starve out a garrison to whom you are bound by such strong ties of sympathy. I wonder that about this time, or say between four and five o'clock in the afternoon, too late for the morning papers and too early for the evening ones, there is not a general explosion heard up and down the street, scattering a legion of antiquated and house-bred notions and whims to the four winds for an airing, — and so the evil cure itself.

How womankind, who are confined to the house still more than men, stand it I do not know; but I have ground to suspect that most of them do not *stand* it at all. When, early in a summer afternoon, we have been shaking the dust of the village from the skirts of our garments, making haste past those houses with purely Doric or Gothic fronts, which have such an air of repose about them, my companion whispers that probably about these times their occupants are all gone to bed. Then it is that I appreciate the beauty and the glory of architecture, which itself never turns in, but forever stands out and erect, keeping watch over the slumberers.

No doubt temperament, and, above all, age, have a good deal to do with it. As a man grows older, his ability to sit still and follow indoor occupations increases. He grows vespertinal in his habits as the evening of life approaches, till at last he comes forth only just before sundown, and gets all the walk that he requires in half an hour.

But the walking of which I speak has nothing in it akin to taking exercise, as it is called, as the sick take medicine at stated hours, — as the

swinging of dumb-bells or chairs; but is itself
the enterprise and adventure of the day. If you
would get exercise, go in search of the springs
of life. Think of a man's swinging dumb-bells
for his health, when those springs are bubbling
up in far-off pastures unsought by him!

Moreover, you must walk like a camel, which
is said to be the only beast which ruminates when
walking. When a traveler asked Wordsworth's
servant to show him her master's study, she
answered, "Here is his library, but his study is
out of doors."

Living much out of doors, in the sun and
wind, will no doubt produce a certain roughness
of character, — will cause a thicker cuticle to
grow over some of the finer qualities of our
nature, as on the face and hands, or as severe
manual labor robs the hands of some of their
delicacy of touch. So staying in the house, on
the other hand, may produce a softness and
smoothness, not to say thinness of skin, accom-
panied by an increased sensibility to certain
impressions. Perhaps we should be more sus-
ceptible to some influences important to our
intellectual and moral growth, if the sun had
shone and the wind blown on us a little less;
and no doubt it is a nice matter to proportion
rightly the thick and thin skin. But methinks
that is a scurf that will fall off fast enough, —

that the natural remedy is to be found in the proportion which the night bears to the day, the winter to the summer, thought to experience. There will be so much the more air and sunshine in our thoughts. The callous palms of the laborer are conversant with finer tissues of self-respect and heroism, whose touch thrills the heart, than the languid fingers of idleness. That is mere sentimentality that lies abed by day and thinks itself white, far from the tan and callus of experience.

When we walk, we naturally go to the fields and woods: what would become of us, if we walked only in a garden or a mall? Even some sects of philosophers have felt the necessity of importing the woods to themselves, since they did not go to the woods. "They planted groves and walks of Platanes," where they took *subdiales ambulationes* in porticos open to the air. Of course it is of no use to direct our steps to the woods, if they do not carry us thither. I am alarmed when it happens that I have walked a mile into the woods bodily, without getting there in spirit. In my afternoon walk I would fain forget all my morning occupations and my obligations to society. But it sometimes happens that I cannot easily shake off the village. The thought of some work will run in my head and I am not where my body is, — I am out of my senses. In my walks I would fain return to my senses. What business have I in the woods, if I am thinking of something out of the woods? I suspect myself, and cannot help a shudder, when I find myself so implicated even in what are called good works, — for this may sometimes happen.

My vicinity affords many good walks; and though for so many years I have walked almost every day, and sometimes for several days together, I have not yet exhausted them. An absolutely new prospect is a great happiness, and I can still get this any afternoon. Two or three hours' walking will carry me to as strange a country as I expect ever to see. A single farm-house which I had not seen before is sometimes as good as the dominions of the King of Dahomey. There is in fact a sort of harmony discoverable between the capabilities of the landscape within a circle of ten miles' radius, or the limits of an afternoon walk, and the threescore years and ten of human life. It will never become quite familiar to you.

Nowadays almost all man's improvements, so called, as the building of houses, and the cutting down of the forest and of all large trees, simply deform the landscape, and make it more and more tame and cheap. A people who would begin by burning the fences and let the forest stand! I saw the fences half consumed, their ends lost in the middle of the prairie, and some worldly miser with a surveyor looking after his bounds, while heaven had taken place around him, and he did not see the angels going to and fro, but was looking for an old post-hole in the midst of paradise. I looked again, and saw him standing in the middle of a boggy stygian fen, surrounded by devils, and he had found his bounds without a doubt, three little stones, where a stake had been driven, and looking nearer, I saw that the Prince of Darkness was his surveyor.

I can easily walk ten, fifteen, twenty, any number of miles, commencing at my own door, without going by any house, without crossing a road except where the fox and the mink do: first along by the river, and then the brook, and then the meadow and the woodside. There are square miles in my vicinity which have no inhabitant. From many a hill I can see civilization and the abodes of man afar. The farmers and their works are scarcely more obvious than woodchucks and their burrows. Man and his affairs, church and state and school, trade and commerce, and manufactures and agriculture, even politics, the most alarming of them all, — I am pleased to see how little space they occupy in the landscape. Politics is but a narrow field,

and that still narrower highway yonder leads to
it. I sometimes direct the traveler thither. If
you would go to the political world, follow the
great road, — follow that market-man, keep his
dust in your eyes, and it will lead you straight
to it; for it, too, has its place merely, and does
not occupy all space. I pass from it as from
a bean-field into the forest, and it is forgotten.
In one half-hour I can walk off to some portion
of the earth's surface where a man does not
stand from one year's end to another, and there,
consequently, politics are not, for they are but
as the cigar-smoke of a man.

The village is the place to which the roads
tend, a sort of expansion of the highway, as a
lake of a river. It is the body of which roads
are the arms and legs, — a trivial or quadrivial
place, the thoroughfare and ordinary of travelers. The word is from the Latin *villa*, which
together with *via*, a way, or more anciently *ved*
and *vella*, Varro derives from *veho*, to carry,
because the villa is the place to and from which
things are carried. They who got their living
by teaming were said *vellaturam facere*. Hence,
too, the Latin word *vilis* and our vile; also
villain. This suggests what kind of degeneracy
villagers are liable to. They are wayworn by
the travel that goes by and over them, without
traveling themselves.

Some do not walk at all; others walk in the highways; a few walk across lots. Roads are made for horses and men of business. I do not travel in them much, comparatively, because I am not in a hurry to get to any tavern or grocery or livery-stable or depot to which they lead. I am a good horse to travel, but not from choice a roadster. The landscape-painter uses the figures of men to mark a road. He would not make that use of my figure. I walk out into a Nature such as the old prophets and poets, Menu, Moses, Homer, Chaucer, walked in. You may name it America, but it is not America; neither Americus Vespucius, nor Columbus, nor the rest were the discoverers of it. There is a truer account of it in mythology than in any history of America, so called, that I have seen.

However, there are a few old roads that may be trodden with profit, as if they led somewhere now that they are nearly discontinued. There is the Old Marlborough Road, which does not go to Marlborough now, methinks, unless that is Marlborough where it carries me. I am the bolder to speak of it here, because I presume that there are one or two such roads in every town.

THE OLD MARLBOROUGH ROAD.

Where they once dug for money,
But never found any;
Where sometimes Martial Miles
Singly files,
And Elijah Wood,
I fear for no good:
No other man,
Save Elisha Dugan, —
O man of wild habits,
Partridges and rabbits,
Who hast no cares
Only to set snares,
Who liv'st all alone,
Close to the bone,
And where life is sweetest
Constantly eatest.
When the spring stirs my blood
    With the instinct to travel
    I can get enough gravel
On the Old Marlborough Road.
Nobody repairs it,
For nobody wears it;
It is a living way,
As the Christians say.
Not many there be
    Who enter therein,
Only the guests of the
    Irishman Quin.
What is it, what is it,
    But a direction out there,
And the bare possibility
    Of going somewhere?
    Great guide-boards of stone,
    But travelers none;

Cenotaphs of the towns
Named on their crowns.
It is worth going to see
Where you *might* be.
What king
Did the thing,
I am still wondering;
Set up how or when,
By what selectmen,
Gourgas or Lee,
Clark or Darby?
They're a great endeavor
To be something forever;
Blank tablets of stone,
Where a traveler might groan,
And in one sentence
Grave all that is known;
Which another might read,
In his extreme need.
I know one or two
Lines that would do,
Literature that might stand
All over the land,
Which a man could remember
Till next December,
And read again in the Spring,
After the thawing.
If with fancy unfurled
You leave your abode,
You may go round the world
By the Old Marlborough Road.

At present, in this vicinity, the best part of the land is not private property; the landscape is not owned, and the walker enjoys comparative freedom. But possibly the day will come when it will be partitioned off into so-called pleasure-grounds, in which a few will take a narrow and exclusive pleasure only, — when fences shall be multiplied, and man-traps and other engines invented to confine men to the *public* road, and walking over the surface of God's earth shall be construed to mean trespassing on some gentleman's grounds. To enjoy a thing exclusively is commonly to exclude yourself from the true enjoyment of it. Let us improve our opportunities, then, before the evil days come.

What is it that makes it so hard sometimes to determine whither we will walk? I believe that there is a subtle magnetism in Nature, which, if we unconsciously yield to it, will direct us aright. It is not indifferent to us which way we walk. There is a right way; but we are very liable from heedlessness and stupidity to take the wrong one. We would fain take that walk, never yet taken by us through this actual world, which is perfectly symbolical of the path which we love to travel in the interior and ideal world; and sometimes, no doubt, we find it difficult to choose our direction, because it does not yet exist distinctly in our idea.

When I go out of the house for a walk, uncertain as yet whither I will bend my steps, and submit myself to my instinct to decide for me, I find, strange and whimsical as it may seem, that I finally and inevitably settle southwest, toward some particular wood or meadow or deserted pasture or hill in that direction. My needle is slow to settle, — varies a few degrees, and does not always point due southwest, it is true, and it has good authority for this variation, but it always settles between west and south-southwest. The future lies that way to me, and the earth seems more unexhausted and richer on that side. The outline which would bound my walks would be, not a circle, but a parabola, or rather like one of those cometary orbits which have been thought to be non-returning curves, in this case opening westward, in which my house occupies the place of the sun. I turn round and round irresolute sometimes for a quarter of an hour, until I decide, for a thousandth time, that I will walk into the southwest or west. Eastward I go only by force; but westward I go free. Thither no business leads me. It is hard for me to believe that I shall find fair landscapes or sufficient wildness and freedom behind the eastern horizon. I am not excited by the prospect of a walk thither; but I believe that the forest which I see in the western horizon stretches uninterruptedly toward the setting sun, and there are no towns

nor cities in it of enough consequence to disturb
me. Let me live where I will, on this side is
the city, on that the wilderness, and ever I am
leaving the city more and more, and withdraw-
ing into the wilderness. I should not lay so
much stress on this fact, if I did not believe that
something like this is the prevailing tendency of
my countrymen. I must walk toward Oregon,
and not toward Europe. And that way the nation is moving, and I may say that mankind progress from east to west. Within a few years we
have witnessed the phenomenon of a southeast-
ward migration, in the settlement of Australia;
but this affects us as a retrograde movement,
and, judging from the moral and physical character of the first generation of Australians, has
not yet proved a successful experiment. The
eastern Tartars think that there is nothing west
beyond Thibet. "The world ends there," say
they; "beyond there is nothing but a shoreless
sea." It is unmitigated East where they live.

We go eastward to realize history and study
the works of art and literature, retracing the
steps of the race; we go westward as into the
future, with a spirit of enterprise and adventure.
The Atlantic is a Lethean stream, in our passage over which we have had an opportunity to
forget the Old World and its institutions. If
we do not succeed this time, there is perhaps one

more chance for the race left before it arrives on the banks of the Styx; and that is in the Lethe of the Pacific, which is three times as wide.

I know not how significant it is, or how far it is an evidence of singularity, that an individual should thus consent in his pettiest walk with the general movement of the race; but I know that something akin to the migratory instinct in birds and quadrupeds, — which, in some instances, is known to have affected the squirrel tribe, impelling them to a general and mysterious movement, in which they were seen, say some, crossing the broadest rivers, each on its particular chip, with its tail raised for a sail, and bridging narrower streams with their dead, — that something like the *furor* which affects the domestic cattle in the spring, and which is referred to a worm in their tails, — affects both nations and individuals, either perennially or from time to time. Not a flock of wild geese cackles over our town, but it to some extent unsettles the value of real estate here, and, if I were a broker, I should probably take that disturbance into account.

> "Than longen folk to gon on pilgrimages,
>   And palmeres for to seken strange strondes."

Every sunset which I witness inspires me with the desire to go to a West as distant and as fair as that into which the sun goes down. He ap-

pears to migrate westward daily, and tempt us
to follow him. He is the Great Western Pioneer
whom the nations follow. We dream all night
of those mountain-ridges in the horizon, though
they may be of vapor only, which were last
gilded by his rays. The island of Atlantis, and
the islands and gardens of the Hesperides, a sort
of terrestrial paradise, appear to have been the
Great West of the ancients, enveloped in mys-
tery and poetry. Who has not seen in imagination, when looking into the sunset sky, the
gardens of the Hesperides, and the foundation of
all those fables?

Columbus felt the westward tendency more
strongly than any before. He obeyed it, and
found a New World for Castile and Leon. The
herd of men in those days scented fresh pastures
from afar.

> " And now the sun had stretched out all the hills,
>   And now was dropped into the western bay ;
>   At last *he* rose, and twitched his mantle blue ;
>   To-morrow to fresh woods and pastures new."

Where on the globe can there be found an
area of equal extent with that occupied by the
bulk of our States, so fertile and so rich and
varied in its productions, and at the same time
so habitable by the European, as this is? Michaux, who knew but part of them, says that
"the species of large trees are much more nu-

merous in North America than in Europe; in the
United States there are more than one hundred
and forty species that exceed thirty feet in
height; in France there are but thirty that attain this size." Later botanists more than confirm his observations. Humboldt came to America to realize his youthful dreams of a tropical
vegetation, and he beheld it in its greatest perfection in the primitive forests of the Amazon,
the most gigantic wilderness on the earth, which
he has so eloquently described. The geographer Guyot, himself a European, goes farther,
— farther than I am ready to follow him; yet
not when he says: "As the plant is made for
the animal, as the vegetable world is made for
the animal world, America is made for the man
of the Old World. . . . The man of the Old
World sets out upon his way. Leaving the
highlands of Asia, he descends from station to
station towards Europe. Each of his steps is
marked by a new civilization superior to the
preceding, by a greater power of development.
Arrived at the Atlantic, he pauses on the shore
of this unknown ocean, the bounds of which he
knows not, and turns upon his footprints for an
instant." When he has exhausted the rich soil
of Europe, and reinvigorated himself, "then
recommences his adventurous career westward as
in the earliest ages." So far Guyot.

From this western impulse coming in contact with the barrier of the Atlantic sprang the commerce and enterprise of modern times. The younger Michaux, in his "Travels West of the Alleghanies in 1802," says that the common inquiry in the newly settled West was, "'From what part of the world have you come?' As if these vast and fertile regions would naturally be the place of meeting and common country of all the inhabitants of the globe."

To use an obsolete Latin word, I might say, *Ex Oriente lux ; ex Occidente* FRUX. From the East light; from the West fruit.

Sir Francis Head, an English traveler and a Governor-General of Canada, tells us that "in both the northern and southern hemispheres of the New World, Nature has not only outlined her works on a larger scale, but has painted the whole picture with brighter and more costly colors than she used in delineating and in beautifying the Old World. . . . The heavens of America appear infinitely higher, the sky is bluer, the air is fresher, the cold is intenser, the moon looks larger, the stars are brighter, the thunder is louder, the lightning is vivider, the wind is stronger, the rain is heavier, the mountains are higher, the rivers longer, the forests bigger, the plains broader." This statement will do at least to set against Buffon's account of this part of the world and its productions.

Linnæus said long ago, "Nescio quæ facies *læta*, *glabra* plantis Americanis: I know not what there is of joyous and smooth in the aspect of American plants;" and I think that in this country there are no, or at most very few, *Africanæ bestiæ*, African beasts, as the Romans called them, and that in this respect also it is peculiarly fitted for the habitation of man. We are told that within three miles of the centre of the East-Indian city of Singapore, some of the inhabitants are annually carried off by tigers; but the traveler can lie down in the woods at night almost anywhere in North America without fear of wild beasts.

These are encouraging testimonies. If the moon looks larger here than in Europe, probably the sun looks larger also. If the heavens of America appear infinitely higher, and the stars brighter, I trust that these facts are symbolical of the height to which the philosophy and poetry and religion of her inhabitants may one day soar. At length, perchance, the immaterial heaven will appear as much higher to the American mind, and the intimations that star it as much brighter. For I believe that climate does thus react on man, — as there is something in the mountain-air that feeds the spirit and inspires. Will not man grow to greater perfection intellectually as well as physically under

these influences? Or is it unimportant how
many foggy days there are in his life? I trust
that we shall be more imaginative, that our
thoughts will be clearer, fresher, and more
ethereal, as our sky, — our understanding more
comprehensive and broader, like our plains, —
our intellect generally on a grander scale, like
our thunder and lightning, our rivers and mountains and forests, — and our hearts shall even
correspond in breadth and depth and grandeur
to our inland seas. Perchance there will appear
to the traveler something, he knows not what,
of *læta* and *glabra*, of joyous and serene, in our
very faces. Else to what end does the world go
on, and why was America discovered?

To Americans I hardly need to say, —

"Westward the star of empire takes its way."

As a true patriot, I should be ashamed to think
that Adam in paradise was more favorably sit-
uated on the whole than the backwoodsman in
this country.

Our sympathies in Massachusetts are not confined to New England; though we may be es-
tranged from the South, we sympathize with the
West. There is the home of the younger sons,
as among the Scandinavians they took to the sea
for their inheritance. It is too late to be study-
ing Hebrew; it is more important to understand
even the slang of to-day.

Some months ago I went to see a panorama of the Rhine. It was like a dream of the Middle Ages. I floated down its historic stream in something more than imagination, under bridges built by the Romans, and repaired by later heroes, past cities and castles whose very names were music to my ears, and each of which was the subject of a legend. There were Ehren-breitstein and Rolandseck and Coblentz, which I knew only in history. They were ruins that interested me chiefly. There seemed to come up from its waters and its vine-clad hills and valleys a hushed music as of Crusaders depart-ing for the Holy Land. I floated along under the spell of enchantment, as if I had been transported to an heroic age, and breathed an atmosphere of chivalry.

Soon after, I went to see a panorama of the Mississippi, and as I worked my way up the river in the light of to-day, and saw the steam-boats wooding up, counted the rising cities, gazed on the fresh ruins of Nauvoo, beheld the In-dians moving west across the stream, and, as before I had looked up the Moselle, now looked up the Ohio and the Missouri and heard the legends of Dubuque and of Wenona's Cliff, — still thinking more of the future than of the past or present, — I saw that this was a Rhine stream of a different kind; that the foundations

of castles were yet to be laid, and the famous
bridges were yet to be thrown over the river;
and I felt that *this was the heroic age itself*,
though we know it not, for the hero is commonly
the simplest and obscurest of men.

The West of which I speak is but another
name for the Wild; and what I have been preparing to say is, that in Wildness is the preser-
vation of the World.   Every tree sends its fibres
forth in search of the Wild.   The cities import
it at any price.   Men plough and sail for it.
From the forest and wilderness come the tonics
and barks which brace mankind.   Our ancestors
were savages.   The story of Romulus and Re-
mus being suckled by a wolf is not a meaningless fable.   The founders of every state which
has risen to eminence have drawn their nourishment and vigor from a similar wild source.   It
was because the children of the Empire were not
suckled by the wolf that they were conquered
and displaced by the children of the northern
forests who were.

I believe in the forest, and in the meadow,
and in the night in which the corn grows.   We
require an infusion of hemlock-spruce or arbor
vitæ in our tea.   There is a difference between
eating and drinking for strength and from mere
gluttony.   The Hottentots eagerly devour the

marrow of the koodoo and other antelopes raw, as a matter of course. Some of our Northern Indians eat raw the marrow of the Arctic reindeer, as well as various other parts, including the summits of the antlers, as long as they are soft. And herein, perchance, they have stolen a march on the cooks of Paris. They get what usually goes to feed the fire. This is probably better than stall-fed beef and slaughter-house pork to make a man of. Give me a wildness whose glance no civilization can endure, — as if we lived on the marrow of koodoos devoured raw.

There are some intervals which border the strain of the wood-thrush, to which I would migrate, — wild lands where no settler has squatted; to which, methinks, I am already acclimated.

The African hunter Cummings tells us that the skin of the eland, as well as that of most other antelopes just killed, emits the most delicious perfume of trees and grass. I would have every man so much like a wild antelope, so much a part and parcel of Nature, that his very person should thus sweetly advertise our senses of his presence, and remind us of those parts of Nature which he most haunts. I feel no disposition to be satirical, when the trapper's coat emits the odor of musquash even; it is a sweeter scent to me than that which commonly exhales from the merchant's or the scholar's garments. When I go into their wardrobes and handle their vestments, I am reminded of no grassy plains and flowery meads which they have frequented, but of dusty merchants' exchanges and libraries rather.

A tanned skin is something more than respectable, and perhaps olive is a fitter color than white for a man, — a denizen of the woods. "The pale white man!" I do not wonder that the African pitied him. Darwin the naturalist says, "A white man bathing by the side of a Tahitian was like a plant bleached by the gardener's art, compared with a fine, dark green one, growing vigorously in the open fields."

Ben Jonson exclaims, —

"How near to good is what is fair!"

So I would say, —

How near to good is what is *wild!*

Life consists with wildness. The most alive is the wildest. Not yet subdued to man, its presence refreshes him. One who pressed forward incessantly and never rested from his labors, who grew fast and made infinite demands on life, would always find himself in a new country or wilderness, and surrounded by the raw material of life. He would be climbing over the prostrate stems of primitive forest-trees.

Hope and the future for me are not in lawns and cultivated fields, not in towns and cities, but in the impervious and quaking swamps. When, formerly, I have analyzed my partiality for some farm which I had contemplated purchasing, I have frequently found that I was attracted solely by a few square rods of impermeable and unfathomable bog, — a natural sink in one corner of it. That was the jewel which dazzled me. I derive more of my subsistence from the swamps which surround my native town than from the cultivated gardens in the village. There are no richer parterres to my eyes than the dense beds of dwarf andromeda (*Cassandra calyculata*) which cover these tender places on the earth's surface. Botany cannot go farther than tell me the names of the shrubs which grow there, — the high-blueberry, panicled andromeda, lamb-kill, azalea, and rhodora, — all standing in the quaking sphagnum. I often think that I should like to have my house front on this mass of dull red bushes, omitting other flower plots and borders, transplanted spruce and trim box, even graveled walks, — to have this fertile spot under my windows, not a few imported barrow-fulls of soil only to cover the sand which was thrown out in digging the cellar. Why not put my house, my parlor, behind this plot, instead of behind that meagre assemblage of curiosities, that poor apology for a Nature and Art, which I call my front yard? It is an effort to clear up and make a decent appearance when the carpenter and mason have departed, though done as much for the passer-by as the dweller within. The most tasteful front-yard fence was never an agreeable object of study to me; the most elaborate ornaments, acorn-tops, or what not, soon wearied and disgusted me. Bring your sills up to the very edge of the swamp, then (though it may not be the best place for a dry cellar), so that there be no access on that side to citizens. Front-yards are not made to walk in, but, at most, through, and you could go in the back way.

Yes, though you may think me perverse, if it were proposed to me to dwell in the neighbor-hood of the most beautiful garden that ever human art contrived, or else of a Dismal Swamp, I should certainly decide for the swamp. How vain, then, have been all your labors, citizens, for me!

My spirits infallibly rise in proportion to the outward dreariness. Give me the ocean, the desert, or the wilderness! In the desert, pure air and solitude compensate for want of moisture and fertility. The traveler Burton says of it: "Your *morale* improves; you become frank and cordial, hospitable and single-minded. . . . In the desert, spirituous liquors excite only disgust. There is a keen enjoyment in a mere animal existence." They who have been traveling long on the steppes of Tartary say: "On reëntering cultivated lands, the agitation, perplexity, and turmoil of civilization oppressed and suffocated us; the air seemed to fail us, and we felt every moment as if about to die of asphyxia." When I would recreate myself, I seek the darkest wood, the thickest and most interminable and, to the citizen, most dismal swamp. I enter a swamp as a sacred place, — a *sanctum sanctorum*. There is the strength, the marrow of Nature. The wild-wood covers the virgin-mould, — and the same soil is good for men and for trees. A man's health requires as many acres of meadow to his prospect as his farm does loads of muck. There are the strong meats on which he feeds. A town is saved, not more by the righteous men in it than by the woods and swamps that surround it. A township where one primitive forest waves above while another primitive forest rots below, — such a town is fitted to raise not only corn and potatoes, but poets and philosophers for the coming ages. In such a soil grew Homer and Confucius and the rest, and out of such a wilderness comes the Reformer eating locusts and wild honey.

To preserve wild animals implies generally

the creation of a forest for them to dwell in or resort to. So it is with man. A hundred years ago they sold bark in our streets peeled from our own woods. In the very aspect of those primitive and rugged trees there was, methinks, a tanning principle which hardened and consolidated the fibres of men's thoughts. Ah! already I shudder for these comparatively degenerate days of my native village, when you cannot collect a load of bark of good thickness, — and we no longer produce tar and turpentine.

The civilized nations — Greece, Rome, England — have been sustained by the primitive forests which anciently rotted where they stand. They survive as long as the soil is not exhausted. Alas for human culture! little is to be expected of a nation, when the vegetable mould is exhausted, and it is compelled to make manure of the bones of its fathers. There the poet sustains himself merely by his own superfluous fat, and the philosopher comes down on his marrow-bones.

It is said to be the task of the American "to work the virgin soil," and that "agriculture here already assumes proportions unknown everywhere else." I think that the farmer displaces the Indian even because he redeems the meadow, and so makes himself stronger and in some respects more natural. I was surveying for a man

the other day a single straight line one hundred
and thirty-two rods long, through a swamp, at
whose entrance might have been written the
words which Dante read over the entrance to the
infernal regions, — "Leave all hope, ye that enter," — that is, of ever getting out again; where
at one time I saw my employer actually up to
his neck and swimming for his life in his property, though it was still winter. He had another similar swamp which I could not survey at
all, because it was completely under water, and
nevertheless, with regard to a third swamp,
which I did *survey* from a distance, he remarked
to me, true to his instincts, that he would not
part with it for any consideration, on account of
the mud which it contained. And that man
intends to put a girdling ditch round the whole
in the course of forty months, and so redeem it
by the magic of his spade. I refer to him only
as the type of a class.

The weapons with which we have gained our
most important victories, which should be
handed down as heirlooms from father to son,
are not the sword and the lance, but the bush-
whack, the turf-cutter, the spade, and the bog-
hoe, rusted with the blood of many a meadow.
and begrimed with the dust of many a hard-
fought field. The very winds blew the Indian's
corn-field into the meadow, and pointed out the

way which he had not the skill to follow. He had no better implement with which to intrench himself in the land than a clam-shell. But the farmer is armed with plough and spade.

In literature it is only the wild that attracts us. Dullness is but another name for tameness. It is the uncivilized free and wild thinking in "Hamlet" and the "Iliad," in all the Scriptures and Mythologies, not learned in the schools, that delights us. As the wild duck is more swift and beautiful than the tame, so is the wild — the mallard — thought, which 'mid falling dews wings its way above the fens. A truly good book is something as natural, and as unexpectedly and unaccountably fair and perfect, as a wild flower discovered on the prairies of the West or in the jungles of the East. Genius is a light which makes the darkness visible, like the lightning's flash, which perchance shatters the temple of knowledge itself, — and not a taper lighted at the hearth-stone of the race, which pales before the light of common day.

English literature, from the days of the minstrels to the Lake Poets, — Chaucer and Spenser and Milton, and even Shakespeare, included, — breathes no quite fresh and, in this sense, wild strain. It is an essentially tame and civilized literature, reflecting Greece and Rome. Her wilderness is a greenwood, her wild man a Robin

Hood. There is plenty of genial love of Nature, but not so much of Nature herself. Her chronicles inform us when her wild animals, but not when the wild man in her, became extinct.

The science of Humboldt is one thing, poetry is another thing. The poet to-day, notwithstanding all the discoveries of science, and the accumulated learning of mankind, enjoys no advantage over Homer.

Where is the literature which gives expression to Nature? He would be a poet who could impress the winds and streams into his service, to speak for him; who nailed words to their primitive senses, as farmers drive down stakes in the spring, which the frost has heaved; who derived his words as often as he used them, — transplanted them to his page with earth adhering to their roots; whose words were so true and fresh and natural that they would appear to expand like the buds at the approach of spring, though they lay half-smothered between two musty leaves in a library, — aye, to bloom and bear fruit there, after their kind, annually, for the faithful reader, in sympathy with surrounding Nature.

I do not know of any poetry to quote which adequately expresses this yearning for the Wild. Approached from this side, the best poetry is tame. I do not know where to find in any literature, ancient or modern, any account which contents me of that Nature with which even I am acquainted. You will perceive that I demand something which no Augustan nor Elizabethan age, which no *culture*, in short, can give. Mythology comes nearer to it than anything. How much more fertile a Nature, at least, has Grecian mythology its root in than English literature! Mythology is the crop which the Old World bore before its soil was exhausted, before the fancy and imagination were affected with blight; and which it still bears, wherever its pristine vigor is unabated. All other literatures endure only as the elms which overshadow our houses; but this is like the great dragon-tree of the Western Isles, as old as mankind, and, whether that does or not, will endure as long; for the decay of other literatures makes the soil in which it thrives.

The West is preparing to add its fables to those of the East. The valleys of the Ganges, the Nile, and the Rhine having yielded their crop, it remains to be seen what the valleys of the Amazon, the Plate, the Orinoco, the St. Lawrence, and the Mississippi will produce. Perchance, when, in the course of ages, American liberty has become a fiction of the past, — as it is to some extent a fiction of the present, — the poets of the world will be inspired by American mythology.

The wildest dreams of wild men, even, are not the less true, though they may not recommend themselves to the sense which is most common among Englishmen and Americans to-day. It is not every truth that recommends itself to the common sense. Nature has a place for the wild clematis as well as for the cabbage. Some expressions of truth are reminiscent, — others merely *sensible*, as the phrase is, — others prophetic. Some forms of disease, even, may prophesy forms of health. The geologist has discovered that the figures of serpents, griffins, flying dragons, and other fanciful embellishments of heraldry, have their prototypes in the forms of fossil species which were extinct before man was created, and hence "indicate a faint and shadowy knowledge of a previous state of organic existence." The Hindoos dreamed that the earth rested on an elephant, and the elephant on a tortoise, and the tortoise on a serpent; and though it may be an unimportant coincidence, it will not be out of place here to state, that a fossil tortoise has lately been discovered in Asia large enough to support an elephant. I confess that I am partial to these wild fancies, which transcend the order of time and development. They are the sublimest recreation of the intellect. The partridge loves peas, but not those that go with her into the pot.

In short, all good things are wild and free. There is something in a strain of music, whether produced by an instrument or by the human voice, — take the sound of a bugle in a summer night, for instance, — which by its wildness, to speak without satire, reminds me of the cries emitted by wild beasts in their native forests. It is so much of their wildness as I can understand. Give me for my friends and neighbors wild men, not tame ones. The wildness of the savage is but a faint symbol of the awful ferity with which good men and lovers meet.

I love even to see the domestic animals reassert their native rights, — any evidence that they have not wholly lost their original wild habits and vigor; as when my neighbor's cow breaks out of her pasture early in the spring and boldly swims the river, a cold, gray tide, twenty-five or thirty rods wide, swollen by the melted snow. It is the buffalo crossing the Mississippi. This exploit confers some dignity on the herd in my eyes, — already dignified. The seeds of instinct are preserved under the thick hides of cattle and horses, like seeds in the bowels of the earth, an indefinite period.

Any sportiveness in cattle is unexpected. I saw one day a herd of a dozen bullocks and cows running about and frisking in unwieldy sport, like huge rats, even like kittens. They shook their heads, raised their tails, and rushed up and down a hill, and I perceived by their horns, as well as by their activity, their relation to the deer tribe. But, alas! a sudden loud *Whoa!* would have damped their ardor at once, reduced them from venison to beef, and stiffened their sides and sinews like the locomotive. Who but the Evil One has cried, " Whoa ! " to mankind ? Indeed, the life of cattle, like that of many men, is but a sort of locomotiveness; they move a side at a time, and man, by his machinery, is meeting the horse and the ox half-way. What-ever part the whip has touched is thenceforth palsied. Who would ever think of a *side* of any of the supple cat tribe, as we speak of a *side* of beef ?

I rejoice that horses and steers have to be broken before they can be made the slaves of men, and that men themselves have some wild oats still left to sow before they become submis-sive members of society. Undoubtedly, all men are not equally fit subjects for civilization; and because the majority, like dogs and sheep, are tame by inherited disposition, this is no reason why the others should have their natures broken that they may be reduced to the same level. Men are in the main alike, but they were made several in order that they might be various. If a low use is to be served, one man will do nearly or quite as well as another; if a high one, individual excellence is to be regarded. Any man can stop a hole to keep the wind away, but no other man could serve so rare a use as the author of this illustration did. Confucius says, "The skins of the tiger and the leopard, when they are tanned, are as the skins of the dog and the sheep tanned." But it is not the part of a true culture to tame tigers, any more than it is to make sheep ferocious; and tanning their skins for shoes is not the best use to which they can be put.

When looking over a list of men's names in a foreign language, as of military officers, or of authors who have written on a particular subject, I am reminded once more that there is nothing in a name. The name Menschikoff, for instance, has nothing in it to my ears more human than a whisker, and it may belong to a rat. As the names of the Poles and Russians are to us, so are ours to them. It is as if they had been named by the child's rigmarole, — *Iery wiery ichery van, tittle-tol-tan*. I see in my mind a herd of wild creatures swarming over the earth, and to each the herdsman has affixed some barbarous sound in his own dialect. The names of men are of course as cheap and meaningless as *Bose* and *Tray*, the names of dogs.

Methinks it would be some advantage to philosophy, if men were named merely in the gross, as they are known. It would be necessary only to know the genus and perhaps the race or variety, to know the individual. We are not prepared to believe that every private soldier in a Roman army had a name of his own, — because we have not supposed that he had a character of his own.

At present our only true names are nicknames. I knew a boy who, from his peculiar energy, was called "Buster" by his playmates, and this rightly supplanted his Christian name. Some travelers tell us that an Indian had no name given him at first, but earned it, and his name was his fame; and among some tribes he acquired a new name with every new exploit. It is pitiful when a man bears a name for convenience merely, who has earned neither name nor fame.

I will not allow mere names to make distinctions for me, but still see men in herds for all them. A familiar name cannot make a man less strange to me. It may be given to a savage who retains in secret his own wild title earned in the woods. We have a wild savage in us, and a savage name is perchance somewhere recorded as ours. I see that my neighbor, who bears the familiar epithet William, or Edwin, takes it off

with his jacket. It does not adhere to him
when asleep or in anger, or aroused by any pas-
sion or inspiration. I seem to hear pronounced
by some of his kin at such a time his original
wild name in some jaw-breaking or else melodious tongue.

Here is this vast, savage, howling mother of
ours, Nature, lying all around, with such beauty,
and such affection for her children, as the leopard; and yet we are so early weaned from her
breast to society, to that culture which is exclusively an interaction of man on man, — a sort of
breeding in and in, which produces at most a
merely English nobility, a civilization destined
to have a speedy limit.

In society, in the best institutions of men, it
is easy to detect a certain precocity. When we
should still be growing children, we are already
little men. Give me a culture which imports
much muck from the meadows, and deepens the
soil, — not that which trusts to heating manures,
and improved implements and modes of culture
only!

Many a poor sore-eyed student that I have
heard of would grow faster, both intellectually
and physically, if, instead of sitting up so very
late, he honestly slumbered a fool's allowance.

There may be an excess even of informing

light. Niepce, a Frenchman, discovered "actinism," that power in the sun's rays which produces a chemical effect; that granite rocks, and stone structures, and statues of metal, "are all alike destructively acted upon during the hours of sunshine, and, but for provisions of Nature no less wonderful, would soon perish under the delicate touch of the most subtile of the agencies of the universe." But he observed that "those bodies which underwent this change during the daylight possessed the power of restoring themselves to their original conditions during the hours of night, when this excitement was no longer influencing them." Hence it has been inferred that "the hours of darkness are as necessary to the inorganic creation as we know night and sleep are to the organic kingdom." Not even does the moon shine every night, but gives place to darkness.

I would not have every man nor every part of a man cultivated, any more than I would have every acre of earth cultivated: part will be tillage, but the greater part will be meadow and forest, not only serving an immediate use, but preparing a mould against a distant future, by the annual decay of the vegetation which it supports.

There are other letters for the child to learn than those which Cadmus invented. The Spaniards have a good term to express this wild and dusky knowledge, *Gramática parda*, tawny grammar, a kind of mother-wit derived from that same leopard to which I have referred.

We have heard of a Society for the Diffusion of Useful Knowledge. It is said that knowledge is power; and the like. Methinks there is equal need of a Society for the Diffusion of Useful Ignorance, what we will call Beautiful Knowledge, a knowledge useful in a higher sense: for what is most of our boasted so-called knowledge but a conceit that we know something, which robs us of the advantage of our actual ignorance? What we call knowledge is often our positive ignorance ; ignorance our negative knowledge. By long years of patient industry and reading of the newspapers, — for what are the libraries of science but files of newspapers? — a man accumulates a myriad facts, lays them up in his memory, and then when in some spring of his life he saunters abroad into the Great Fields of thought, he, as it were, goes to grass like a horse and leaves all his harness behind in the stable. I would say to the Society for the Diffusion of Useful Knowledge, sometimes, — Go to grass. You have eaten hay long enough. The spring has come with its green crop. The very cows are driven to their country pastures before the end of May; though I have heard of one unnatural farmer who kept his cow in the barn and fed her on hay all the year round. So, frequently, the Society for the Diffusion of Useful Knowledge treats its cattle.

A man's ignorance sometimes is not only useful, but beautiful, — while his knowledge, so called, is oftentimes worse than useless, besides being ugly. Which is the best man to deal with, — he who knows nothing about a subject, and, what is extremely rare, knows that he knows nothing, or he who really knows something about it, but thinks that he knows all?

My desire for knowledge is intermittent; but my desire to bathe my head in atmospheres unknown to my feet is perennial and constant. The highest that we can attain to is not Knowledge, but Sympathy with Intelligence. I do not know that this higher knowledge amounts to anything more definite than a novel and grand surprise on a sudden revelation of the insufficiency of all that we called Knowledge before, — a discovery that there are more things in heaven and earth than are dreamed of in our philosophy. It is the lighting up of the mist by the sun. Man cannot *know* in any higher sense than this, any more than he can look serenely and with impunity in the face of the sun: Ὡς τὶ νοῶν, οὐ κεῖνον νοήσεις, — "You will not perceive that, as perceiving a particular thing," say the Chaldean Oracles.

There is something servile in the habit of seeking after a law which we may obey. We may study the laws of matter at and for our convenience, but a successful life knows no law. It is an unfortunate discovery certainly, that of a law which binds us where we did not know before that we were bound. Live free, child of the mist, — and with respect to knowledge we are all children of the mist. The man who takes the liberty to live is superior to all the laws, by virtue of his relation to the law-maker. "That is active duty," says the Vishnu Purana, "which is not for our bondage; that is knowledge which is for our liberation: all other duty is good only unto weariness; all other knowledge is only the cleverness of an artist."

It is remarkable how few events or crises there are in our histories; how little exercised we have been in our minds; how few experiences we have had. I would fain be assured that I am growing apace and rankly, though my very growth disturb this dull equanimity, — though it be with struggle through long, dark, muggy nights or seasons of gloom. It would be well, if all our lives were a divine tragedy even, instead of this trivial comedy or farce. Dante, Bunyan, and others appear to have been exercised in their minds more than we: they were subjected to a kind of culture such as our district schools and colleges do not contemplate. Even Mahomet, though many may scream at his name, had a good deal more to live for, aye, and to die for, than they have commonly.

When, at rare intervals, some thought visits one, as perchance he is walking on a railroad, then indeed the cars go by without his hearing them. But soon, by some inexorable law, our life goes by and the cars return.

> " Gentle breeze, that wanderest unseen,
>   And bendest the thistles round Loira of storms,
>   Traveler of the windy glens,
>   Why hast thou left my ear so soon ? "

While almost all men feel an attraction drawing them to society, few are attracted strongly to Nature. In their reaction to Nature men appear to me for the most part, notwithstanding their arts, lower than the animals. It is not often a beautiful relation, as in the case of the animals. How little appreciation of the beauty of the landscape there is among us! We have to be told that the Greeks called the world Κόσμος, Beauty, or Order, but we do not see clearly why they did so, and we esteem it at best only a curious philological fact.

For my part, I feel that with regard to Nature I live a sort of border life, on the confines of a world into which I make occasional and tran-

sient forays only, and my patriotism and allegiance to the State into whose territories I seem
to retreat are those of a moss-trooper. Unto
a life which I call natural I would gladly follow even a will-o'-the-wisp through bogs and
sloughs unimaginable, but no moon nor firefly
has shown me the causeway to it. Nature is a
personality so vast and universal that we have
never seen one of her features. The walker in
the familiar fields which stretch around my native town sometimes finds himself in another
land than is described in their owners' deeds,
as it were in some far-away field on the confines
of the actual Concord, where her jurisdiction
ceases, and the idea which the word Concord
suggests ceases to be suggested. These farms
which I have myself surveyed, these bounds
which I have set up, appear dimly still as
through a mist; but they have no chemistry
to fix them; they fade from the surface of the
glass; and the picture which the painter painted
stands out dimly from beneath. The world
with which we are commonly acquainted leaves
no trace, and it will have no anniversary.

I took a walk on Spaulding's Farm the other
afternoon. I saw the setting sun lighting up
the opposite side of a stately pine wood. Its
golden rays straggled into the aisles of the wood
as into some noble hall. I was impressed as if

some ancient and altogether admirable and shining family had settled there in that part of the
land called Concord, unknown to me, — to
whom the sun was servant, — who had not gone
into society in the village, — who had not been
called on. I saw their park, their pleasure-
ground, beyond through the wood, in Spaulding's cranberry-meadow. The pines furnished
them with gables as they grew. Their house
was not obvious to vision; the trees grew through
it. I do not know whether I heard the sounds
of a suppressed hilarity or not. They seemed
to recline on the sunbeams. They have sons
and daughters. They are quite well. The
farmer's cart-path, which leads directly through
their hall, does not in the least put them out, as
the muddy bottom of a pool is sometimes seen
through the reflected skies. They never heard
of Spaulding, and do not know that he is their
neighbor, — notwithstanding I·heard him whistle as he drove his team through the house.
Nothing can equal the serenity of their lives.
Their coat of arms is simply a lichen. I saw
it painted on the pines and oaks. Their attics
were in the tops of the trees. They are of no
politics. There was no noise of labor. I did
not perceive that they were weaving or spinning.
Yet I did detect, when the wind lulled and
hearing was done away, the finest imaginable

sweet musical hum, — as of a distant hive in May, which perchance was the sound of their thinking. They had no idle thoughts, and no one without could see their work, for their industry was not as in knots and excrescences embayed.

But I find it difficult to remember them. They fade irrevocably out of my mind even now while I speak, and endeavor to recall them and recollect myself. It is only after a long and serious effort to recollect my best thoughts that I become again aware of their cohabitancy. If it were not for such families as this, I think I should move out of Concord.

We are accustomed to say in New England that few and fewer pigeons visit us every year. Our forests furnish no mast for them. So, it would seem, few and fewer thoughts visit each growing man from year to year, for the grove in our minds is laid waste, — sold to feed unnecessary fires of ambition, or sent to mill, and there is scarcely a twig left for them to perch on. They no longer build nor breed with us. In some more genial season, perchance, a faint shadow flits across the landscape of the mind, cast by the *wings* of some thought in its vernal or autumnal migration, but, looking up, we are unable to detect the substance of the thought it-

self. Our winged thoughts are turned to poul-
try. They no longer soar, and they attain only
to a Shanghai and Cochin - China grandeur.
Those *gra-a-ate thoughts*, those *gra-a-ate men*
you hear of!

We hug the earth, — how rarely we mount!
Methinks we might elevate ourselves a little
more. We might climb a tree, at least. I
found my account in climbing a tree once. It
was a tall white pine, on the top of a hill; and
though I got well pitched, I was well paid for
it, for I discovered new mountains in the horizon which I had never seen before, — so much
more of the earth and the heavens. I might
have walked about the foot of the tree for threescore years and ten, and yet I certainly should
never have seen them. But, above all, I discovered around me, — it was near the end of
June, — on the ends of the topmost branches
only, a few minute and delicate red cone-like
blossoms, the fertile flower of the white pine
looking heavenward. I carried straightway to
the village the topmost spire, and showed it to
stranger jurymen who walked the streets, — for
it was court-week, — and to farmers and lum-
ber-dealers and wood-choppers and hunters, and
not one had ever seen the like before, but they
wondered as at a star dropped down. Tell of

ancient architects finishing their works on the tops of columns as perfectly as on the lower and more visible parts! Nature has from the first expanded the minute blossoms of the forest only toward the heavens, above men's heads and unobserved by them. We see only the flowers that are under our feet in the meadows. The pines have developed their delicate blossoms on the highest twigs of the wood every summer for ages, as well over the heads of Nature's red children as of her white ones; yet scarcely a farmer or hunter in the land has ever seen them.

Above all, we cannot afford not to live in the present. He is blessed over all mortals who loses no moment of the passing life in remembering the past. Unless our philosophy hears the cock crow in every barn-yard within our horizon, it is belated. That sound commonly reminds us that we are growing rusty and antique in our employments and habits of thought. His philosophy comes down to a more recent time than ours. There is something suggested by it that is a newer testament, — the gospel according to this moment. He has not fallen astern; he has got up early and kept up early, and to be where he is is to be in season, in the foremost rank of time. It is an expression of the health and soundness of Nature, a brag for

all the world, — healthiness as of a spring burst
forth, a new fountain of the Muses, to celebrate
this last instant of time. Where he lives no
fugitive slave laws are passed. Who has not
betrayed his master many times since last he
heard that note?

The merit of this bird's strain is in its freedom from all plaintiveness. The singer can
easily move us to tears or to laughter, but where
is he who can excite in us a pure morning joy?
When, in doleful dumps, breaking the awful
stillness of our wooden sidewalk on a Sunday,
or, perchance, a watcher in the house of mourning, I hear a cockerel crow far or near, I think
to myself, "There is one of us well, at any
rate," — and with a sudden gush return to my
senses.

We had a remarkable sunset one day last
November. I was walking in a meadow, the
source of a small brook, when the sun at last,
just before setting, after a cold gray day,
reached a clear stratum in the horizon, and the
softest, brightest morning sunlight fell on the
dry grass and on the stems of the trees in the
opposite horizon and on the leaves of the shrub-
oaks on the hillside, while our shadows stretched
long over the meadow eastward, as if we were
the only motes in its beams. It was such a

light as we could not have imagined a moment before, and the air also was so warm and serene that nothing was wanting to make a paradise of that meadow. When we reflected that this was not a solitary phenomenon, never to happen again, but that it would happen forever and ever an infinite number of evenings, and cheer and reassure the latest child that walked there, it was more glorious still.

The sun sets on some retired meadow, where no house is visible, with all the glory and splendor that it lavishes on cities, and perchance as it has never set before, — where there is but a solitary marsh-hawk to have his wings gilded by it, or only a musquash looks out from his cabin, and there is some little black-veined brook in the midst of the marsh, just beginning to meander, winding slowly round a decaying stump. We walked in so pure and bright a light, gilding the withered grass and leaves, so softly and serenely bright, I thought I had never bathed in such a golden flood, without a ripple or a murmur to it. The west side of every wood and rising ground gleamed like the boundary of Elysium, and the sun on our backs seemed like a gentle herdsman driving us home at evening.

So we saunter toward the Holy Land, till one day the sun shall shine more brightly than

ever he has done, shall perchance shine into our
minds and hearts, and light up our whole lives
with a great awakening light, as warm and
serene and golden as on a bankside in autumn.

AUTUMNAL TINts

EUROPEANS coming to America are surprised
by the brilliancy of our autumnal foliage.   There
is no account of such a phenomenon in English
poetry, because the trees acquire but few bright
colors there.   The most that Thomson says on
this subject in his "Autumn" is contained in the
lines, —

> "But see the fading many-colored woods,
>   Shade deepening over shade, the country round
>   Imbrown; a crowded umbrage, dusk and dun,
>   Of every hue, from wan declining green to sooty dark ; "

and in the line in which he speaks of

> "Autumn beaming o'er the yellow woods."

The autumnal change of our woods has not
made a deep impression on our own literature
yet.   October has hardly tinged our poetry.

A great many, who have spent their lives in
cities, and have never chanced to come into the
country at this season, have never seen this, the
flower, or rather the ripe fruit, of the year.   I
remember riding with one such citizen, who,
though a fortnight too late for the most brilliant
tints, was taken by surprise, and would not be-

lieve that there had been any brighter. He had never heard of this phenomenon before. Not only many in our towns have never witnessed it, but it is scarcely remembered by the majority from year to year.

Most appear to confound changed leaves with withered ones, as if they were to confound ripe apples with rotten ones. I think that the change to some higher color in a leaf is an evidence that it has arrived at a late and perfect maturity, answering to the maturity of fruits. It is generally the lowest and oldest leaves which change first. But as the perfect winged and usually bright-colored insect is short-lived, so the leaves ripen but to fall.

Generally, every fruit, on ripening, and just before it falls, when it commences a more independent and individual existence, requiring less nourishment from any source, and that not so much from the earth through its stem as from the sun and air, acquires a bright tint. So do leaves. The physiologist says it is "due to an increased absorption of oxygen." That is the scientific account of the matter, — only a reassertion of the fact. But I am more interested in the rosy cheek than I am to know what particular diet the maiden fed on. The very forest and herbage, the pellicle of the earth, must acquire a bright color, an evidence of its ripeness, — as if the globe itself were a fruit on its stem, with ever a cheek toward the sun.

Flowers are but colored leaves, fruits but ripe ones. The edible part of most fruits is, as the physiologist says, "the parenchyma or fleshy tissue of the leaf," of which they are formed.

Our appetites have commonly confined our views of ripeness and its phenomena, color, mellowness, and perfectness, to the fruits which we eat, and we are wont to forget that an immense harvest which we do not eat, hardly use at all, is annually ripened by Nature. At our annual Cattle Shows and Horticultural Exhibitions, we make, as we think, a great show of fair fruits, destined, however, to a rather ignoble end, fruits not valued for their beauty chiefly. But round about and within our towns there is annually another show of fruits, on an infinitely grander scale, fruits which address our taste for beauty alone.

October is the month for painted leaves. Their rich glow now flashes round the world. As fruits and leaves and the day itself acquire a bright tint just before they fall, so the year near its setting. October is its sunset sky; November the later twilight.

I formerly thought that it would be worth the while to get a specimen leaf from each changing tree, shrub, and herbaceous plant, when it had acquired its brightest characteristic color, in its transition from the green to the brown state, outline it, and copy its color exactly, with paint, in a book, which should be entitled, "October, or Autumnal Tints;" — beginning with the earliest reddening, Woodbine and the lake of radical leaves, and coming down through the Maples, Hickories, and Sumachs, and many beautifully freckled leaves less generally known, to the latest Oaks and Aspens. What a memento such a book would be! You would need only to turn over its leaves to take a ramble through the autumn woods whenever you pleased. Or if I could preserve the leaves themselves, unfaded, it would be better still. I have made but little progress toward such a book, but I have endeavored, instead, to describe all these bright tints in the order in which they present themselves. The following are some extracts from my notes.

THE PURPLE GRASSES.

By the twentieth of August, everywhere in woods and swamps we are reminded of the fall, both by the richly spotted Sarsaparilla leaves and Brakes, and the withering and blackened Skunk-Cabbage and Hellebore, and, by the riverside, the already blackening Pontederia.

The Purple Grass (*Eragrostis pectinacea*) is now in the height of its beauty. I remember still when I first noticed this grass particularly. Standing on a hillside near our river, I saw, thirty or forty rods off, a stripe of purple half a dozen rods long, under the edge of a wood, where the ground sloped toward a meadow. It was as high-colored and interesting, though not quite so bright, as the patches of Rhexia, being a darker purple, like a berry's stain laid on close and thick. On going to and examining it, I found it to be a kind of grass in bloom, hardly a foot high, with but few green blades, and a fine spreading panicle of purple flowers, a shallow, purplish mist trembling around me. Close at hand it appeared but a dull purple, and made little impression on the eye; it was even difficult to detect; and if you plucked a single plant, you were surprised to find how thin it was, and how little color it had. But viewed at a distance in a favorable light, it was of a fine lively purple, flower-like, enriching the earth. Such puny causes combine to produce these decided effects. I was the more surprised and charmed because grass is commonly of a sober and humble color.

With its beautiful purple blush it reminds me, and supplies the place, of the Rhexia, which is now leaving off, and it is one of the most

interesting phenomena of August. The finest
patches of it grow on waste strips or selvages of
land at the base of dry hills, just above the edge
of the meadows, where the greedy mower does
not deign to swing his scythe; for this is a thin
and poor grass, beneath his notice. Or, it may
be, because it is so beautiful he does not know
that it exists; for the same eye does not see this
and Timothy. He carefully gets the meadow
hay and the more nutritious grasses which grow
next to that, but he leaves this fine purple mist
for the walker's harvest, — fodder for his fancy
stock. Higher up the hill, perchance, grow also
Blackberries, John's - Wort, and neglected,
withered, and wiry June-Grass. How fortunate
that it grows in such places, and not in the
midst of the rank grasses which are annually
cut! Nature thus keeps use and beauty distinct.
I know many such localities, where it does not
fail to present itself annually, and paint the
earth with its blush. It grows on the gentle
slopes, either in a continuous patch or in scattered and rounded tufts a foot in diameter, and
it lasts till it is killed by the first smart frosts.

In most plants the corolla or calyx is the
part which attains the highest color, and is the
most attractive; in many it is the seed-vessel or
fruit; in others, as the Red Maple, the leaves;
and in others still it is the very culm itself
which is the principal flower or blooming part.

The last is especially the case with the Poke
or Garget (*Phytolacca decandra*). Some which
stand under our cliffs quite dazzle me with their
purple stems now and early in September. They
are as interesting to me as most flowers, and
one of the most important fruits of our autumn.
Every part is flower (or fruit), such is its superfluity of color, — stem, branch, peduncle, pedi-
cel, petiole, and even the at length yellowish
purple-veined leaves. Its cylindrical racemes of
berries of various hues, from green to dark purple, six or seven inches long, are gracefully
drooping on all sides, offering repasts to the
birds; and even the sepals from which the birds
have picked the berries are a brilliant lake-red,
with crimson flame-like reflections, equal to anything of the kind, — all on fire with ripeness.
Hence the *lacca*, from *lac*, lake. There are at
the same time flower-buds, flowers, green berries,
dark purple or ripe ones, and these flower-like
sepals, all on the same plant.

We love to see any redness in the vegetation
of the temperate zone. It is the color of colors.
This plant speaks to our blood. It asks a
bright sun on it to make it show to best advantage, and it must be seen at this season of the
year. On warm hillsides its stems are ripe by
the twenty-third of August. At that date I
walked through a beautiful grove of them, six or

seven feet high, on the side of one of our cliffs, where they ripen early. Quite to the ground they were a deep, brilliant purple, with a bloom contrasting with the still clear green leaves. It appears a rare triumph of Nature to have produced and perfected such a plant, as if this were enough for a summer. What a perfect maturity it arrives at! It is the emblem of a successful life concluded by a death not premature, which is an ornament to Nature. What if we were to mature as perfectly, root and branch, glowing in the midst of our decay, like the Poke! I confess that it excites me to behold them. I cut one for a cane, for I would fain handle and lean on it. I love to press the berries between my fingers, and see their juice staining my hand. To walk amid these upright, branching casks of purple wine, which retain and diffuse a sunset glow, tasting each one with your eye, instead of counting the pipes on a London dock, what a privilege! For Nature's vintage is not confined to the vine. Our poets have sung of wine, the product of a foreign plant which commonly they never saw, as if our own plants had no juice in them more than the singers. Indeed, this has been called by some the American Grape, and, though a native of America, its juices are used in some foreign countries to improve the color of the wine; so

that the poetaster may be celebrating the virtues
of the Poke without knowing it. Here are berries enough to paint afresh the western sky, and
play the bacchanal with, if you will. And what
flutes its ensanguined stems would make, to be
used in such a dance! It is truly a royal plant.
I could spend the evening of the year musing
amid the Poke - stems. And perchance amid
these groves might arise at last a new school of
philosophy or poetry. It lasts all through September.

At the same time with this, or near the end
of August, a to me very interesting genus of
grasses, Andropogons, or Beard-Grasses, is in
its prime: *Andropogon furcatus*, Forked Beard-
Grass, or call it Purple-Fingered Grass; *Andropogon scoparius*, Purple Wood-Grass; and
Andropogon (now called *Sorghum*) *nutans*, Indian-Grass. The first is a very tall and slen-
der-culmed grass, three to seven feet high, with
four or five purple finger-like spikes raying upward from the top. The second is also quite
slender, growing in tufts two feet high by one
wide, with culms often somewhat curving, which,
as the spikes go out of bloom, have a whitish
fuzzy look. These two are prevailing grasses at
this season on dry and sandy fields and hillsides.
The culms of both, not to mention their pretty
flowers, reflect a purple tinge, and help to de-

clare the ripeness of the year. Perhaps I have the more sympathy with them because they are despised by the farmer, and occupy sterile and neglected soil. They are high-colored, like ripe grapes, and express a maturity which the spring did not suggest. Only the August sun could have thus burnished these culms and leaves. The farmer has long since done his upland haying, and he will not condescend to bring his scythe to where these slender wild grasses have at length flowered thinly; you often see spaces of bare sand amid them. But I walk encouraged between the tufts of Purple Wood-Grass over the sandy fields, and along the edge of the Shrub-Oaks, glad to recognize these simple contemporaries. With thoughts cutting a broad swathe I "get" them, with horse-raking thoughts I gather them into windrows. The fine-eared poet may hear the whetting of my scythe. These two were almost the first grasses that I learned to distinguish, for I had not known by how many friends I was surrounded; I had seen them simply as grasses standing. The purple of their culms also excites me like that of the Poke-Weed stems.

Think what refuge there is for one, before August is over, from college commencements and society that isolates! I can skulk amid the tufts of Purple Wood-Grass on the borders of

the "Great Fields." Wherever I walk these
afternoons, the Purple - Fingered Grass also
stands like a guide - board, and points my
thoughts to more poetic paths than they have
lately·traveled.

A man shall perhaps rush by and trample
down plants as high as his head, and cannot be
said to know that they exist, though he may
have cut many tons of them, littered his stables
with them, and fed them to his cattle for years.
Yet, if he ever favorably attends to them, he
may be overcome by their beauty. Each humblest plant, or weed, as we call it, stands there
to express some thought or mood of ours; and
yet how long it stands in vain! I had walked
over those Great Fields so many Augusts, and
never yet distinctly recognized these purple companions that I had there. I had brushed against
them and trodden on them, forsooth; and now,
at last, they, as it were, rose up and blessed me.
Beauty and true wealth are always thus cheap
and despised. Heaven might be defined as the
place which men avoid. Who can doubt that
these grasses, which the farmer says are of no
account to him, find some compensation in your
appreciation of them? I may say that I never
saw them before; though, when I came to look
them face to face, there did come down to me
a purple gleam from previous years; and now,

wherever I go, I see hardly anything else. It is the reign and presidency of the Andropogons.

Almost the very sands confess the ripening influence of the August sun, and methinks, together with the slender grasses waving over them, reflect a purple tinge. The impurpled sands! Such is the consequence of all this sunshine absorbed into the pores of plants and of the earth. All sap or blood is now wine-colored. At last we have not only the purple sea, but the purple land.

The Chestnut Beard-Grass, Indian-Grass, or Wood-Grass, growing here and there in waste places, but more rare than the former (from two to four or five feet high), is still handsomer and of more vivid colors than its congeners, and might well have caught the Indian's eye. It has a long, narrow, one - sided, and slightly nodding panicle of bright purple and yellow flowers, like a banner raised above its reedy leaves. These bright standards are now advanced on the distant hillsides, not in large armies, but in scattered troops or single file, like the red men. They stand thus fair and bright, representative of the race which they are named after, but for the most part unobserved as they. The expression of this grass haunted me for a week, after I first passed and noticed it, like the glance of an eye. It stands like an Indian chief taking a last look at his favorite hunting-grounds.

THE RED MAPLE.

By the twenty-fifth of September, the Red Maples generally are beginning to be ripe. Some large ones have been conspicuously changing for a week, and some single trees are now very brilliant. I notice a small one, half a mile off across a meadow, against the green woodside there, a far brighter red than the blossoms of any tree in summer, and more conspicuous. I have observed this tree for several autumns invariably changing earlier than its fellows, just as one tree ripens its fruit earlier than another. It might serve to mark the season, perhaps. I should be sorry, if it were cut down. I know of two or three such trees in different parts of our town, which might, perhaps, be propagated from, as early ripeners or September trees, and their seed be advertised in the market, as well as that of radishes, if we cared as much about them.

At present these burning bushes stand chiefly along the edge of the meadows, or I distinguish them afar on the hillsides here and there. Sometimes you will see many small ones in a swamp turned quite crimson when all other trees around are still perfectly green, and the

former appear so much the brighter for it.
They take you by surprise, as you are going by
on one side, across the fields, thus early in the
season, as if it were some gay encampment of
the red men, or other foresters, of whose arrival
you had not heard.

Some single trees, wholly bright scarlet, seen
against others of their kind still freshly green,
or against evergreens, are more memorable than
whole groves will be by and by. How beautiful, when a whole tree is like one great scarlet
fruit full of ripe juices, every leaf, from lowest
limb to topmost spire, all aglow, especially if
you look toward the sun! What more remarkable object can there be in the landscape?
Visible for miles, too fair to be believed. If
such a phenomenon occurred. but once, it would
be handed down by tradition to posterity, and
get into the mythology at last.

The whole tree thus ripening in advance of
its fellows attains a singular preëminence, and
sometimes maintains it for a week or two. I
am thrilled at the sight of it, bearing aloft its
scarlet standard for the regiment of green-clad
foresters around, and I go half a mile out of my
way to examine it. A single tree becomes thus
the crowning beauty of some meadowy vale, and
the expression of the whole surrounding forest
is at once more spirited for it.

A small Red Maple has grown, perchance, far away at the head of some retired valley, a mile from any road, unobserved. It has faithfully discharged the duties of a Maple there, all winter and summer, neglected none of its economies, but added to its stature in the virtue which belongs to a Maple, by a steady growth for so many months, never having gone gadding abroad, and is nearer heaven than it was in the spring. It has faithfully husbanded its sap, and afforded a shelter to the wandering bird, has long since ripened its seeds and committed them to the winds, and has the satisfaction of knowing, perhaps, that a thousand little well-behaved Maples are already settled in life somewhere. It deserves well of Mapledom. Its leaves have been asking it from time to time, in a whisper, "When shall we redden?" And now, in this month of September, this month of traveling, when men are hastening to the seaside, or the mountains, or the lakes, this modest Maple, still without budging an inch, travels in its reputation, — runs up its scarlet flag on that hillside, which shows that it has finished its summer's work before all other trees, and withdraws from the contest. At the eleventh hour of the year, the tree which no scrutiny could have detected here when it was most industrious is thus, by the tint of its maturity, by its very

blushes, revealed at last to the careless and distant traveler, and leads his thoughts away from
the dusty road into those brave solitudes which
it inhabits.   It flashes out conspicuous with all
the virtue and beauty of a Maple, — *Acer ru-
brum*.   We may now read its title, or *rubric*,
clear.   Its *virtues*, not its sins, are as scarlet.

Notwithstanding the Red Maple is the most
intense scarlet of any of our trees, the Sugar-
Maple has been the most celebrated, and Michaux in his "Sylva" does not speak of the autumnal color of the former.   About the second
of October, these trees, both large and small,
are most brilliant, though many are still green.
In "sprout-lands" they seem to vie with one
another, and ever some particular one in the
midst of the crowd will be of a peculiarly pure
scarlet, and by its more intense color attract
our eye even at a distance, and carry off the
palm.   A large Red-Maple swamp, when at the
height of its change, is the most obviously brilliant of all tangible things, where I dwell, so
abundant is this tree with us.   It varies much
both in form and color.   A great many are
merely yellow; more, scarlet; others, scarlet
deepening into crimson, more red than common.
Look at yonder swamp of Maples mixed with
Pines, at the base of a Pine-clad hill, a quarter
of a mile off, so that you get the full effect of

the bright colors, without detecting the imperfections of the leaves, and see their yellow, scarlet, and crimson fires, of all tints, mingled and contrasted with the green. Some Maples are yet green, only yellow or crimson-tipped on the edges of their flakes, like the edges of a Hazel-Nut bur ; some are wholly brilliant scarlet, raying out regularly and finely every way, bilaterally, like the veins of a leaf; others, of more irregular form, when I turn my head slightly, emptying out some of its earthiness and concealing the trunk of the tree, seem to rest heavily flake on flake, like yellow and scarlet clouds, wreath upon wreath, or like snowdrifts driving through the air, stratified by the wind. It adds greatly to the beauty of such a swamp at this season, that, even though there may be no other trees interspersed, it is not seen as a simple mass of color, but, different trees being of different colors and hues, the outline of each crescent tree-top is distinct, and where one laps on to another. Yet a painter would hardly venture to make them thus distinct a quarter of a mile off.

As I go across a meadow directly toward a low rising ground this bright afternoon, I see, some fifty rods off toward the sun, the top of a Maple swamp just appearing over the sheeny russet edge of the hill, a stripe apparently twenty rods long by ten feet deep, of the most intensely brilliant scarlet, orange, and yellow, equal to any flowers or fruits, or any tints ever painted. As I advance, lowering the edge of the hill which makes the firm foreground or lower frame of the picture, the depth of the brilliant grove revealed steadily increases, suggesting that the whole of the inclosed valley is filled with such color. One wonders that the tithing-men and fathers of the town are not out to see what the trees mean by their high colors and exuberance of spirits, fearing that some mischief is brewing. I do not see what the Puritans did at this season, when the Maples blaze out in scarlet. They certainly could not have worshiped in groves then. Perhaps that is what they built meeting-houses and fenced them round with horse-sheds for.

THE ELM.

Now too, the first of October, or later, the Elms are at the height of their autumnal beauty, — great brownish yellow masses, warm from their September oven, hanging over the highway. Their leaves are perfectly ripe. I wonder if there is any answering ripeness in the lives of the men who live beneath them. As I look down our street, which is lined with them, they remind me both by their form and color of yellowing sheaves of grain, as if the harvest had indeed come to the village itself, and we might expect to find some maturity and *flavor* in the thoughts of the villagers at last. Under those bright rustling yellow piles just ready to fall on the heads of the walkers, how can any crudity or greenness of thought or act prevail? When I stand where half a dozen large Elms droop over a house, it is as if I stood within a ripe pumpkin-rind, and I feel as mellow as if I were the pulp, though I may be somewhat stringy and seedy withal. What is the late greenness of the English Elm, like a cucumber out of season, which does not know when to have done, compared with the early and golden maturity of the American tree? The street is the scene of a great harvest-home. It would be worth the while to set out these trees, if only for their autumnal value. Think of these great yellow canopies or parasols held over our heads and houses by the mile together, making the village all one and compact, — an *ulmarium*, which is at the same time a nursery of men! And then how gently and unobserved they drop their burden and let in the sun when it is wanted, their leaves not heard when they fall on our roofs and in our streets; and thus the village parasol is shut up and put away! I see the market-man driving into the village, and disappear-

ing under its canopy of Elm-tops, with *his* crop,
as into a great granary or barn-yard. I am
tempted to go thither as to a husking of
thoughts, now dry and ripe, and ready to be
separated from their integuments; but, alas! I
foresee that it will be chiefly husks and little
thought, blasted pig-corn, fit only for cob-meal,
—for, as you sow, so shall you reap.

FALLEN LEAVES.

By the sixth of October the leaves generally
begin to fall, in successive showers, after frost
or rain; but the principal leaf-harvest, the acme
of the *Fall*, is commonly about the sixteenth.
Some morning at that date there is perhaps a
harder frost than we have seen, and ice formed
under the pump, and now, when the morning
wind rises, the leaves come down in denser
showers than ever. They suddenly form thick
beds or carpets on the ground, in this gentle air,
or even without wind, just the size and form of
the tree above. Some trees, as small Hickories,
appear to have dropped their leaves instanta-
neously, as a soldier grounds arms at a signal;
and those of the Hickory, being bright yellow
still, though withered, reflect a blaze of light
from the ground where they lie. Down they
have come on all sides, at the first earnest touch
of autumn's wand, making a sound like rain.

Or else it is after moist and rainy weather that we notice how great a fall of leaves there has been in the night, though it may not yet be the touch that loosens the Rock-Maple leaf. The streets are thickly strewn with the trophies, and fallen Elm-leaves make a dark brown pavement under our feet. After some remarkably warm Indian-summer day or days, I perceive that it is the unusual heat which, more than anything, causes the leaves to fall, there having been, perhaps, no frost nor rain for some time. The intense heat suddenly ripens and wilts them, just as it softens and ripens peaches and other fruits, and causes them to drop.

The leaves of late Red Maples, still bright, strew the earth, often crimson-spotted on a yellow ground, like some wild apples, — though they preserve these bright colors on the ground but a day or two, especially if it rains. On causeways I go by trees here and there all bare and smoke-like, having lost their brilliant clothing; but there it lies, nearly as bright as ever on the ground on one side, and making nearly as regular a figure as lately on the tree. I would rather say that I first observe the trees thus flat on the ground like a permanent colored shadow, and they suggest to look for the boughs that bore them. A queen might be proud to walk where these gallant trees have spread their bright cloaks in the mud. I see wagons roll over them as a shadow or a reflection, and the drivers heed them just as little as they did their shadows before.

Birds'-nests, in the Huckleberry and other shrubs, and in trees, are already being filled with the withered leaves. So many have fallen in the woods that a squirrel cannot run after a falling nut without being heard. Boys are raking them in the streets, if only for the pleasure of dealing with such clean crisp substances. Some sweep the paths scrupulously neat, and then stand to see the next breath strew them with new trophies. The swamp-floor is thickly covered, and the *Lycopodium lucidulum* looks suddenly greener amid them. In dense woods they half cover pools that are three or four rods long. The other day I could hardly find a well-known spring, and even suspected that it had dried up, for it was completely concealed by freshly fallen leaves; and when I swept them aside and revealed it, it was like striking the earth, with Aaron's rod, for a new spring. Wet grounds about the edges of swamps look dry with them. At one swamp, where I was surveying, thinking to step on a leafy shore from a rail, I got into the water more than a foot deep.

When I go to the river the day after the

principal fall of leaves, the sixteenth, I find my
boat all covered, bottom and seats, with the
leaves of the Golden Willow under which it is
moored, and I set sail with a cargo of them
rustling under my feet. If I empty it, it will
be full again to-morrow. I do not regard them
as litter, to be swept out, but accept them as
suitable straw or matting for the bottom of my
carriage. When I turn up into the mouth of
the Assabet, which is wooded, large fleets of
leaves are floating on its surface, as it were getting out to sea, with room to tack; but next the
shore, a little farther up, they are thicker than
foam, quite concealing the water for a rod in
width, under and amid the Alders, Button-
Bushes, and Maples, still perfectly light and
dry, with fibre unrelaxed; and at a rocky bend
where they are met and stopped by the morning
wind, they sometimes form a broad and dense
crescent quite across the river. When I turn
my prow that way, and the wave which it makes
strikes them, list what a pleasant rustling from
these dry substances getting on one another!
Often it is their undulation only which reveals
the water beneath them. Also every motion of
the wood-turtle on the shore is betrayed by their
rustling there. Or even in mid-channel, when
the wind rises, I hear them blown with a rustling sound. Higher up they are slowly moving

round and round in some great eddy which the
river makes, as that at the "Leaning Hemlocks,"
where the water is deep, and the current is
wearing into the bank.

Perchance, in the afternoon of such a day,
when the water is perfectly calm and full of reflections, I paddle gently down the main stream,
and, turning up the Assabet, reach a quiet
cove, where I unexpectedly find myself surrounded by myriads of leaves, like fellow-voy-
agers, which seem to have the same purpose, or
want of purpose, with myself. See this great
fleet of scattered leaf-boats which we paddle
amid, in this smooth river-bay, each one curled
up on every side by the sun's skill, each nerve
a stiff spruce-knee, — like boats of hide, and of
all patterns, Charon's boat probably among the
rest, and some with lofty prows and poops, like
the stately vessels of the ancients, scarcely moving in the sluggish current, — like the great
fleets, the dense Chinese cities of boats, with
which you mingle on entering some great mart,
some New York or Canton, which we are all
steadily approaching together. How gently
each has been deposited on the water! No violence has been used towards them yet, though,
perchance, palpitating hearts were present at
the launching. And painted ducks, too, the
splendid wood-duck among the rest, often come

to sail and float amid the painted leaves, — barks of a nobler model still!

What wholesome herb-drinks are to be had in the swamps now! What strong medicinal, but rich scents from the decaying leaves! The rain falling on the freshly dried herbs and leaves, and filling the pools and ditches into which they have dropped thus clean and rigid, will soon convert them into tea, — green, black, brown, and yellow teas, of all degrees of strength, enough to set all Nature a-gossiping. Whether we drink them or not, as yet, before their strength is drawn, these leaves, dried on great Nature's coppers, are of such various pure and delicate tints as might make the fame of Oriental teas.

How they are mixed up, of all species, Oak and Maple and Chestnut and Birch! But Nature is not cluttered with them; she is a perfect husbandman; she stores them all. Consider what a vast crop is thus annually shed on the earth! This, more than any mere grain or seed, is the great harvest of the year. The trees are now repaying the earth with interest what they have taken from it. They are discounting. They are about to add a leaf's thickness to the depth of the soil. This is the beautiful way in which Nature gets her muck, while I chaffer with this man and that, who talks to me about sulphur and the cost of carting. We are all the richer for their decay. I am more interested in this crop than in the English grass alone or in the corn. It prepares the virgin mould for future cornfields and forests, on which the earth fattens. It keeps our homestead in good heart.

For beautiful variety no crop can be compared with this. Here is not merely the plain yellow of the grains, but nearly all the colors that we know, the brightest blue not excepted: the early blushing Maple, the Poison-Sumach blazing its sins as scarlet, the mulberry Ash, the rich chrome yellow of the Poplars, the brilliant red Huckleberry, with which the hills' backs are painted, like those of sheep. The frost touches them, and, with the slightest breath of returning day or jarring of earth's axle, see in what showers they come floating down! The ground is all party-colored with them. But they still live in the soil, whose fertility and bulk they increase, and in the forests that spring from it. They stoop to rise, to mount higher in coming years, by subtle chemistry, climbing by the sap in the trees, and the sapling's first fruits thus shed, transmuted at last, may adorn its crown, when, in after-years, it has become the monarch of the forest.

It is pleasant to walk over the beds of these

fresh, crisp, and rustling leaves. How beautifully they go to their graves! how gently lay themselves down and turn to mould! — painted of a thousand hues, and fit to make the beds of us living. So they troop to their last resting-place, light and frisky. They put on no weeds, but merrily they go scampering over the earth, selecting the spot, choosing a lot, ordering no iron fence, whispering all through the woods about it, — some choosing the spot where the bodies of men are mouldering beneath, and meeting them half-way. How many flutterings before they rest quietly in their graves! They that soared so loftily, how contentedly they return to dust again, and are laid low, resigned to lie and decay at the foot of the tree, and afford nourishment to new generations of their kind, as well as to flutter on high! They teach us how to die. One wonders if the time will ever come when men, with their boasted faith in immortality, will lie down as gracefully and as ripe, — with such an Indian-summer serenity will shed their bodies, as they do their hair and nails.

When the leaves fall, the whole earth is a cemetery pleasant to walk in. I love to wander and muse over them in their graves. Here are no lying nor vain epitaphs. What though you own no lot at Mount Auburn? Your lot is surely cast somewhere in this vast cemetery, which has been consecrated from of old. You need attend no auction to secure a place. There is room enough here. The Loose-strife shall bloom and the Huckleberry-bird sing over your bones. The woodman and hunter shall be your sextons, and the children shall tread upon the borders as much as they will. Let us walk in the cemetery of the leaves, — this is your true Greenwood Cemetery.

THE SUGAR—MAPLE.

But think not that the splendor of the year is over; for as one leaf does not make a summer, neither does one falling leaf make an autumn. The smallest Sugar-Maples in our streets make a great show as early as the fifth of October, more than any other trees there. As I look up the Main Street, they appear like painted screens standing before the houses; yet many are green. But now, or generally by the seventeenth of October, when almost all Red Maples, and some White Maples, are bare, the large Sugar-Maples also are in their glory, glowing with yellow and red, and show unexpectedly bright and delicate tints. They are remarkable for the contrast they often afford of deep blushing red on one half and green on the other. They become at length dense masses of rich yellow with a deep scarlet blush, or more than blush, on the exposed surfaces. They are the brightest trees now in the street.

The large ones on our Common are particularly beautiful. A delicate, but warmer than golden yellow is now the prevailing color, with scarlet cheeks. Yet, standing on the east side of the Common just before sundown, when the western light is transmitted through them, I see that their yellow even, compared with the pale lemon yellow of an Elm close by, amounts to a scarlet, without noticing the bright scarlet portions. Generally, they are great regular oval masses of yellow and scarlet. All the sunny warmth of the season, the Indian-summer, seems to be absorbed in their leaves. The lowest and inmost leaves next the bole are, as usual, of the most delicate yellow and green, like the complexion of young men brought up in the house. There is an auction on the Common to-day, but its red flag is hard to be discerned amid this blaze of color.

Little did the fathers of the town anticipate this brilliant success, when they caused to be imported from farther in the country some straight poles with their tops cut off, which they called Sugar-Maples; and, as I remember, after they were set out, a neighboring merchant's clerk, by way of jest, planted beans about them.

Those which were then jestingly called bean-poles are to-day far the most beautiful objects noticeable in our streets. They are worth all and more than they have cost, — though one of the selectmen, while setting them out, took the cold which occasioned his death, — if only be-cause they have filled the open eyes of children with their rich color unstintedly so many Octo-bers. We will not ask them to yield us sugar in the spring, while they afford us so fair a prospect in the autumn. Wealth indoors may be the inheritance of few, but it is equally dis-tributed on the Common. All children alike can revel in this golden harvest.

Surely trees should be set in our streets with a view to their October splendor; though I doubt whether this is ever considered by the "Tree Society." Do you not think it will make some odds to these children that they were brought up under the Maples? Hundreds of eyes are steadily drinking in this color, and by these teachers even the truants are caught and educated the moment they step abroad. Indeed, neither the truant nor the studious is at present taught color in the schools. These are instead of the bright colors in apothecaries' shops and city windows. It is a pity that we have no more *Red* Maples, and some Hickories, in our streets as well. Our paint-box is very imperfectly filled. Instead of, or beside, supplying such paint-boxes as we do, we might supply these natural colors to the young. Where else will they study color under greater advantages? What School of Design can vie with this? Think how much the eyes of painters of all kinds, and of manufacturers of cloth and paper, and paper-stainers, and countless others, are to be educated by these autumnal colors. The stationer's envelopes may be of very various tints, yet not so various as those of the leaves of a single tree. If you want a different shade or tint of a particular color, you have only to look farther within or without the tree or the wood. These leaves are not many dipped in one dye, as at the dye-house, but they are dyed in light of infinitely various degrees of strength, and left to set and dry there.

Shall the names of so many of our colors continue to be derived from those of obscure foreign localities, as Naples yellow, Prussian blue, raw Sienna, burnt Umber, Gamboge? — (surely the Tyrian purple must have faded by this time), — or from comparatively trivial articles of commerce, — chocolate, lemon, coffee, cinnamon, claret? — (shall we compare our Hickory to a lemon, or a lemon to a Hickory?) — or from ores and oxides which few ever see? Shall we so often, when describing to our neigh-

bors the color of something we have seen, refer
them, not to some natural object in our neighborhood, but perchance to a bit of earth fetched
from the other side of the planet, which possibly they may find at the apothecary's, but which
probably neither they nor we ever saw? Have
we not an *earth* under our feet, — aye, and a sky
over our heads? Or is the last *all* ultramarine?
What do we know of sapphire, amethyst, emer-
ald, ruby, amber, and the like, — most of us
who take these names in vain? Leave these
precious words to cabinet keepers, virtuosos,
and maids-of-honor, — to the Nabobs, Begums,
and Chobdars of Hindostan, or wherever else.
I do not see why, since America and her autumn
woods have been discovered, our leaves should
not compete with the precious stones in giving
names to colors; and, indeed, I believe that in
course of time the names of some of our trees
and shrubs, as well as flowers, will get into our
popular chromatic nomenclature.

But of much more importance than a knowledge of the names and distinctions of color is
the joy and exhilaration which these colored
leaves excite. Already these brilliant trees
throughout the street, without any more variety,
are at least equal to an annual festival and holiday, or a week of such. These are cheap and
innocent gala-days, celebrated by one and all

without the aid of committees or marshals, such
a show as may safely be licensed, not attracting
gamblers or rum - sellers, not requiring any
special police to keep the peace. And poor
indeed must be that New - England village's
October which has not the Maple in its streets.
This October festival costs no powder, nor ringing of bells, but every tree is a living liberty-
pole on which a thousand bright flags are waving.

No wonder that we must have our annual
Cattle-Show, and Fall Training, and perhaps
Cornwallis, our September Courts, and the
like. Nature herself holds her annual fair in
October, not only in the streets, but in every
hollow and on every hillside. When lately we
looked into that Red-Maple swamp all ablaze,
where the trees were clothed in their vestures of
most dazzling tints, did it not suggest a thousand gypsies beneath, — a race capable of wild
delight, — or even the fabled fauns, satyrs, and
wood-nymphs come back to earth? Or was it
only a congregation of wearied wood-choppers,
or of proprietors come to inspect their lots, that
we thought of? Or, earlier still, when we paddled on the river through that fine-grained September air, did there not appear to be something new going on under the sparkling surface
of the stream, a shaking of props, at least, so

that we made haste in order to be up in time? Did not the rows of yellowing Willows and Button-Bushes on each side seem like rows of booths, under which, perhaps, some fluviatile egg-pop equally yellow was effervescing? Did not all these suggest that man's spirits should rise as high as Nature's, — should hang out their flag, and the routine of his life be interrupted by an analogous expression of joy and hilarity?

No annual training or muster of soldiery, no celebration with its scarfs and banners, could import into the town a hundredth part of the annual splendor of our October. We have only to set the trees, or let them stand, and Nature will find the colored drapery, — flags of all her nations, some of whose private signals hardly the botanist can read, — while we walk under the triumphal arches of the Elms. Leave it to Nature to appoint the days, whether the same as in neighboring States or not, and let the clergy read her proclamations, if they can understand them. Behold what a brilliant drapery is her Woodbine flag! What public-spirited merchant, think you, has contributed this part of the show? There is no handsomer shingling and paint than this vine, at present covering a whole side of some houses. I do not believe that the Ivy *never sere* is comparable

to it. No wonder it has been extensively introduced into London. Let us have a good many
Maples and Hickories and Scarlet Oaks, then,
I say. Blaze away! Shall that dirty roll of
bunting in the gun-house be all the colors a village can display? A village is not complete,
unless it have these trees to mark the season in
it. They are important, like the town-clock.
A village that has them not will not be found
to work well. It has a screw loose, an essen-
tial part is wanting. Let us have Willows for
spring, Elms for summer, Maples and Walnuts and Tupeloes for autumn, Evergreens for
winter, and Oaks for all seasons. What is a
gallery in a house to a gallery in the streets,
which every market-man rides through, whether
he will or not? Of course, there is not a pic-
ture-gallery in the country which would be
worth so much to us as is the western view
at sunset under the Elms of our main street.
They are the frame to a picture which is daily
painted behind them. An avenue of Elms as
large as our largest and three miles long would
seem to lead to some admirable place, though
only C—— were at the end of it.

A village needs these innocent stimulants of
bright and cheering prospects to keep off melancholy and superstition. Show me two villages,
one embowered in trees and blazing with all the

glories of October, the other a merely trivial and treeless waste, or with only a single tree or two for suicides, and I shall be sure that in the latter will be found the most starved and bigoted religionists and the most desperate drinkers. Every wash-tub and milk-can and gravestone will be exposed. The inhabitants will disappear abruptly behind their barns and houses, like desert Arabs amid their rocks, and I shall look to see spears in their hands. They will be ready to accept the most barren and forlorn doctrine, — as that the world is speedily coming to an end, or has already got to it, or that they themselves are turned wrong side outward. They will perchance crack their dry joints at one another and call it a spiritual communication.

But to confine ourselves to the Maples. What if we were to take half as much pains in protecting them as we do in setting them out, — not stupidly tie our horses to our dahlia-stems?

What meant the fathers by establishing this *perfectly living* institution before the church, — this institution which needs no repairing nor repainting, which is continually enlarged and repaired by its growth? Surely they

" Wrought in a sad sincerity ;
Themselves from God they could not free ;

> They *planted* better than they knew ; —
> The conscious *trees* to beauty grew."

Verily these Maples are cheap preachers, permanently settled, which preach their half-century, and century, aye, and century-and-a-half sermons, with constantly increasing unction and influence, ministering to many generations of men; and the least we can do is to supply them with suitable colleagues as they grow infirm.

THE SCARLET OAK.

Belonging to a genus which is remarkable for the beautiful form of its leaves, I suspect that some Scarlet-Oak leaves surpass those of all other Oaks in the rich and wild beauty of their outlines. I judge from an acquaintance with twelve species, and from drawings which I have seen of many others.

Stand under this tree and see how finely its leaves are cut against the sky, — as it were, only a few sharp points extending from a mid-rib. They look like double, treble, or quadruple crosses. They are far more ethereal than the less deeply scalloped Oak-leaves. They have so little leafy *terra firma* that they appear melting away in the light, and scarcely obstruct our view. The leaves of very young plants are, like those of full-grown Oaks of other species, more entire, simple, and lumpish in their outlines, but these, raised high on old trees, have solved the leafy problem. Lifted higher and higher, and sublimated more and more, putting off some earthiness and cultivating more intimacy with the light each year, they have at length the least possible amount of earthy matter, and the greatest spread and grasp of skyey influences. There they dance, arm in arm with the light, — tripping it on fantastic points, fit partners in those aërial halls. So intimately mingled are they with it, that, what with their slenderness and their glossy surfaces, you can hardly tell at last what in the dance is leaf and what is light. And when no zephyr stirs, they are at most but a rich tracery to the forest-windows.

I am again struck with their beauty, when, a month later, they thickly strew the ground in the woods, piled one upon another under my feet. They are then brown above, but purple beneath. With their narrow lobes and their bold deep scallops reaching almost to the middle, they suggest that the material must be cheap, or else there has been a lavish expense in their creation, as if so much had been cut out. Or else they seem to us the remnants of the stuff out of which leaves have been cut with a die. Indeed, when they lie thus one upon another, they remind me of a pile of scrap-tin.

Or bring one home, and study it closely at
your leisure, by the fireside. It is a type, not
from any Oxford font, not in the Basque nor
the arrow-headed character, not found on the
Rosetta Stone, but destined to be copied in
sculpture one day, if they ever get to whittling
stone here. What a wild and pleasing outline,
a combination of graceful curves and angles!
The eye rests with equal delight on what is not
leaf and on what is leaf, — on the broad, free,
open sinuses, and on the long, sharp, bristle-
pointed lobes. A simple oval outline would in-
clude it all, if you connected the points of the
leaf; but how much richer is it than that, with
its half dozen deep scallops, in which the eye
and thought of the beholder are embayed! If
I were a drawing-master, I would set my pupils
to copying these leaves, that they might learn
to draw firmly and gracefully.

Regarded as water, it is like a pond with half
a dozen broad rounded promontories extending
nearly to its middle, half from each side, while
its watery bays extend far inland, like sharp
friths, at each of whose heads several fine
streams empty in, — almost a leafy archipelago.

But it oftener suggests land, and, as Diony-
sius and Pliny compared the form of the Morea
to that of the leaf of the Oriental Plane-tree,
so this leaf reminds me of some fair wild island

in the ocean, whose extensive coast, alternate rounded bays with smooth strands, and sharp-pointed rocky capes, mark it as fitted for the habitation of man, and destined to become a centre of civilization at last. To the sailor's eye, it is a much-indented shore. Is it not, in fact, a shore to the aërial ocean, on which the windy surf beats? At sight of this leaf we are all mariners, — if not vikings, buccaneers, and filibusters. Both our love of repose and our spirit of adventure are addressed. In our most casual glance, perchance, we think that if we succeed in doubling those sharp capes we shall find deep, smooth, and secure havens in the ample bays. How different from the White-Oak leaf, with its rounded headlands, on which no lighthouse need be placed! That is an England, with its long civil history, that may be read. This is some still unsettled New-found Island or Celebes. Shall we go and be rajahs there?

By the twenty-sixth of October the large Scarlet Oaks are in their prime, when other Oaks are usually withered. They have been kindling their fires for a week past, and now generally burst into a blaze. This alone of *our* indigenous deciduous trees (excepting the Dog-wood, of which I do not know half a dozen, and they are but large bushes) is now in its glory.

The two Aspens and the Sugar-Maple come nearest to it in date, but they have lost the greater part of their leaves. Of evergreens, only the Pitch-Pine is still commonly bright.

But it requires a particular alertness, if not devotion to these phenomena, to appreciate the wide-spread, but late and unexpected glory of the Scarlet Oaks. I do not speak here of the small trees and shrubs, which are commonly observed, and which are now withered, but of the large trees. Most go in and shut their doors, thinking that bleak and colorless November has already come, when some of the most brilliant and memorable colors are not yet lit.

This very perfect and vigorous one, about forty feet high, standing in an open pasture, which was quite glossy green on the twelfth, is now, the twenty-sixth, completely changed to bright dark scarlet, — every leaf, between you and the sun, as if it had been dipped into a scarlet dye. The whole tree is much like a heart in form, as well as color. Was not this worth waiting for? Little did you think, ten days ago, that that cold green tree would assume such color as this. Its leaves are still firmly attached, while those of other trees are falling around it. It seems to say, — "I am the last to blush, but I blush deeper than any of ye. I bring up the rear in my red coat.

We Scarlet ones, alone of Oaks, have not given up the fight."

The sap is now, and even far into November, frequently flowing fast in these trees, as in Maples in the spring ; and apparently their bright tints, now that most other Oaks are withered, are connected with this phenomenon. They are full of life. It has a pleasantly astringent, acorn-like taste, this strong Oak-wine, as I find on tapping them with my knife.

Looking across this woodland valley, a quarter of a mile wide, how rich those Scarlet Oaks embosomed in Pines, their bright red branches intimately intermingled with them! They have their full effect there. The Pine-boughs are the green calyx to their red petals. Or, as we go along a road in the woods, the sun striking endwise through it, and lighting up the red tents of the Oaks, which on each side are mingled with the liquid green of the Pines, makes a very gorgeous scene. Indeed, without the evergreens for contrast, the autumnal tints would lose much of their effect.

The Scarlet Oak asks a clear sky and the brightness of late October days. These bring out its colors. If the sun goes into a cloud they become comparatively indistinct. As I sit on a cliff in the southwest part of our town, the sun is now getting low, and the woods in Lin-

coln, south and east of me, are lit up by its
more level rays; and in the Scarlet Oaks, scattered so equally over the forest, there is brought
out a more brilliant redness than I had believed
was in them.   Every tree of this species which
is visible in those directions, even to the horizon, now stands out distinctly red.   Some great
ones lift their red backs high above the woods,
in the next town, like huge roses with a myriad
of fine petals; and some more slender ones, in a
small grove of White Pines on Pine Hill in the
east, on the very verge of the horizon, alternating with the Pines on the edge of the grove,
and shouldering them with their red coats, look
like soldiers in red amid hunters in green.
This time it is Lincoln green, too.   Till the
sun got low, I did not believe that there were
so many red coats in the forest army.   Theirs
is an intense burning red, which would lose
some of its strength, methinks, with every step
you might take toward them; for the shade that
lurks amid their foliage does not report itself at
this distance, and they are unanimously red.
The focus of their reflected color is in the atmosphere far on this side.   Every such tree becomes a nucleus of red, as it were, where, with
the declining sun, that color grows and glows.
It is partly borrowed fire, gathering strength
from the sun on its way to your eye.   It has

only some comparatively dull red leaves for a
rallying-point, or kindling-stuff, to start it, and
it becomes an intense scarlet or red mist, or
fire, which finds fuel for itself in the very atmosphere. So vivacious is redness. The very
rails reflect a rosy light at this hour and season.
You see a redder tree than exists.

If you wish to count the Scarlet Oaks, do it
now. In a clear day stand thus on a hill-top
in the woods, when the sun is an hour high,
and every one within range of your vision, excepting in the west, will be revealed. You
might live to the age of Methuselah and never
find a tithe of them, otherwise. Yet sometimes
even in a dark day I have thought them as
bright as I ever saw them. Looking westward,
their colors are lost in a blaze of light; but in
other directions the whole forest is a flower-gar-
den, in which these late roses burn, alternating
with green, while the so-called "gardeners,"
walking here and there, perchance, beneath,
with spade and water-pot, see only a few little
asters amid withered leaves.

These are *my* China-asters, *my* late garden-
flowers. It costs me nothing for a gardener.
The falling leaves, all over the forest, are protecting the roots of my plants. Only look at
what is to be seen, and you will have garden
enough, without deepening the soil in your

yard. We have only to elevate our view a little, to see the whole forest as a garden. The
blossoming of the Scarlet Oak, — the forest-
flower, surpassing all in splendor (at least since
the Maple)! · I do not know but they interest
me more than the Maples, they are so widely
and equally dispersed throughout the forest;
they are so hardy, a nobler tree on the whole;
— our chief November flower, abiding the approach of winter with us, imparting warmth to
early November prospects. It is remarkable
that the latest bright color that is general
should be this deep, dark scarlet and red, the
intensest of colors. The ripest fruit of the
year; like the cheek of a hard, glossy, red apple, from the cold Isle of Orleans, which will
not be mellow for eating till next spring!
When I rise to a hill-top, a thousand of these
great Oak roses, distributed on every side, as
far as the horizon! I admire them four or five
miles off! This my unfailing prospect for a
fortnight past! This late forest-flower sur-
passes all that spring or summer could do.
Their colors were but rare and dainty specks
comparatively (created for the near - sighted,
who walk amid the humblest herbs and under-
woods), and made no impression on a distant
eye. Now it is an extended forest or a moun-
tain-side, through or along which we journey

from day to day, that bursts into bloom. Comparatively, our gardening is on a petty scale, — the gardener still nursing a few asters amid dead weeds, ignorant of the gigantic asters and roses which, as it were, overshadow him, and ask for none of his care. It is like a little red paint ground on a saucer, and held up against the sunset sky. Why not take more elevated and broader views, walk in the great garden, not skulk in a little "debauched" nook of it? consider the beauty of the forest, and not merely of a few impounded herbs?

Let your walks now be a little more adventurous; ascend the hills. If, about the last of October, you ascend any hill in the outskirts of our town, and probably of yours, and look over the forest, you may see — well, what I have endeavored to describe. All this you surely *will* see, and much more, if you are prepared to see it, — if you *look* for it. Otherwise, regular and universal as this phenomenon is, whether you stand on the hill-top or in the hollow, you will think for threescore years and ten that all the wood is, at this season, sere and brown. Objects are concealed from our view, not so much because they are out of the course of our visual ray as because we do not bring our minds and eyes to bear on them; for there is no power to see in the eye itself, any more than in any other jelly. We do not realize how far and widely, or how near and narrowly, we are to look. The greater part of the phenomena of Nature are for this reason concealed from us all our lives. The gardener sees only the gardener's garden. Here, too, as in political economy, the supply answers to the demand. Nature does not cast pearls before swine. There is just as much beauty visible to us in the landscape as we are prepared to appreciate, — not a grain more. The actual objects which one man will see from a particular hill-top are just as different from those which another will see as the beholders are different. The Scarlet Oak must, in a sense, be in your eye when you go forth. We cannot see anything until we are possessed with the idea of it, take it into our heads, — and then we can hardly see anything else. In my botanical rambles I find that, first, the idea, or image, of a plant occupies my thoughts, though it may seem very foreign to this locality, — no nearer than Hudson's Bay, — and for some weeks or months I go thinking of it, and expecting it, unconsciously, and at length I surely see it. This is the history of my finding a score or more of rare plants, which I could name. A man sees only what concerns him. A botanist absorbed in the study of grasses does not distinguish the grandest Pas-

ture Oaks. He, as it were, tramples down
Oaks unwittingly in his walk, or at most sees
only their shadows. I have found that it required a different intention of the eye, in the
same locality, to see different plants, even
when they were closely allied, as *Juncaceæ* and
Gramineæ: when I was looking for the former,
I did not see the latter in the midst of them.
How much more, then, it requires different in-
tentions of the eye and of the mind to attend to
different departments of knowledge! How differently the poet and the naturalist look at
objects!

Take a New-England selectman, and set him
on the highest of our hills, and tell him to look,
— sharpening his sight to the utmost, and putting
on the glasses that suit him best (aye, using
a spy-glass, if he likes), — and make a full
report. What, probably, will he *spy?* — what
will he *select* to look at? Of course, he will
see a Brocken spectre of himself. He will see
several meeting-houses, at least, and, perhaps,
that somebody ought to be assessed higher than
he is, since he has so handsome a wood-lot.
Now take Julius Cæsar, or Emanuel Sweden-
borg, or a Fiji Islander, and set him up there.
Or suppose all together, and let them compare
notes afterward. Will it appear that they have
enjoyed the same prospect? What they will

see will be as different as Rome was from Heaven or Hell, or the last from the Fiji Islands. For aught we know, as strange a man as any of these is always at our elbow.

Why, it takes a sharp-shooter to bring down even such trivial game as snipes and wood-cocks; he must take very particular aim, and know what he is aiming at. He would stand a very small chance, if he fired at random into the sky, being told that snipes were flying there. And so is it with him that shoots at beauty; though he wait till the sky falls, he will not bag any, if he does not already know its seasons and haunts, and the color of its wing, — if he has not dreamed of it, so that he can *anticipate* it; then, indeed, he flushes it at every step, shoots double and on the wing, with both barrels, even in cornfields. The sportsman trains himself, dresses and watches unweariedly, and loads and primes for his particular game. He prays for it, and offers sacrifices, and so he gets it. After due and long preparation, schooling his eye and hand, dreaming awake and asleep, with gun and paddle and boat, he goes out after meadow-hens, which most of his townsmen never saw nor dreamed of, and paddles for miles against a head-wind, and wades in water up to his knees, being out all day without his dinner, and *therefore* he gets them. He had them half-way into his bag when he started, and has only to shove them down. The true sportsman can shoot you almost any of his game from his windows: what else has he windows or eyes for? It comes and perches at last on the barrel of his gun; but the rest of the world never see it *with the feathers on*. The geese fly exactly under his zenith, and honk when they get there, and he will keep himself supplied by firing up his chimney; twenty musquash have the refusal of each one of his traps before it is empty. If he lives, and his game-spirit increases, heaven and earth shall fail him sooner than game; and when he dies, he will go to more extensive and, perchance, happier hunting-grounds. The fisherman, too, dreams of fish; sees a bobbing cork in his dreams, till he can almost catch them in his sink-spout. I knew a girl who, being sent to pick huckleberries, picked wild gooseberries by the quart, where no one else knew that there were any, because she was accustomed to pick them up country where she came from. The astronomer knows where to go star-gathering, and sees one clearly in his mind before any have seen it with a glass. The hen scratches and finds her food right under where she stands; but such is not the way with the hawk.

These bright leaves which I have mentioned

are not the exception, but the rule; for I believe that all leaves, even grasses and mosses,
acquire brighter colors just before their fall.
When you come to observe faithfully the
changes of each humblest plant, you find that
each has, sooner or later, its peculiar autumnal
tint; and if you undertake to make a complete
list of the bright tints, it will be nearly as long
as a catalogue of the plants in your vicinity.

WILD APPLES

THE HISTORY OF THE APPLE-TREE

It is remarkable how closely the history of the apple-tree is connected with that of man. The geologist tells us that the order of the *Rosaceæ*, which includes the Apple, also the true Grasses, and the *Labiatæ*, or Mints, were introduced only a short time previous to the appearance of man on the globe.

It appears that apples made a part of the food of that unknown primitive people whose traces have lately been found at the bottom of the Swiss lakes, supposed to be older than the foundation of Rome, so old that they had no metallic implements. An entire black and shriveled Crab-Apple has been recovered from their stores.

Tacitus says of the ancient Germans, that they satisfied their hunger with wild apples (*agrestia poma*), among other things.

Niebuhr observes that "the words for a house, a field, a plough, ploughing, wine, oil, milk, sheep, apples, and others relating to agriculture and the gentler way of life, agree in

Latin and Greek, while the Latin words for all objects pertaining to war or the chase are utterly alien from the Greek." Thus the apple-tree may be considered a symbol of peace no less than the olive.

The apple was early so important, and generally distributed, that its name traced to its root in many languages signifies fruit in general. Μῆλον, in Greek, means an apple, also the fruit of other trees, also a sheep and any cattle, and finally riches in general.

The apple-tree has been celebrated by the Hebrews, Greeks, Romans, and Scandinavians. Some have thought that the first human pair were tempted by its fruit. Goddesses are fabled to have contended for it, dragons were set to watch it, and heroes were employed to pluck it.

The tree is mentioned in at least three places in the Old Testament, and its fruit in two or three more. Solomon sings, — "As the apple-tree among the trees of the wood, so is my beloved among the sons." And again, — "Stay me with flagons, comfort me with apples." The noblest part of man's noblest feature is named from this fruit, "the apple of the eye."

The apple-tree is also mentioned by Homer and Herodotus. Ulysses saw in the glorious garden of Alcinoüs "pears and pomegranates,

and apple-trees bearing beautiful fruit" (καὶ
μηλέαι ἀγλαόκαρποι). And according to Homer,
apples were among the fruits which Tantalus
could not pluck, the wind ever blowing their
boughs away from him. Theophrastus knew
and described the apple-tree as a botanist.

According to the Prose Edda, "Iduna keeps
in a box the apples which the gods, when they
feel old age approaching, have only to taste of
to become young again. It is in this manner
that they will be kept in renovated youth until
Ragnarök" (or the destruction of the gods).

I learn from Loudon that "the ancient
Welsh bards were rewarded for excelling in
song by the token of the apple-spray;" and
"in the Highlands of Scotland the apple-tree
is the badge of the clan Lamont."

The apple-tree (*Pyrus malus*) belongs chiefly
to the northern temperate zone. Loudon says
that "it grows spontaneously in every part of
Europe except the frigid zone, and throughout
Western Asia, China, and Japan." We have
also two or three varieties of the apple indigenous in North America. The cultivated apple-
tree was first introduced into this country by the
earliest settlers, and is thought to do as well or
better here than anywhere else. Probably some
of the varieties which are now cultivated were
first introduced into Britain by the Romans.

Pliny, adopting the distinction of Theophrastus, says, — "Of trees there are some which are altogether wild (*sylvestres*), some more civilized (*urbaniores*)." Theophrastus includes the apple among the last; and, indeed, it is in this sense the most civilized of all trees. It is as harmless as a dove, as beautiful as a rose, and as valuable as flocks and herds. It has been longer cultivated than any other, and so is more humanized; and who knows but, like the dog, it will at length be no longer traceable to its wild original? It migrates with man, like the dog and horse and cow: first, perchance, from Greece to Italy, thence to England, thence to America; and our Western emigrant is still marching steadily toward the setting sun with the seeds of the apple in his pocket, or perhaps a few young trees strapped to his load. At least a million apple-trees are thus set farther westward this year than any cultivated ones grew last year. Consider how the Blossom-Week, like the Sabbath, is thus annually spreading over the prairies; for when man migrates, he carries with him not only his birds, quadrupeds, insects, vegetables, and his very sward, but his orchard also.

The leaves and tender twigs are an agreeable food to many domestic animals, as the cow, horse, sheep, and goat; and the fruit is sought

after by the first, as well as by the hog. Thus
there appears to have existed a natural alliance
between these animals and this tree from the
first. "The fruit of the Crab in the forests of
France" is said to be "a great resource for the
wild boar."

Not only the Indian, but many indigenous
insects, birds, and quadrupeds, welcomed the
apple-tree to these shores. The tent-caterpillar
saddled her eggs on the very first twig that was
formed, and it has since shared her affections
with the wild cherry; and the canker-worm also
in a measure abandoned the elm to feed on it.
As it grew apace, the blue-bird, robin, cherry-
bird, king-bird, and many more came with
haste and built their nests and warbled in its
boughs, and so became orchard-birds, and multiplied more than ever. It was an era in the
history of their race. The downy woodpecker
found such a savory morsel under its bark that
he perforated it in a ring quite round the tree,
before he left it, — a thing which he had never
done before, to my knowledge. It did not take
the partridge long to find out how sweet its
buds were, and every winter eve she flew, and
still flies, from the wood, to pluck them, much
to the farmer's sorrow. The rabbit, too, was
not slow to learn the taste of its twigs and bark;
and when the fruit was ripe, the squirrel half

rolled, half carried it to his hole; and even the musquash crept up the bank from the brook at evening, and greedily devoured it, until he had worn a path in the grass there; and when it was frozen and thawed, the crow and the jay were glad to taste it occasionally. The owl crept into the first apple-tree that became hollow, and fairly hooted with delight, finding it just the place for him; so, settling down into it, he has remained there ever since.

My theme being the Wild Apple, I will merely glance at some of the seasons in the annual growth of the cultivated apple, and pass on to my special province.

The flowers of the apple are perhaps the most beautiful of any tree's, so copious and so delicious to both sight and scent. The walker is frequently tempted to turn and linger near some more than usually handsome one, whose blossoms are two thirds expanded. How superior it is in these respects to the pear, whose blossoms are neither colored nor fragrant!

By the middle of July, green apples are so large as to remind us of coddling, and of the autumn. The sward is commonly strewed with little ones which fall still-born, as it were, — Nature thus thinning them for us. The Roman writer Palladius said, — "If apples are inclined to fall before their time, a stone placed in a split root will retain them." Some such notion, still surviving, may account for some of the stones which we see placed, to be overgrown, in the forks of trees. They have a saying in Suffolk, England, —

> "At Michaelmas time, or a little before,
> Half an apple goes to the core."

Early apples begin to be ripe about the first of August; but I think that none of them are so good to eat as some to smell. One is worth more to scent your handkerchief with than any perfume which they sell in the shops. . The fragrance of some fruits is not to be forgotten, along with that of flowers. Some gnarly apple which I pick up in the road reminds me by its fragrance of all the wealth of Pomona, — carrying me forward to those days when they will be collected in golden and ruddy heaps in the orchards and about the cider-mills.

A week or two later, as you are going by orchards or gardens, especially in the evenings, you pass through a little region possessed by the fragrance of ripe apples, and thus enjoy them without price, and without robbing anybody.

There is thus about all natural products a certain volatile and ethereal quality which represents their highest value, and which cannot be vulgarized, or bought and sold. No mortal has

ever enjoyed the perfect flavor of any fruit, and
only the godlike among men begin to taste its
ambrosial qualities. For nectar and ambrosia
are only those fine flavors of every earthly fruit
which our coarse palates fail to perceive, — just
as we occupy the heaven of the gods without
knowing it. When I see a particularly mean
man carrying a load of fair and fragrant early
apples to market, I seem to see a contest going
on between him and his horse, on the one side,
and the apples on the other, and, to my mind,
the apples always gain it. Pliny says that
apples are the heaviest of all things, and that
the oxen begin to sweat at the mere sight of a
load of them. Our driver begins to lose his
load the moment he tries to transport them to
where they do not belong, that is, to any but
the most beautiful. Though he gets out from
time to time, and feels of them, and thinks they
are all there, I see the stream of their evanescent and celestial qualities going to heaven from
his cart, while the pulp and skin and core only
are going to market. They are not apples, but
pomace. Are not these still Iduna's apples,
the taste of which keeps the gods forever
young? and think you that they will let Loki
or Thjassi carry them off to Jötunheim, while
they grow wrinkled and gray? No, for Ragnarök, or the destruction of the gods, is not yet.

There is another thinning of the fruit, commonly near the end of August or in September, when the ground is strewn with windfalls; and this happens especially when high winds occur after rain. In some orchards you may see fully three quarters of the whole crop on the ground, lying in a circular form beneath the trees, yet hard and green, — or, if it is a hillside, rolled far down the hill. However, it is an ill wind that blows nobody any good. All the country over, people are busy picking up the windfalls, and this will make them cheap for early apple-pies.

In October, the leaves falling, the apples are more distinct on the trees. I saw one year in a neighboring town some trees fuller of fruit than I remember to have ever seen before, small yellow apples hanging over the road. The branches were gracefully drooping with their weight, like a barberry-bush, so that the whole tree acquired a new character. Even the topmost branches, instead of standing erect, spread and drooped in all directions; and there were so many poles supporting the lower ones that they looked like pictures of banian-trees. As an old English manuscript says, "The mo appelen the tree bereth the more sche boweth to the folk."

Surely the apple is the noblest of fruits.

Let the most beautiful or the swiftest have it. That should be the "going" price of apples.

Between the 5th and 20th of October I see the barrels lie under the trees. And perhaps I talk with one who is selecting some choice barrels to fulfill an order. He turns a specked one over many times before he leaves it out. If I were to tell what is passing in my mind, I should say that every one was specked which he had handled; for he rubs off all the bloom, and those fugacious ethereal qualities leave it. Cool evenings prompt the farmers to make haste, and at length I see only the ladders here and there left leaning against the trees.

It would be well, if we accepted these gifts with more joy and gratitude, and did not think it enough simply to put a fresh load of compost about the tree. Some old English customs are suggestive at least. I find them described chiefly in Brand's "Popular Antiquities." It appears that "on Christmas Eve the farmers and their men in Devonshire take a large bowl of cider, with a toast in it, and carrying it in state to the orchard, they salute the apple-trees with much ceremony, in order to make them bear well the next season." This salutation consists in "throwing some of the cider about the roots of the tree, placing bits of the toast on the branches," and then, "encircling one of the

best bearing trees in the orchard, they drink
the following toast three several times: —

> ' Here's to thee, old apple-tree,
> Whence thou mayst bud, and whence thou mayst blow,
> And whence thou mayst bear apples enow!
> Hats-full! caps-full!
> Bushel, bushel, sacks-full!
> And my pockets full, too! Hurra!'"

Also what was called "apple-howling" used
to be practiced in various counties of England
on New Year's Eve. A troop of boys visited
the different orchards, and, encircling the apple-trees, repeated the following words: —

> "Stand fast, root! bear well, top!
> Pray God send us a good howling crop:
> Every twig, apples big;
> Every bow, apples enow!"

"They then shout in chorus, one of the boys
accompanying them on a cow's horn. During
this ceremony they rap the trees with their
sticks." This is called "wassailing" the trees,
and is thought by some to be "a relic of the
heathen sacrifice to Pomona."

Herrick sings, —

> "Wassaile the trees that they may beare
> You many a plum and many a peare;
> For more or less fruits they will bring
> As you so give them wassailing."

Our poets have as yet a better right to sing
of cider than of wine; but it behooves them to

sing better than English Phillips did, else they
will do no credit to their Muse.

THE WILD APPLE.

So much for the more civilized apple-trees
(*urbaniores*, as Pliny calls them). I love better
to go through the old orchards of ungrafted apple-trees, at whatever season of the year, — so
irregularly planted: sometimes two trees standing close together; and the rows so devious that
you would think that they not only had grown
while the owner was sleeping, but had been set
out by him in a somnambulic state. The rows
of grafted fruit will never tempt me to wander
amid them like these. But I now, alas, speak
rather from memory than from any recent experience, such ravages have been made!

Some soils, like a rocky tract called the Easterbrooks Country in my neighborhood, are so
suited to the apple, that it will grow faster in
them without any care, or if only the ground is
broken up once a year, than it will in many
places with any amount of care. The owners
of this tract allow that the soil is excellent for
fruit, but they say that it is so rocky that they
have not patience to plough it, and that, together with the distance, is the reason why it is
not cultivated. There are, or were recently,
extensive orchards there standing without or-

der. Nay, they spring up wild and bear well
there in the midst of pines, birches, maples,
and oaks. I am often surprised to see rising
amid these trees the rounded tops of apple-trees
glowing with red or yellow fruit, in harmony
with the autumnal tints of the forest.

Going up the side of a cliff about the first of
November, I saw a vigorous young apple-tree,
which, planted by birds or cows, had shot up
amid the rocks and open woods there, and had
now much fruit on it, uninjured by the frosts,
when all cultivated apples were gathered. It
was a rank wild growth, with many green leaves
on it still, and made an impression of thorniness. The fruit was hard and green, but looked
as if it would be palatable in the winter. Some
was dangling on the twigs, but more half buried in the wet leaves under the tree, or rolled
far down the hill amid the rocks. The owner
knows nothing of it. The day was not observed
when it first blossomed, nor when it first bore
fruit, unless by the chickadee. There was no
dancing on the green beneath it in its honor,
and now there is no hand to pluck its fruit, —
which is only gnawed by squirrels, as I perceive. It has done double duty, — not only
borne this crop, but each twig has grown a foot
into the air. And this is *such* fruit! bigger
than many berries, we must admit, and carried

home will be sound and palatable next spring.
What care I for Iduna's apples so long as I
can get these?

When I go by this shrub thus late and hardy,
and see its dangling fruit, I respect the tree,
and I am grateful for Nature's bounty, even
though I cannot eat it. Here on this rugged
and woody hillside has grown an apple - tree,
not planted by man, no relic of a former orchard, but a natural growth, like the pines and
oaks. Most fruits which we prize and use depend entirely on our care. Corn and grain,
potatoes, peaches, melons, etc., depend altogether on our planting; but the apple emulates
man's independence and enterprise. It is not
simply carried, as I have said, but, like him, to
some extent, it has migrated to this New World,
and is even, here and there, making its way
amid the aboriginal trees; just as the ox and
dog and horse sometimes run wild and maintain themselves.

Even the sourest and crabbedest apple, growing in the most unfavorable position, suggests
such thoughts as these, it is so noble a fruit.

THE CRAB.

Nevertheless, *our* wild apple is wild only
like myself, perchance, who belong not to the
aboriginal race here, but have strayed into the

woods from the cultivated stock. Wilder still, as I have said, there grows elsewhere in this country a native and aboriginal Crab-Apple, *Malus coronaria*, "whose nature has not yet been modified by cultivation." It is found from Western New York to Minnesota, and southward. Michaux says that its ordinary height "is fifteen or eighteen feet, but it is sometimes found twenty-five or thirty feet high," and that the large ones "exactly resemble the common apple-tree." "The flowers are white mingled with rose color, and are collected in corymbs." They are remarkable for their delicious odor. The fruit, according to him, is about an inch and a half in diameter, and is intensely acid. Yet they make fine sweetmeats and also cider of them. He concludes that "if, on being cultivated, it does not yield new and palatable varieties, it will at least be celebrated for the beauty of its flowers, and for the sweetness of its perfume."

I never saw the Crab-Apple till May, 1861. I had heard of it through Michaux, but more modern botanists, so far as I know, have not treated it as of any peculiar importance. Thus it was a half-fabulous tree to me. I contemplated a pilgrimage to the "Glades," a portion of Pennsylvania where it was said to grow to perfection. I thought of sending to a nursery

for it, but doubted if they had it, or would distinguish it from European varieties. At last I
had occasion to go to Minnesota, and on entering Michigan I began to notice from the cars a
tree with handsome rose-colored flowers. At
first I thought it some variety of thorn; but it
was not long before the truth flashed on me,
that this was my long-sought Crab-Apple. It
was the prevailing flowering shrub or tree to be
seen from the cars at that season of the year, —
about the middle of May. But the cars never
stopped before one, and so I was launched on
the bosom of the Mississippi without having
touched one, experiencing the fate of Tantalus.
On arriving at St. Anthony's Falls, I was sorry
to be told that I was too far north for the Crab-
Apple. Nevertheless I succeeded in finding it
about eight miles west of the Falls; touched it
and smelled it, and secured a lingering corymb
of flowers for my herbarium. This must have
been near its northern limit.

HOW THE WILD APPLE GROWS.

But though these are indigenous, like the
Indians, I doubt whether they are any hardier
than those backwoodsmen among the apple-
trees, which, though descended from cultivated
stocks, plant themselves in distant fields and
forests, where the soil is favorable to them. I

know of no trees which have more difficulties to
contend with, and which more sturdily resist
their foes. These are the ones whose story we
have to tell. It oftentimes reads thus: —

Near the beginning of May, we notice little
thickets of apple-trees just springing up in the
pastures where cattle have been, — as the rocky
ones of our Easterbrooks Country, or the top
of Nobscot Hill, in Sudbury. One or two of
these perhaps survive the drought and other accidents, — their very birthplace defending them
against the encroaching grass and some other
dangers, at first.

> In two years' time 't had thus
>   Reached the level of the rocks,
> Admired the stretching world,
>   Nor feared the wandering flocks.
>
> But at this tender age
>   Its sufferings began:
> There came a browsing ox
>   And cut it down a span.

This time, perhaps, the ox does not notice it
amid the grass; but the next year, when it has
grown more stout, he recognizes it for a fellow-
emigrant from the old country, the flavor of
whose leaves and twigs he well knows; and
though at first he pauses to welcome it, and express his surprise, and gets for answer, "The
same cause that brought you here brought me,"

he nevertheless browses it again, reflecting, it may be, that he has some title to it.

Thus cut down annually, it does not despair; but, putting forth two short twigs for every one cut off, it spreads out low along the ground in the hollows or between the rocks, growing more stout and scrubby, until it forms, not a tree as yet, but a little pyramidal, stiff, twiggy mass, almost as solid and impenetrable as a rock. Some of the densest and most impenetrable clumps of bushes that I have ever seen, as well on account of the closeness and stubbornness of their branches as of their thorns, have been these wild-apple scrubs. They are more like the scrubby fir and black spruce on which you stand, and sometimes walk, on the tops of mountains, where cold is the demon they contend with, than anything else. No wonder they are prompted to grow thorns at last, to defend themselves against such foes. In their thorniness, however, there is no malice, only some malic acid.

The rocky pastures of the tract I have referred to, — for they maintain their ground best in a rocky field, — are thickly sprinkled with these little tufts, reminding you often of some rigid gray mosses or lichens, and you see thousands of little trees just springing up between them, with the seed still attached to them.

Being regularly clipped all around each year
by the cows, as a hedge with shears, they are
often of a perfect conical or pyramidal form,
from one to four feet high, and more or less
sharp, as if trimmed by the gardener's art. In
the pastures on Nobscot Hill and its spurs,
they make fine dark shadows when the sun is
low. They are also an excellent covert from
hawks for many small birds that roost and build
in them. Whole flocks perch in them at night,
and I have seen three robins' nests in one which
was six feet in diameter.

No doubt many of these are already old trees,
if you reckon from the day they were planted,
but infants still when you consider their development and the long life before them. I
counted the annual rings of some which were
just one foot high, and as wide as high, and
found that they were about twelve years old,
but quite sound and thrifty! They were so low
that they were unnoticed by the walker, while
many of their contemporaries from the nurseries
were already bearing considerable crops. But
what you gain in time is perhaps in this case,
too, lost in power, — that is, in the vigor of the
tree. This is their pyramidal state.

The cows continue to browse them thus for
twenty years or more, keeping them down and
compelling them to spread, until at last they

are so broad that they become their own fence, when some interior shoot, which their foes cannot reach, darts upward with joy: for it has not forgotten its high calling, and bears its own peculiar fruit in triumph.

Such are the tactics by which it finally defeats its bovine foes. Now, if you have watched the progress of a particular shrub, you will see that it is no longer a simple pyramid or cone, but that out of its apex there rises a sprig or two, growing more lustily perchance than an orchard-tree, since the plant now devotes the whole of its repressed energy to these upright parts. In a short time these become a small tree, an inverted pyramid resting on the apex of the other, so that the whole has now the form of a vast hour-glass. The spreading bottom, having served its purpose, finally disappears, and the generous tree permits the now harmless cows to come in and stand in its shade, and rub against and redden its trunk, which has grown in spite of them, and even to taste a part of its fruit, and so disperse the seed.

Thus the cows create their own shade and food; and the tree, its hour-glass being inverted, lives a second life, as it were.

It is an important question with some nowadays, whether you should trim young apple-trees as high as your nose or as high as your eyes. The ox trims them up as high as he can reach, and that is about the right height, I think.

In spite of wandering kine, and other adverse circumstances, that despised shrub, valued only by small birds as a covert and shelter from hawks, has its blossom-week at last, and in course of time its harvest, sincere, though small.

By the end of some October, when its leaves have fallen, I frequently see such a central sprig, whose progress I have watched, when I thought it had forgotten its destiny, as I had, bearing its first crop of small green or yellow or rosy fruit, which the cows cannot get at over the bushy and thorny hedge which surrounds it, and I make haste to taste the new and undescribed variety. We have all heard of the numerous varieties of fruit invented by Van Mons and Knight. This is the system of Van Cow, and she has invented far more and more memorable varieties than both of them.

Through what hardships it may attain to bear a sweet fruit! Though somewhat small, it may prove equal, if not superior, in flavor to that which has grown in a garden, — will perchance be all the sweeter and more palatable for the very difficulties it has had to contend with. Who knows but this chance wild fruit, planted by a cow or a bird on some remote and rocky hillside, where it is as yet unobserved by man, may be the choicest of all its kind, and foreign potentates shall hear of it, and royal societies seek to propagate it, though the virtues of the perhaps truly crabbed owner of the soil may never be heard of, — at least, beyond the limits of his village? It was thus the Porter and the Baldwin grew.

Every wild-apple shrub excites our expectation thus, somewhat as every wild child. It is, perhaps, a prince in disguise. What a lesson to man! So are human beings, referred to the highest standard, the celestial fruit which they suggest and aspire to bear, browsed on by fate; and only the most persistent and strongest genius defends itself and prevails, sends a tender scion upward at last, and drops its perfect fruit on the ungrateful earth. Poets and philosophers and statesmen thus spring up in the country pastures, and outlast the hosts of unoriginal men.

Such is always the pursuit of knowledge. The celestial fruits, the golden apples of the Hesperides, are ever guarded by a hundred-headed dragon which never sleeps, so that it is an Herculean labor to pluck them.

This is one, and the most remarkable way in which the wild apple is propagated; but commonly it springs up at wide intervals in woods and swamps, and by the sides of roads, as the soil may suit it, and grows with comparative rapidity. Those which grow in dense woods are very tall and slender. I frequently pluck from these trees a perfectly mild and tamed fruit. As Palladius says, "*Et injussu consternitur ubere mali:*" And the ground is strewn with the fruit of an unbidden apple-tree.

It is an old notion that, if these wild trees do not bear a valuable fruit of their own, they are the best stocks by which to transmit to posterity the most highly prized qualities of others. However, I am not in search of stocks, but the wild fruit itself, whose fierce gust has suffered no "inteneration." It is not my

> " highest plot
> To plant the Bergamot."

THE FRUIT, AND ITS FLAVOR.

The time for wild apples is the last of October and the first of November. They then get to be palatable, for they ripen late, and they are still perhaps as beautiful as ever. I make a great account of these fruits, which the farmers do not think it worth the while to gather, — wild flavors of the Muse, vivacious and inspiriting. The farmer thinks that he has better in his barrels, but he is mistaken, unless he has a walker's appetite and imagination, neither of which can he have.

Such as grow quite wild, and are left out till the first of November, I presume that the owner does not mean to gather. They belong to children as wild as themselves, — to certain active boys that I know, — to the wild-eyed woman of the fields, to whom nothing comes amiss, who gleans after all the world, and, moreover, to us walkers. We have met with them, and they are ours. These rights, long enough insisted upon, have come to be an institution in some old countries, where they have learned how to live. I hear that "the custom of grippling, which may be called apple-gleaning, is, or was formerly, practiced in Herefordshire. It consists in leaving a few apples, which are called the gripples, on every tree, after the general gathering, for the boys, who go with climbing-poles and bags to collect them."

As for those I speak of, I pluck them as a wild fruit, native to this quarter of the earth, — fruit of old trees that have been dying ever since I was a boy and are not yet dead, frequented only by the woodpecker and the squirrel, deserted now by the owner, who has not faith enough to look under their boughs. From the appearance of the tree-top, at a little distance, you would expect nothing but lichens to drop from it, but your faith is rewarded by finding the ground strewn with spirited fruit,

— some of it, perhaps, collected at squirrel-holes, with the marks of their teeth by which they carried them, — some containing a cricket or two silently feeding within, and some, especially in damp days, a shell-less snail. The very sticks and stones lodged in the tree-top might have convinced you of the savoriness of the fruit which has been so eagerly sought after in past years.

I have seen no account of these among the "Fruits and Fruit-Trees of America," though they are more memorable to my taste than the grafted kinds; more racy and wild American flavors do they possess when October and November, when December and January, and perhaps February and March even, have assuaged them somewhat. An old farmer in my neighborhood, who always selects the right word, says that "they have a kind of bow-arrow tang."

Apples for grafting appear to have been selected commonly, not so much for their spirited flavor, as for their mildness, their size, and bearing qualities, — not so much for their beauty, as for their fairness and soundness. Indeed, I have no faith in the selected lists of pomological gentlemen. Their "Favorites" and "None-suches" and "Seek-no-farthers," when I have fruited them, commonly turn out very tame and forgettable. They are eaten with comparatively little zest, and have no real *tang* nor *smack* to them.

What if some of these wildings are acrid and puckery, genuine *verjuice*, do they not still belong to the *Pomaceœ*, which are uniformly innocent and kind to our race? I still begrudge them to the cider-mill. Perhaps they are not fairly ripe yet.

No wonder that these small and high-colored apples are thought to make the best cider. Loudon quotes from the "Herefordshire Report," that "apples of a small size are always, if equal in quality, to be preferred to those of a larger size, in order that the rind and kernel may bear the greatest proportion to the pulp, which affords the weakest and most watery juice." And he says that, "to prove this, Dr. Symonds, of Hereford, about the year 1800, made one hogshead of cider entirely from the rinds and cores of apples, and another from the pulp only, when the first was found of extraordinary strength and flavor, while the latter was sweet and insipid."

Evelyn says that the "Red-strake" was the favorite cider-apple in his day; and he quotes one Dr. Newburg as saying, "In Jersey 't is a general observation, as I hear, that the more of red any apple has in its rind, the more proper it is for this use. Pale-faced apples they ex-

clude as much as may be from their cider-vat."
This opinion still prevails.

All apples are good in November. Those
which the farmer leaves out as unsalable and
unpalatable to those who frequent the markets
are choicest fruit to the walker. But it is remarkable that the wild apple, which I praise as
so spirited and racy when eaten in the fields or
woods, being brought into the house, has frequently a harsh and crabbed taste. The Saunterer's Apple not even the saunterer can eat in
the house. The palate rejects it there, as it
does haws and acorns, and demands a tamed
one; for there you miss the November air,
which is the sauce it is to be eaten with. Accordingly, when Tityrus, seeing the lengthening
shadows, invites Melibœus to go home and pass
the night with him, he promises him *mild* apples and soft chestnuts, — *mitia poma, castaneæ
molles.* I frequently pluck wild apples of so
rich and spicy a flavor that I wonder all or-
chardists do not get a scion from that tree, and
I fail not to bring home my pockets full. But
perchance, when I take one out of my desk and
taste it in my chamber, I find it unexpectedly
crude, — sour enough to set a squirrel's teeth
on edge and make a jay scream.

These apples have hung in the wind and frost
and rain till they have absorbed the qualities of

the weather or season, and thus are highly *sea-soned*, and they *pierce* and *sting* and *permeate* us with their spirit. They must be eaten in *season*, accordingly, — that is, out-of-doors.

To appreciate the wild and sharp flavors of these October fruits, it is necessary that you be breathing the sharp October or November air. The out-door air and exercise which the walker gets give a different tone to his palate, and he craves a fruit which the sedentary would call harsh and crabbed. They must be eaten in the fields, when your system is all aglow with exercise, when the frosty weather nips your fingers, the wind rattles the bare boughs or rustles the few remaining leaves, and the jay is heard screaming around. What is sour in the house a bracing walk makes sweet. Some of these apples might be labeled, "To be eaten in the wind."

Of course no flavors are thrown away; they are intended for the taste that is up to them. Some apples have two distinct flavors, and perhaps one half of them must be eaten in the house, the other out-doors. One Peter Whitney wrote from Northborough in 1782, for the Proceedings of the Boston Academy, describing an apple-tree in that town "producing fruit of opposite qualities, part of the same apple being frequently sour and the other sweet;" also some all sour, and others all sweet, and this diversity on all parts of the tree.

There is a wild apple on Nawshawtuck Hill in my town which has to me a peculiarly pleasant bitter tang, not perceived till it is three quarters tasted. It remains on the tongue. As you eat it, it smells exactly like a squash-bug. It is a sort of triumph to eat and relish it.

I hear that the fruit of a kind of plum-tree in Provence is "called *Prunes sibarelles*, because it is impossible to whistle after having eaten them, from their sourness." But perhaps they were only eaten in the house and in summer, and if tried out-of-doors in a stinging atmosphere, who knows but you could whistle an octave higher and clearer?

In the fields only are the sours and bitters of Nature appreciated; just as the wood-chopper eats his meal in a sunny glade, in the middle of a winter day, with content, basks in a sunny ray there, and dreams of summer in a degree of cold which, experienced in a chamber, would make a student miserable. They who are at work abroad are not cold, but rather it is they who sit shivering in houses. As with temperatures, so with flavors; as with cold and heat, so with sour and sweet. This natural raciness, the sours and bitters which the diseased palate refuses, are the true condiments.

Let your condiments be in the condition of your senses. To appreciate the flavor of these wild apples requires vigorous and healthy senses, *papillæ* firm and erect on the tongue and palate, not easily flattened and tamed.

From my experience with wild apples, I can understand that there may be reason for a savage's preferring many kinds of food which the civilized man rejects. The former has the palate of an out-door man. It takes a savage or wild taste to appreciate a wild fruit.

What a healthy out-of-door appetite it takes to relish the apple of life, the apple of the world, then!

> " Nor is it every apple I desire,
>   Nor that which pleases every palate best;
> 'T is not the lasting Deuxan I require,
>   Nor yet the red-cheeked Greening I request,
> Nor that which first beshrewed the name of wife,
> Nor that whose beauty caused the golden strife:
> No, no! bring me an apple from the tree of life."

So there is one *thought* for the field, another for the house. I would have my thoughts, like wild apples, to be food for walkers, and will not warrant them to be palatable if tasted in the house.

THEIR BEAUTY.

Almost all wild apples are handsome. They cannot be too gnarly and crabbed and rusty to look at. The gnarliest will have some redeeming traits even to the eye. You will discover some evening redness dashed or sprinkled on some protuberance or in some cavity. It is rare that the summer lets an apple go without streaking or spotting it on some part of its sphere. It will have some red stains, commemorating the mornings and evenings it has witnessed; some dark and rusty blotches, in memory of the clouds and foggy, mildewy days that have passed over it; and a spacious field of green reflecting the general face of Nature, — green even as the fields; or a yellow ground, which implies a milder flavor, — yellow as the harvest, or russet as the hills.

Apples, these I mean, unspeakably fair, — apples not of Discord, but of Concord! Yet not so rare but that the homeliest may have a share. Painted by the frosts, some a uniform clear bright yellow, or red, or crimson, as if their spheres had regularly revolved, and enjoyed the influence of the sun on all sides alike, — some with the faintest pink blush imaginable, — some brindled with deep red streaks like a cow, or with hundreds of fine blood-red rays running regularly from the stem-dimple to the blossom-end, like meridional lines, on a straw-colored ground, — some touched with a greenish rust, like a fine lichen, here and there, with crimson blotches or eyes more or less confluent and fiery when wet, — and others gnarly, and freckled or peppered all over on the stem side with fine crimson spots on a white ground, as if accidentally sprinkled from the brush of Him who paints the autumn leaves. Others, again, are sometimes red inside, perfused with a beautiful blush, fairy food, too beautiful to eat, — apple of the Hesperides, apple of the evening sky! But like shells and pebbles on the seashore, they must be seen as they sparkle amid the withering leaves in some dell in the woods, in the autumnal air, or as they lie in the wet grass, and not when they have wilted and faded in the house.

THE NAMING OF THEM.

It would be a pleasant pastime to find suitable names for the hundred varieties which go to a single heap at the cider-mill. Would it not tax a man's invention, — no one to be named after a man, and all in the *lingua vernacula?* Who shall stand godfather at the christening of the wild apples? It would exhaust the Latin and Greek languages, if they were used, and make the *lingua vernacula* flag. We should have to call in the sunrise and the sunset, the rainbow and the autumn woods and the wild flowers, and the woodpecker and the purple finch and the squirrel and the jay and the but-

terfly, the November traveler and the truant
boy, to our aid.

In 1836 there were in the garden of the London Horticultural Society more than fourteen
hundred distinct sorts. But here are species
which they have not in their catalogue, not to
mention the varieties which our Crab might
yield to cultivation.

Let us enumerate a few of these. I find myself compelled, after all, to give the Latin
names of some for the benefit of those who live
where English is not spoken, — for they are
likely to have a world-wide reputation.

There is, first of all, the Wood-Apple (*Malus
sylvatica*) ; the Blue-Jay Apple; the Apple
which grows in Dells in the Woods (*sylvestri-
vallis*), also in Hollows in Pastures (*campestri-
vallis*) ; the Apple that grows in an old Cellar-
Hole (*Malus cellaris*) ; the Meadow-Apple; the
Partridge - Apple; the Truant's Apple (*cessa-
toris*), which no boy will ever go by without
knocking off some, however *late* it may be; the
Saunterer's Apple, — you must lose yourself
before you can find the way to that; the Beauty
of the Air (*Decus Aëris*); December-Eating;
the Frozen-Thawed (*gelato-soluta*), good only
in that state; the Concord Apple, possibly the
same with the *Musketaquidensis ;* the Assabet
Apple; the Brindled Apple; Wine of New

England; the Chickaree Apple; the Green
Apple (*Malus viridis*), — this has many syno-
nyms: in an imperfect state, it is the *Cholera
morbifera aut dysenterifera, puerulis dilectis-
sima ;* the Apple which Atalanta stopped to
pick up; the Hedge-Apple (*Malus Sepium*);
the Slug-Apple (*limacea*) ; the Railroad-Apple,
which perhaps came from a core thrown out of
the cars; the Apple whose Fruit we tasted in
our Youth; our Particular Apple, not to be
found in any catalogue, — *Pedestrium Sola-
tium ;* also the Apple where hangs the Forgotten Scythe; Iduna's Apples, and the Apples
which Loki found in the Wood; and a great
many more I have on my list, too numerous to
mention, — all of them good. As Bodæus exclaims, referring to the cultivated kinds, and
adapting Virgil to his case, so I, adapting Bodæus, —

"Not if I had a hundred tongues, a hundred mouths,
    An iron voice, could I describe all the forms
    And reckon up all the names of these *wild apples*."

THE LAST GLEANING.

By the middle of November the wild apples
have lost some of their brilliancy, and have
chiefly fallen. A great part are decayed on the
ground, and the sound ones are more palatable
than before. The note of the chickadee sounds

now more distinct, as you wander amid the old
trees, and the autumnal dandelion is half closed
and tearful. But still, if you are a skillful
gleaner, you may get many a pocketful even
of grafted fruit, long after apples are supposed
to be gone out-of-doors. I know a Blue-Pearmain tree, growing within the edge of a swamp,
almost as good as wild. You would not suppose that there was any fruit left there, on the
first survey, but you must look according to system. Those which lie exposed are quite brown
and rotten now, or perchance a few still show
one blooming cheek here and there amid the
wet leaves. Nevertheless, with experienced
eyes, I explore amid the bare alders and the
huckleberry-bushes and the withered sedge, and
in the crevices of the rocks, which are full of
leaves, and pry under the fallen and decaying
ferns, which, with apple and alder leaves,
thickly strew the ground. For I know that
they lie concealed, fallen into hollows long since
and covered up by the leaves of the tree itself,
— a proper kind of packing. From these lurking-places, anywhere within the circumference
of the tree, I draw forth the fruit, all wet and
glossy, may be nibbled by rabbits and hollowed
out by crickets, and perhaps with a leaf or two
cemented to it (as Curzon an old manuscript
from a monastery's mouldy cellar), but still

with a rich bloom on it, and at least as ripe and well kept, if not better than those in barrels, more crisp and lively than they. If these resources fail to yield anything, I have learned to look between the bases of the suckers which spring thickly from some horizontal limb, for now and then one lodges there, or in the very midst of an alder-clump, where they are covered by leaves, safe from cows which may have smelled them out. If I am sharp-set, for I do not refuse the Blue-Pearmain, I fill my pockets on each side; and as I retrace my steps in the frosty eve, being perhaps four or five miles from home, I eat one first from this side, and then from that, to keep my balance.

I learn from Topsell's Gesner, whose authority appears to be Albertus, that the following is the way in which the hedgehog collects and carries home his apples. He says, — "His meat is apples, worms, or grapes: when he findeth apples or grapes on the earth, he rolleth himself upon them, until he have filled all his prickles, and then carrieth them home to his den, never bearing above one in his mouth; and if it fortune that one of them fall off by the way, he likewise shaketh off all the residue, and walloweth upon them afresh, until they be all settled upon his back again. So, forth he goeth, making a noise like a cart-wheel; and if

he have any young ones in his nest, they pull
off his load wherewithal he is loaded, eating
thereof what they please, and laying up the
residue for the time to come."

THE "FROZEN-THAWED" APPLE.

Toward the end of November, though some
of the sound ones are yet more mellow and perhaps more edible, they have generally, like the
leaves, lost their beauty, and are beginning to
freeze. It is finger-cold, and prudent farmers
get in their barreled apples, and bring you the
apples and cider which they have engaged; for
it is time to put them into the cellar. Perhaps
a few on the ground show their red cheeks above
the early snow, and occasionally some even preserve their color and soundness under the snow
throughout the winter. But generally at the
beginning of the winter they freeze hard, and
soon, though undecayed, acquire the color of a
baked apple.

Before the end of December, generally, they
experience their first thawing. Those which a
month ago were sour, crabbed, and quite unpalatable to the civilized taste, such at least as
were frozen while sound, let a warmer sun come
to thaw them, for they are extremely sensitive
to its rays, are found to be filled with a rich
sweet cider, better than any bottled cider that I

know of, and with which I am better acquainted
than with wine. All apples are good in this
state, and your jaws are the cider-press. Others, which have more substance, are a sweet
and luscious food, — in my opinion of more
worth than the pineapples which are imported
from the West Indies. Those which lately
even I tasted only to repent of it, — for I am
semi-civilized, — which the farmer willingly left
on the tree, I am now glad to find have the property of hanging on like the leaves of the young
oaks. It is a way to keep cider sweet without
boiling. Let the frost come to freeze them
first, solid as stones, and then the rain or a
warm winter day to thaw them, and they will
seem to have borrowed a flavor from heaven
through the medium of the air in which they
hang. Or perchance you find, when you get
home, that those which rattled in your pocket
have thawed, and the ice is turned to cider.
But after the third or fourth freezing and thawing they will not be found so good.

What are the imported half-ripe fruits of the
torrid South, to this fruit matured by the cold
of the frigid North? These are those crabbed
apples with which I cheated my companion, and
kept a smooth face that I might tempt him to
eat. Now we both greedily fill our pockets
with them, — bending to drink the cup and save

our lappets from the overflowing juice, — and grow more social with their wine. Was there one that hung so high and sheltered by the tangled branches that our sticks could not dislodge it?

It is a fruit never carried to market, that I am aware of, — quite distinct from the apple of the markets, as from dried apple and cider, — and it is not every winter that produces it in perfection.

The era of the Wild Apple will soon be past. It is a fruit which will probably become extinct in New England. You may still wander through old orchards of native fruit of great extent, which for the most part went to the cider-mill, now all gone to decay. I have heard of an orchard in a distant town, on the side of a hill, where the apples rolled down and lay four feet deep against a wall on the lower side, and this the owner cut down for fear they should be made into cider. Since the temperance reform and the general introduction of grafted fruit, no native apple-trees, such as I see everywhere in deserted pastures, and where the woods have grown up around them, are set out. I fear that he who walks over these fields a century hence will not know the pleasure of knocking off wild apples. Ah, poor man, there are many pleasures which he will not know! Notwithstanding the prevalence of the Baldwin and the Porter, I doubt if so extensive orchards are set out to-day in my town as there were a century ago, when those vast straggling cider-orchards were planted, when men both ate and drank apples, when the pomace-heap was the only nursery, and trees cost nothing but the trouble of setting them out. Men could afford then to stick a tree by every wall-side and let it take its chance. I see nobody planting trees to-day in such out of the way places, along the lonely roads and lanes, and at the bottom of dells in the wood. Now that they have grafted trees, and pay a price for them, they collect them into a plat by their houses, and fence them in, — and the end of it all will be that we shall be compelled to look for our apples in a barrel.

This is "The word of the Lord that came to Joel the son of Pethuel.

"Hear this, ye old men, and give ear, all ye inhabitants of the land! Hath this been in your days, or even in the days of your fathers? . . .

"That which the palmerworm hath left hath the locust eaten; and that which the locust hath left hath the cankerworm eaten; and that which the cankerworm hath left hath the caterpillar eaten.

"Awake, ye drunkards, and weep! and howl, all ye drinkers of wine, because of the new wine! for it is cut off from your mouth.

"For a nation is come up upon my land, strong, and without number, whose teeth are the teeth of a lion, and he hath the cheek teeth of a great lion.

"He hath laid my vine waste, and barked my fig-tree; he hath made it clean bare, and cast it away; the branches thereof are made white. . . .

"Be ye ashamed, O ye husbandmen! howl, O ye vinedressers! . . .

"The vine is dried up, and the fig-tree languisheth; the pomegranate-tree, the palm-tree also, and the apple-tree, even all the trees of the field, are withered: because joy is withered away from the sons of men."

NIGHT AND MOONLIGHT

CHANCING to take a memorable walk by moonlight some years ago, I resolved to take more such walks, and make acquaintance with another side of nature: I have done so.

According to Pliny, there is a stone in Arabia called Selenites, "wherein is a white, which increases and decreases with the moon." My journal for the last year or two has been *selenitic* in this sense.

Is not the midnight like Central Africa to most of us? Are we not tempted to explore it, — to penetrate to the shores of its lake Tchad, and discover the source of its Nile, perchance the Mountains of the Moon? Who knows what fertility and beauty, moral and natural, are there to be found? In the Mountains of the Moon, in the Central Africa of the night, there is where all Niles have their hidden heads. The expeditions up the Nile as yet extend but to the Cataracts, or perchance to the mouth of the White Nile; but it is the Black Nile that concerns us.

I shall be a benefactor if I conquer some

realms from the night, if I report to the gazettes anything transpiring about us at that season worthy of their attention, — if I can show men that there is some beauty awake while they are asleep, — if I add to the domains of poetry.

Night is certainly more novel and less profane than day. I soon discovered that I was acquainted only with its complexion, and as for the moon, I had seen her only as it were through a crevice in a shutter, occasionally. Why not walk a little way in her light?

Suppose you attend to the suggestions which the moon makes for one month, commonly in vain, will it not be very different from anything in literature or religion? But why not study this Sanskrit? What if one moon has come and gone with its world of poetry, its weird teachings, its oracular suggestions, — so divine a creature freighted with hints for me, and I have not used her? One moon gone by unnoticed?

I think it was Dr. Chalmers who said, criticising Coleridge, that for his part he wanted ideas which he could see all round, and not such as he must look at away up in the heavens. Such a man, one would say, would never look at the moon, because she never turns her other side to us. The light which comes from ideas which have their orbit as distant from the earth,

and which is no less cheering and enlightening
to the benighted traveler than that of the moon
and stars, is naturally reproached or nicknamed
as moonshine by such. They are moonshine,
are they? Well, then do your night-traveling
when there is no moon to light you; but I will
be thankful for the light that reaches me from
the star of least magnitude. Stars are lesser or
greater only as they appear to us so. I will
be thankful that I see so much as one side of a
celestial idea, — one side of the rainbow, — and
the sunset sky.

Men talk glibly enough about moonshine, as
if they knew its qualities very well, and despised
them; as owls might talk of sunshine. None
of your sunshine, — but this word commonly
means merely something which they do not understand, — which they are abed and asleep to,
however much it may be worth their while to
be up and awake to it.

It must be allowed that the light of the moon,
sufficient though it is for the pensive walker,
and not disproportionate to the inner light we
have, is very inferior in quality and intensity to
that of the sun. But the moon is not to be
judged alone by the quantity of light she sends
to us, but also by her influence on the earth and
its inhabitants. "The moon gravitates toward
the earth, and the earth reciprocally toward the

moon." The poet who walks by moonlight is conscious of a tide in his thought which is to be referred to lunar influence. I will endeavor to separate the tide in my thoughts from the current distractions of the day. I would warn my hearers that they must not try my thoughts by a daylight standard, but endeavor to realize that I speak out of the night. All depends on your point of view. In Drake's "Collection of Voyages," Wafer says of some Albinoes among the Indians of Darien, "They are quite white, but their whiteness is like that of a horse, quite different from the fair or pale European, as they have not the least tincture of a blush or sanguine complexion. . . . Their eyebrows are milk-white, as is likewise the hair of their heads, which is very fine. . . . They seldom go abroad in the daytime, the sun being disagreeable to them, and causing their eyes, which are weak and poring, to water, especially if it shines towards them, yet they see very well by moonlight, from which we call them moon-eyed."

Neither in our thoughts in these moonlight walks, methinks, is there "the least tincture of a blush or sanguine complexion," but we are intellectually and morally Albinoes, — children of Endymion, — such is the effect of conversing much with the moon.

I complain of Arctic voyagers that they do

not enough remind us of the constant peculiar
dreariness of the scenery, and the perpetual twilight of the Arctic night. So he whose theme
is moonlight, though he may find it difficult,
must, as it were, illustrate it with the light of
the moon alone.

Many men walk by day; few walk by night.
It is a very different season. Take a July
night, for instance. About ten o'clock, —
when man is asleep, and day fairly forgotten,
— the beauty of moonlight is seen over lonely
pastures where cattle are silently feeding. On
all sides novelties present themselves. Instead
of the sun there are the moon and stars, instead
of the wood-thrush there is the whip-poor-will,
— instead of butterflies in the meadows, fireflies, winged sparks of fire! who would have
believed it? What kind of cool deliberate life
dwells in those dewy abodes associated with a
spark of fire? So man has fire in his eyes, or
blood, or brain. Instead of singing birds, the
half-throttled note of a cuckoo flying over, the
croaking of frogs, and the intenser dream of
crickets. But above all, the wonderful trump
of the bullfrog, ringing from Maine to Geor-
gia. The potato-vines stand upright, the corn
grows apace, the bushes loom, the grain-fields
are boundless. On our open river terraces once
cultivated by the Indian, they appear to occupy

the ground like an army, — their heads nodding
in the breeze.   Small trees and shrubs are seen
in the midst overwhelmed as by an inundation.
The shadows of rocks and trees, and shrubs and
hills, are more conspicuous than the objects
themselves.   The slightest irregularities in the
ground are revealed by the shadows, and what
the feet find comparatively smooth appears
rough and diversified in consequence.   For the
same reason the whole landscape is more varie-
gated and picturesque than by day.   The smallest recesses in the rocks are dim and cavernous;
the ferns in the wood appear of tropical size.
The sweet fern and indigo in overgrown wood-
paths wet you with dew up to your middle.
The leaves of the shrub-oak are shining as if a
liquid were flowing over them.   The pools seen
through the trees are as full of light as the sky.
"The light of the day takes refuge in their bos-
oms," as the Purana says of the ocean.   All
white objects are more remarkable than by day.
A distant cliff looks like a phosphorescent space
on a hillside.   The woods are heavy and dark.
Nature slumbers.   You see the moonlight reflected from particular stumps in the recesses of
the forest, as if she selected what to shine on.
These small fractions of her light remind one of
the plant called moon-seed, — as if the moon
were sowing it in such places.

In the night the eyes are partly closed or re-
tire into the head. Other senses take the lead.
The walker is guided as well by the sense of
smell. Every plant and field and forest emits
its odor now, swamp-pink in the meadow and
tansy in the road; and there is the peculiar dry
scent of corn which has begun to show its tas-
sels. The senses both of hearing and smelling
are more alert. We hear the tinkling of rills
which we never detected before. From time to
time, high up on the sides of hills, you pass
through a stratum of warm air. A blast which
has come up from the sultry plains of noon. It
tells of the day, of sunny noon-tide hours and
banks, of the laborer wiping his brow and the
bee humming amid flowers. It is an air in
which work has been done, — which men have
breathed. It circulates about from woodside
to hillside like a dog that has lost its master,
now that the sun is gone. The rocks retain all
night the warmth of the sun which they have
absorbed. And so does the sand. If you dig
a few inches into it you find a warm bed. You
lie on your back on a rock in a pasture on the
top of some bare hill at midnight, and speculate
on the height of the starry canopy. The stars
are the jewels of the night, and perchance surpass anything which day has to show. A companion with whom I was sailing one very windy

but bright moonlight night, when the stars were few and faint, thought that a man could get along with *them*, — though he was considerably reduced in his circumstances, — that they were a kind of bread and cheese that never failed.

No wonder that there have been astrologers, that some have conceived that they were personally related to particular stars. Dubartas, as translated by Sylvester, says he 'll

> " not believe that the great architect
> With all these fires the heavenly arches decked
> Only for show, and with these glistering shields,
> T' awake poor shepherds, watching in the fields."
> He 'll " not believe that the least flower which pranks
> Our garden borders, or our common banks,
> And the least stone, that in her warming lap
> Our mother earth doth covetously wrap,
> Hath some peculiar virtue of its own,
> And that the glorious stars of heav'n have none."

And Sir Walter Raleigh well says, "The stars are instruments of far greater use than to give an obscure light, and for men to gaze on after sunset;" and he quotes Plotinus as affirming that they "are significant, but not efficient;" and also Augustine as saying, "*Deus regit inferiora corpora per superiora:*" God rules the bodies below by those above. But best of all is this which another writer has expressed: "*Sapiens adjuvabit opus astrorum quemadmodum agricola terræ naturam:*" a wise man assisteth the work of the stars as the husbandman helpeth the nature of the soil.

It does not concern men who are asleep in their beds, but it is very important to the traveler, whether the moon shines brightly or is obscured. It is not easy to realize the serene joy of all the earth, when she commences to shine unobstructedly, unless you have often been abroad alone in moonlight nights. She seems to be waging continual war with the clouds in your behalf. Yet we fancy the clouds to be *her* foes also. She comes on magnifying her dangers by her light, revealing, displaying them in all their hugeness and blackness, then suddenly casts them behind into the light concealed, and goes her way triumphant through a small space of clear sky.

In short, the moon traversing, or appearing to traverse, the small clouds which lie in her way, now obscured by them, now easily dissipating and shining through them, makes the drama of the moonlight night to all watchers and night-travelers. Sailors speak of it as the moon eating up the clouds. The traveler all alone, the moon all alone, except for his sympathy, overcoming with incessant victory whole squadrons of clouds above the forests and lakes and hills. When she is obscured he so sympathizes with her that he could whip a dog for her relief, as Indians do. When she enters on a clear field of great extent in the heavens, and shines unobstructedly, he is glad. And when she has fought her way through all the squadron of her foes, and rides majestic in a clear sky unscathed, and there are no more any obstructions in her path, he cheerfully and confidently pursues his way, and rejoices in his heart, and the cricket also seems to express joy in its song.

How insupportable would be the days, if the night with its dews and darkness did not come to restore the drooping world. As the shades begin to gather around us, our primeval instincts are aroused, and we steal forth from our lairs, like the inhabitants of the jungle, in search of those silent and brooding thoughts which are the natural prey of the intellect.

Richter says that "the earth is every day overspread with the veil of night for the same reason as the cages of birds are darkened, viz.: that we may the more readily apprehend the higher harmonies of thought in the hush and quiet of darkness. Thoughts which day turns into smoke and mist stand about us in the night as light and flames; even as the column which fluctuates above the crater of Vesuvius, in the daytime appears a pillar of cloud, but by night a pillar of fire."

There are nights in this climate of such serene and majestic beauty, so medicinal and fertilizing to the spirit, that methinks a sensitive nature would not devote them to oblivion, and perhaps there is no man but would be better and wiser for spending them out - of - doors, though he should sleep all the next day to pay for it; should sleep an Endymion sleep, as the ancients expressed it, — nights which warrant the Grecian epithet ambrosial, when, as in the land of Beulah, the atmosphere is charged with dewy fragrance, and with music, and we take our repose and have our dreams awake, — when the moon, not secondary to the sun, —

> " gives us his blaze again,
> Void of its flame, and sheds a softer day.
> Now through the passing cloud she seems to stoop,
> Now up the pure cerulean rides sublime."

Diana still hunts in the New England sky.

> " In Heaven queen she is among the spheres.
> She, mistress-like, makes all things to be pure.
> Eternity in her oft change she bears ;
> She Beauty is ; by her the fair endure.

> " Time wears her not ; she doth his chariot guide ;
> Mortality below her orb is placed ;
> By her the virtues of the stars down slide ;
> By her is Virtue's perfect image cast."

The Hindoos compare the moon to a saintly being who has reached the last stage of bodily existence.

Great restorer of antiquity, great enchanter. In a mild night when the harvest or hunter's moon shines unobstructedly, the houses in our village, whatever architect they may have had by day, acknowledge only a master. The village street is then as wild as the forest. New and old things are confounded. I know not whether I am sitting on the ruins of a wall, or on the material which is to compose a new one. Nature is an instructed and impartial teacher, spreading no crude opinions, and flattering none; she will be neither radical nor conservative. Consider the moonlight, so civil, yet so savage!

The light is more proportionate to our knowledge than that of day. It is no more dusky in ordinary nights than our mind's habitual atmosphere, and the moonlight is as bright as our most illuminated moments are.

> "In such a night let me abroad remain
> Till morning breaks, and all's confused again."

Of what significance the light of day, if it is not the reflection of an inward dawn? — to what purpose is the veil of night withdrawn, if the morning reveals nothing to the soul? It is merely garish and glaring.

When Ossian in his address to the sun exclaims, —

" Where has darkness its dwelling ?
  Where is the cavernous home of the stars,
  When thou quickly followest their steps,
  Pursuing them like a hunter in the sky, —
  Thou climbing the lofty hills,
  They descending on barren mountains ? "

who does not in his thought accompany the
stars to their "cavernous home," "descending"
with them "on barren mountains"?

Nevertheless, even by night the sky is blue
and not black, for we see through the shadow of
the earth into the distant atmosphere of day,
where the sunbeams are reveling.

MAY DAYS

MAY 1, 1841. Life in gardens and parlors is unpalatable to me. It wants rudeness and necessity to give it relish. I would at least strike my spade into the earth with as good-will as the woodpecker his bill into a tree.

May 1, 1851. Khaled would have his weary soldiers vigilant still. Apprehending a midnight sally from the enemy, "Let no man sleep," said he; "we shall have rest enough after death."

May 1, 1852. Five A. M. To Cliffs. A smart frost in the night. The ploughed ground and platforms white with it. I hear the little forked-tailed chipping-sparrow (*Fringilla socialis*) shaking out his rapid "tchi-tchi-tchi-tchi-tchi-tchi," — a little jingle from the oak behind the depot. I hear the note of that plump bird with a dark streaked breast, that runs and hides in the grass, whose note sounds so like a cricket's in the grass. I used to hear it when I walked by moonlight last summer. I hear it now from deep in the sod, for there is hardly grass yet. The bird keeps so low you do not see it. You do not suspect how many there are till their heads appear. The word *seringo* reminds me of its note, as if it were produced by some kind of fine metallic spring. It is an earth sound.

It is a moist, lowering morning for the Mayers. The sun now shines under a cloud in the horizon, and his still yellow light falls on the western fields as sometimes on the eastern after a shower in a summer afternoon. Nuttall says the note of the chipping-sparrow is "given from time to time in the night, like the reverie of a dream." Have I not heard it when spearing? Found the first violet which would open to-day, *V. sagittata* var. *ovata*, — or *cucullata?* for the leaves are not toothed at base nor arrow-shaped as in the first, yet they are hairy, and, I should say, petiole-margined; still, like the latter, they are rolled in at base, and the scape is four-angled. . . . The woods have a damp smell this morning. I hear a robin amid them. Yet there are fewer singers to be heard than on a very pleasant morning some weeks ago. The low early blueberry (June berry) is well budded. The grass ground — low ground, at least — wears a good green tinge; there are no leaves on the woods; the river is high over the meadows. There is a thin, gauze-like veil over the village (I am on Fairhaven Hill), probably formed of the smokes. As yet we have had no

morning fogs, to my knowledge. I hear the
first to-wee finch; he says, "to-wee-to-wee;"
and another, much farther off than I supposed
when I went in search of him, says, "whip your
chr-r-r-r-r-r," with a metallic ring. I hear the
first cat-bird, also, mewing, and the wood-
thrush, which still thrills me, — a sound to be
heard in a new country from one side of a clearing. I heard a black and white creeper just
now, "wicher-wicher-wicher-wich." I am on
the Cliff. It is about six. The flicker cackles.
I hear a woodpecker tapping. The tinkle of
the huckleberry bird comes up from the shrub-
oak plain. He commonly lives away from the
habitations of men, in retired bushy fields and
sprout lands. We have thus flowers and the
song of birds before the woods leave out, like
poetry. When leaving the woods I heard the
hooting of an owl, which sounded very much
like a clown calling to his team. Saw two large
woodpeckers on an oak. I am tempted to say
that they were other and larger than the flicker;
but I have been deceived in him before. . . .

The little peeping frogs which I got last night
resemble the description of the *Hylodes Picker-
ingii*, and in some respects the peeping hyla;
but they are probably the former, though every
way considerably smaller. Mine are about
three fourths of an inch long as they sit, seven

eighths if stretched; four-fingered and five-toed, with small tubercles on the ends of them. Some difference in their color. One is like a pale oak leaf at this season, streaked with brown. Two others more ashy. Two have crosses on back, of dark brown, with transverse bands on the legs. I keep them in a tumbler. They peep at twilight and evening; occasionally at other times. One that got out in the evening on to the carpet was found soon after, by his peeping, on the piano. They easily ascend the glass of the window. Jump eighteen inches or more. When they peep, the loose, wrinkled skin of the throat is swelled up into a globular bubble, very large and transparent, and quite round, except on the throat side, behind which their little heads are lost, mere protuberances on the side of this sphere. The peeping wholly absorbs them, their mouths being shut, or apparently so. Will sit half a day on the side of a smooth tumbler. Made that trilling note in the house. Remain many hours at the bottom of the water in the tumbler, or sit as long on the leaves above. A pulse in the throat always, except in one for an hour or two, apparently asleep. They change their color to a darker or lighter shade, chameleon-like.

May 1, 1853. To Cliffs. The oak leaves on the plain are fallen. The colors are now

light blue above (where is my cyanometer?
Saussure invented one, and Humboldt used it
in his travels); the landscape russet and greenish, spotted with fawn-colored ploughed lands,
with green pine and gray or reddish oak woods
intermixed, and dark blue or slate-colored water
here and there. It is greenest in the meadows
and where water has lately stood, and a strong,
invigorating scent comes up from the fresh
meadows. It is like the greenness of an apple
faintly or dimly appearing through the russet.

May 1, 1854. Early starlight by river-side.
The water smooth and broad. I hear the loud
and incessant cackling of probably the pigeon
woodpecker, what some time since I thought to
be a different kind. Thousands of robins are
filling the air with their trills, mingling with
the peeping of hylodes and ringing of frogs;
and now the snipes have just begun their win-
nowing sounds and squeaks.

May 1, 1855. P. M. By boat with S——
to Conantum a-maying.

The myrtle bird is one of the commonest and
tamest birds now. It catches insects like a
pewee, darting off from its perch and returning
to it, and sings something like "a-chill chill,
chill chill, chill chill, a-twear, twill twill twee,"
or it may be all *tw* (not loud, a little like the
Fringilla hiemalis, or more like the pine war-

bler), rapid, and more and more intense as it advances. There is an unaccountable sweetness as of flowers in the air. A true May day, — raw and drizzling in the morning. The grackle still. What various brilliant and evanescent colors on the surface of this agitated water, — now, as we are crossing Willow Bay, looking toward the half-concealed sun over the foam-spotted flood! It reminds me of the sea. . . .

Went to G——'s for the hawk of yesterday. It was nailed to the barn *in terrorem*, and as a trophy. He gave it to me, with an egg. He called it the female, and probably was right, it was so large. He tried in vain to shoot the male, which I saw circling about just out of gunshot, and screaming, while he robbed the nest. He climbed the tree when I was there yesterday P. M., and found two young, which he thought not more than a fortnight old, with only down, at least no feathers, and one addled egg; also three or four white-bellied or deer mice (*Mus leucopus*), a perch and a sucker, and a gray rabbit's skin. I think they must have found the fish dead. They were now stale. I found the remains of a partridge under the tree. G—— had seen squirrels, etc., in other nests.

May 1, 1857. Two P. M. First notice the ring of the toad as I am crossing the common in front of the meeting-house. There is a cool

and breezy south wind, and the ring of the first
toad leaks into the general stream of sound unnoticed by most, as the mill brook empties into
the river, and the voyager cannot tell if he is
above or below its mouth.   The bell was ringing for town meeting, and every one heard it,
but none heard this older and more universal
bell, rung by more native Americans all the
land over.   It is a sound from amid the waves
of the aerial sea, that breaks on our ears with
the surf of the air, — a sound that is almost
breathed with the wind, taken into the lungs
instead of being heard by the ears.   It comes
from far over and through the troughs of the
aerial sea, like a petrel; and who can guess by
what pool the singer sits? — whether behind the
meeting-house sheds, or over the burying-
ground hill, or by the river-side.   A new reign
has commenced.   Bufo the first has ascended
his throne, the surface of the earth, marshaled
into office by the south wind.   Bufo, the double-
chinned, inflates his throat.   Attend to his mes-
sage.   Take off your great coats, swains, and
prepare for the summer campaign.   Hop a few
paces farther toward your goals.   The measures
which I shall advocate are warmth, moisture,
and low-flying insects. . . .

It is foolish for a man to accumulate material
wealth chiefly, houses and lands.   Our stock in

life, our real estate, is that amount of thought
which we have had, which we have thought out.
The ground we have thus created is forever pas-
turage for our thoughts. I fall back on to vis-
ions which I have had. What else adds to my
possessions, and makes me rich in all lands? If
you have ever done any work with those finest
tools, the Imagination and Fancy and Reason,
it is a new creation, independent of the world,
and a possession forever. You have laid up
something against a rainy day. You have, to
that extent, cleared the wilderness.

May 1, 1859. We accuse savages of worshiping only the bad spirit or devil. Though
they may distinguish both a good and a bad,
they regard only that one which they fear, worship the devil only. We too are savages in
this, doing precisely the same thing. This occurred to me yesterday, as I sat in the woods
admiring the beauty of the blue butterfly. We
are not chiefly interested in birds and insects,
for example, as they are ornamental to the earth
and cheering to man, but we spare the lives of
the former only on condition that they eat more
grubs than they do cherries, and the only account of the insects which the State encourages
is of the insects injurious to vegetation. We
too admit both a good and bad spirit, but we
worship chiefly the bad spirit whom we fear.

We do not think first of the good, but of the
harm things will do us. The catechism says
that the chief end of man is to glorify God and
enjoy him forever, which of course is applicable
mainly to God as seen in his works. Yet the
only account of the beautiful insects, butterflies,
etc., which God has made and set before us,
which the State ever thinks of spending any
money on is the account of those which are injurious to vegetation ! This is the way we
glorify God and enjoy him forever. . . .

We have attended to the evil, and said nothing about the good. This is looking a gift
horse in the mouth, with a vengeance. Children are attracted by the beauty of butterflies,
but their parents and legislators deem it an idle
pursuit. The parents remind one of the devil,
but the children of God. Though God may
have pronounced his work good, we ask, Is it
not poisonous?

Science is *inhuman*. Things seen with a
microscope begin to be insignificant. So described, they are monstrous, as if they should
be magnified a thousand diameters. Suppose
I should see and describe men and horses and
trees and birds as if they were a thousand times
larger than they are. With our prying instruments we disturb the harmony and balance of
nature.

May 2, 1852. Reptiles must not be omitted, especially frogs. Their croaking is the
most earthy sound now, a rustling of the scurf
of the earth, not to be overlooked in the awakening of the year. . . .

The commonplaces of one age or nation make
the poetry of another. . . .

The handsome, blood-red, lacquered marks on
the edge and under the edge of the painted tortoise's shell, like the marks on a waiter, concen-
tric. Few colors like it in nature. This tortoise, too, like the guttata, painted on thin
parts of the shell, and on legs and tail in this
style, but on throat bright yellow stripes.
Sternum dull yellowish or buff. It hisses like
the spotted tortoise. Is the male the larger and
flatter, with depressed sternum? There is *some*
regularity in the guttata's spots, generally a
straight row on back. Some of the spots are
orange sometimes on the head. . . .

If you would obtain insight, avoid anat-
omy. . . .

May 2, 1855. The anemone is well named,
for see now the nemorosa amid the fallen brush
and leaves, trembling in the wind, so fragile.

May 2, 1859. A peetweet and its mate.
The river seems really inhabited when the peetweet is back. This bird does not return to our
stream until the weather is decidedly pleasant

and warm. He is perched on the accustomed
rock. His note peoples the river like the prat-
tle of children once more in the yard of a house
that has stood empty. . . .

I am surprised by the tender yellowish green
of the aspen leaves, just expanded suddenly,
even like a fire, seen in the sun against the dark
brown twigs of the wood, though these leaflets
are yet but thinly dispersed. It is very enlivening.

I feel no desire to go to California or Pike's
Peak, but I often think at night, with inexpressible satisfaction and yearning, of the arrow-
headiferous sands of Concord. I have often
spent whole afternoons, especially in the spring,
pacing back and forth over a sandy field, looking for these relics of a race. This is the gold
which our sands yield. The soil of that rocky
spot of Simon Brown's land is quite ash-colored
(now that the sod is turned up) from Indian
fires, with numerous pieces of coal in it. There
is a great deal of this ash-colored soil in the
country. We do literally plough up the hearths
of a people, and plant in their ashes. The
ashes of their fires colors much of our soil.

May 2, 1860. I observed on the 29th that
the clams had not only been moving much, fur-
rowing the sandy bottom near the shore, but
generally, or almost invariably, had moved

toward the middle of the river. Perhaps it had
something to do with the low stage of the water.
I saw one making his way, — or perhaps it had
rested since morning, — over that sawdust bar
just below Turtle Bar, toward the river, the
surface of the bar being an inch or two higher
than the water. Probably the water falling left
it thus on moist land.

A crowd of men seems to generate vermin
even of the human kind. In great towns there
is degradation undreamed of elsewhere, gamblers, dog-killers, rag-pickers. Some live by
robbing or by luck. There was the Concord
muster of last September. I see still a well-
dressed man carefully and methodically searching for money on the muster field far off across
the river. I turn my glass upon him and notice
how he proceeds. (I saw them searching in the
fall till the snow came.) He walks, regularly
and slowly, back and forth over the ground
where the soldiers had their tents, still marked
by the straw, with his head prone, and picking
in the straw with a stick, now and then turning
back or aside to examine something more closely.
He is dressed, methinks, better than the aver-
age man whom you meet in the streets. How
can he pay for his board thus? He dreams of
finding a few coppers, or perchance half a dime,
which have fallen from the soldiers' pockets,

and no doubt he will find something of the kind, having dreamed of it. Having knocked, this door will be opened to him.

May 3, 1841. We are all pilots of the most intricate Bahama channels. Beauty may be the sky overhead, but duty is the water underneath. When I see a man with serene countenance in garden or parlor, it looks like a great inward leisure that he enjoys, but in reality he sails on no summer's sea. This steady sailing comes of a heavy hand on the tiller. We do not attend to larks and bluebirds so leisurely but that conscience is as erect as the attitude of the listener. The man of principle gets never a holiday. Our true character underlies all our words and actions, as the granite underlies the other strata. Its steady pulse does not cease for any deed of ours, as the sap is still ascending in the stalk of the fairest flower.

May 3, 1852. Five A. M. To Cliffs. A great brassy moon going down in the west. . . . Looking from the Cliff, now about six A. M., the landscape is as if seen in a mirage, the Cliff being in shadow, and that in the cool sunlight. The earth and water smell fresh and new, and the latter is marked by a few smooth streaks. The atmosphere suits the grayish-brown landscape, the still, ashy maple swamps, and now nearly bare shrub oaks. The white pine, left here and there over the sprout land, is never more beautiful than with the morning light, before the water is rippled and the morning song of the birds is quenched.

Hear the first brown thrasher, two of them. They drown all the rest. He says, "cherruwit, cherruwit, go ahead, go ahead, give it to him, give it to him," etc. Plenty of birds in the woods this morning. The huckleberry birds and the chickadees are as numerous, if not as loud, as any. The flicker taps a dead tree somewhat as one uses a knocker on a door in the village street. In his note he begins low, rising higher and higher.

Anursnack looks green three miles off. This is an important epoch, when the distant bare hills begin to show green or verdurous to the eye. The earth wears a new aspect. Not tawny or russet now, but green are such bare hills. Some of the notes, the trills of the lark sitting amid the tussocks and stubble, are like the notes of my seringo bird. May these birds that live so low in the grass be called the cricket birds ? and does their song resemble that of the cricket, an earth song ?

Evening. The moon is full. The air is filled with a certain luminous, liquid white light. You can see the moonlight, as it were

reflected from the atmosphere, which some
might mistake for a haze, — a glow of mellow
light, somewhat like the light I saw in the afternoon sky some weeks ago, as if the air were
a very thin but transparent liquid, not dry as
in winter, nor gross as in summer. The sky
has depth, and not merely distance. Going
through the depot field, I hear the dream frog
at a distance. The little peeping frogs make a
background of sound in the horizon, which you
do not hear unless you attend. The former is
a trembling note, some higher, some lower,
along the edge of the earth, — an all-pervading
sound. Nearer, it is a blubbering or rather
bubbling sound, such as children, who stand
nearer to nature, can and do often make. . . .
The little peeper prefers a pool on the edge of
a wood, which mostly dries up at midsummer,
whose shore is covered with leaves, and where
there are twigs in the water, as where choppers
have worked. Theirs is a clear, sharp, ear-
piercing peep, not shrill, sometimes a squeak
from one whose pipe is out of order. . . . They
have much the greatest apparatus for peeping
of any frogs that I know. . . . I go along the
side of Fairhaven Hill. The clock strikes distinctly, showing the wind is easterly. There is
a grand, rich, musical echo trembling in the air
long after the clock has ceased to strike, like a

vast organ, filling the air with a trembling
music, like a flower of sound. Nature adopts
it. The water is so calm, the woods and single
trees are doubled by the reflection, and in this
light you cannot divide them as you walk along
the river. See the spearer's lights, one northeast, one southwest, toward Sudbury, beyond
Lee's Bridge, — scarlet-colored fires. From
the hill, the river is a broad blue stream exactly
the color of the heavens which it reflects. Sit
on the Cliff with comfort in great-coat. All
the tawny and russet earth (for no green is seen
upon the ground at this hour) sending only this
faint, multitudinous sound (of frogs) to heaven.
The vast, wild earth. The first whip-poor-will
startles me; I hear three. Summer is coming
apace. Within three or four days the birds
have come so fast I can hardly keep the run of
them, — much faster than the flowers.

Sunday, May 3, 1857. A remarkably warm
and pleasant morning. A. M. To battle ground
by river. I heard the ring of toads at six
A. M. The flood on the meadows, still high,
is quite smooth, and many are out this still and
suddenly very warm morning, pushing about
in boats. Now, thinks many a one, is the
time to paddle or push gently far up or down
the river, along the still, warm meadow's edge,
and perhaps we may see some large turtles, or

musk-rats, or otter, or rare fish or fowl. It will be a grand forenoon for a cruise, to explore these meadow shores and inundated maple swamps which we have never explored. Now we shall be recompensed for the week's confinement in shop or garden. We will spend our Sabbath exploring these smooth, warm vernal waters. Up or down shall we go, — to Fairhaven Bay and the Sudbury meadows, or to Ball's Hill and Carlisle Bridge? Along the meadow's edge, lined with willows and alders and maples; underneath the catkins of the early willow, and brushing those of the sweet-gale with our prow; where the sloping pasture and the ploughed ground submerged are fast drinking up the flood, what fair isles, what remote coast, shall we explore? what San Salvador or Bay of All Saints arrive at? All are tempted forth, like flies into the sun. All isles seem Fortunate and blessed to-day, all capes are of Good Hope. The same sun and calm that tempt the turtles out tempt the voyagers. It is an opportunity to explore their own natures, to float along their own shores. The woodpecker cackles and the crow blackbird utters his jarring chatter from the oaks and maples. All well men and women who are not restrained by superstitious custom come abroad this morning, by land or water, and such as have boats launch them and put

forth in search of adventure. Others, less free
or it may be less fortunate, take their station
on bridges, watching the rush of waters through
them and the motions of the departing voyagers,
and listening to the note of blackbirds from over
the smooth water. Perhaps they see a swimming
snake or a musk-rat dive, — airing and sunning
themselves there till the first bell rings. Up
and down the town men and boys that are under subjection are polishing their shoes and
brushing their go-to-meeting clothes.

I sympathize not to-day with those who go to
church in newest clothes, and sit quietly in
straight-backed pews. I sympathize rather
with the boy who has none to look after him,
who borrows a boat and paddle, and in common
clothes sets out to explore these temporary vernal lakes. I meet one paddling along under a
sunny bank, with bare feet and his pants rolled
up above his knees, ready to leap into the water
at a moment's warning. Better for him to
read Robinson Crusoe than Baxter's Saints'
Rest. . . .

The pine-warbler is perhaps the commonest
bird heard now from the wood sides. It seems
left to it almost alone to fill the empty aisles.

May 4, 1852. This excitement about Kossuth is not interesting to me, it is so superficial.

. . . Men are making speeches to him all over the country, but each expresses only the thought or the want of thought of the multitude. No man stands on truth. They are merely banded together as usual, one leaning on another, and all together on nothing, as the Hindoos made the world rest on an elephant, and the elephant on a tortoise, and had nothing to put under the tortoise. You can pass your hand under the largest mob, a nation in revolution even, and however solid a bulk they may make, like a hail cloud in the atmosphere, you may not meet so much as a cobweb of support. They may not rest, even by a point, on eternal foundations. But an individual standing on truth you cannot pass your hand under, for his foundations reach to the centre of the universe. So superficial these men and their doings. It is life on a leaf, or a chip, which has nothing but air or water beneath. I love to see a man with a tap-root, though it make him difficult to transplant. It is unimportant what these men do. Let them try forever, they can effect nothing. Of what significance are the things you can forget?

May 4, 1853. Cattle are going up country. Hear the "tull-lull" of the white-throated sparrow.

Eight A. M. To Walden and Cliffs. The sound of the oven-bird. . . . The woods and

fields next the Cliffs now ring with the silver
jingle of the field sparrow, the medley of the
brown thrasher, the honest *qui vive* of the chewink, or his jingle from the top of a low copse
tree, while his mate scratches in the dry leaves
beneath. The black and white creeper is hop-
ping along the oak boughs, head downward,
pausing from time to time to utter its note, like
a fine, delicate saw sharpening, and ever and
anon rises, clear over all, the smooth rich melody of the wood-thrush. Could that have been
a jay? I think it was some large, uncommon
woodpecker that uttered that very loud, strange,
cackling note. The dry woods have the smell
of fragrant everlasting. I am surprised by the
cool drops which now at ten o'clock fall from
the flowers of the amelanchier, while other
plants are dry, as if these had attracted more
moisture. The white pines have started. The
indigo bird and its mate, dark throat, light beneath, white spot on wings which is not described, a hoarse note and rapid, the first two
or three syllables "twe, twe, twee," the last
being dwelt upon, or "twe, twe, twe, tweee,"
or as if there were an *r* in it, "tre," etc., not
musical. . . .

It is stated in the "Life of Humboldt" that he
proved "that the expression, 'The ocean reflects
the sky,' was a purely poetical, not a scientifi-

cally correct one, as the sea is often blue when the sky is almost totally covered with light, white clouds." He used Saussure's cyanometer even to measure the color of the sea. This might probably be used to measure the intensity of blue flowers, like lupines, at a distance.

May 4, 1855. A robin sings, when I in the house cannot distinguish the earliest dawning from the full moonlight. His song first advertises me of the daybreak when I thought it was night, as I lay looking out into the full moonlight. I heard a robin begin his strain, and yielded the point to him, believing that he was better acquainted with the signs of day than I.

May 4, 1858. P. M. By boat to Holden swamp. To go among the willows now and hear the bees hum is equal to going some hundreds of miles southward toward summer.

Go into Holden swamp to hear warblers. See a little blue butterfly (or moth) (saw one yesterday) fluttering about on the dry brown leaves in a warm place by the swamp side, making a pleasant contrast. From time to time have seen the large *Vanessa antiopa* resting on the black willows, like a leaf still adhering. As I sit by the swamp side this warm summery afternoon I hear the crows cawing hoarsely, and from time to time see one flying toward the top of a tall white pine. At length I distinguish a hen-hawk perched on the top. The crow repeatedly stoops toward him, now from this side, now from that, passing near his head each time, but he pays not the least attention to it.

I hear the "veer-e, ver-e, ver-e" of the creeper continually in the swamp. It is the prevailing note there, and methought I heard a redstart's note, but oftener than the last the tweezer or screeper note of the party-colored warbler, bluish above, throat and breast yellow or orange, white on wings, and neck above yellowish, going restlessly over the trees (maples, etc.) by the swamp, in creeper fashion; and as you may hear at the same time the true creeper's note without seeing it, you might think this bird uttered the creeper's note also.

The redwings, though here and there in flocks, are apparently beginning to build. I infer this from their shyness and alarm in the bushes along the river, and their richer solitary warbling.

May 4, 1859. P. M. To Lee's Cliff on foot. . . . Crossing the first Conantum field I perceive a peculiar fragrance in the air (not the meadow fragrance), like that of vernal flowers or of expanding buds. The ground is covered with the mouse-ear in full bloom, and it may be that in part. It is a temperate southwest breeze, and this is a scent of willows (flowers and leaflets), bluets, violets, shad-bush, mouse-ear, etc., combined, or perhaps the last chiefly. At any rate, it is very perceptible. The air is more genial, laden with the fragrance of spring flowers. I, sailing on the spring ocean, getting in from my winter voyage, begin to smell the land. Such a scent perceived by a mariner would be very exciting. I not only smell the land breeze, but I perceive in it the fragrance of spring flowers. I come out expecting to see the redstart or the party-colored warbler, and as soon as I get within a dozen rods of the Holden wood I hear the screeper note of the tweezer bird, that is, the party-colored warbler, which also I see, but not distinctly. Two or three are flitting from tree-top to tree-top about the swamp there, and you have only to sit still on one side and wait for them to come round. The water has what you may call a summer ripple and sparkle on it; that is, the ripple does not suggest coldness in the breeze that raises it. It is a hazy day; the air is made hazy, you might fancy, with a myriad expanding buds. After crossing the arrow-head fields, we see a woodchuck run along and climb to the top of a wall and sit erect there, — our first. It is almost exactly the color of the ground, the wall, and the bare brown twigs altogether. When in the Miles swamp field we see two, one chas-

ing the other, coming very fast down the lilac-
field hill, straight toward us, while we squat
still in the middle of the field. The foremost
is a small gray or slaty-colored one; the other,
two or three times as heavy, and a warm tawny,
decidedly yellowish in the sun, a very large and
fat one, pursuing the first. . . . Suddenly the
foremost, when thirty or forty rods off, per-
ceives us, and tries, as it were, to sink into the
earth, and finally gets behind a low tuft of grass
and peeps out. Also the other (which at first
appears to fondle the earth, inclining his cheek
to it and dragging his body a little along it)
tries to hide himself, and at length gets behind
an apple-tree and peeps out on one side in an
amusing manner. This makes three that we
see. They are clumsy runners, with their short
legs and heavy bodies, — run with an undulating or wabbling motion, jerking up their hind
quarters. They can run pretty fast, however.
Their tails were dark-tipped. They are low
when the animal is running.

Looking up through this soft and warm southwest wind I notice the conspicuous shadow of
mid-Conantum Cliff, now at three P. M., and
elsewhere the shade of a few apple-trees, trunks
and boughs. Through this warm and hazy
air the sheeny surface of the hill, now considerably greened, looks soft as velvet, and

June is suggested to my mind. It is remarkable that shadow should only be noticed now when decidedly warm weather comes, though before the leaves have expanded, that is, when it begins to be grateful to our senses. The shadow of the Cliff is like a dark pupil on the side of the hill. The first shadow is as noticeable and memorable as a flower. I observe annually the first shadow of this cliff, when we begin to pass from sunshine into shade for our refreshment; when we look on shade with yearning, as on a friend. That cliff and its shade suggest dark eyes and eyelashes, and overhanging brows. Few things are more suggestive of heat than this first shade, though now we see only the tracery of tree boughs on the greening grass and the sandy street. This I notice at the same time with the first humble-bee; when the *Rana palustris* purrs in the meadow generally; when the white willow and the aspen display their tender green, full of yellow light; when the party-colored warbler is first heard over the swamp; the woodchuck, who loves warmth, is out on the hill-sides in numbers; the jingle of the chipbird and the song of the thrasher are heard incessantly; the first cricket is heard in a warm, rocky place; and that scent of vernal flowers is in the air. This is an intenser expression of that same influence or aspect of nature which I began to perceive ten days ago, the same *Lieferung*.

These days we begin to think in earnest of bathing in the river and to sit at an open window. Life out-of-doors begins.

It would require a good deal of time and patience to study the habits of woodchucks, they are so shy and watchful. They hear the least sound of a footstep on the ground, and are quick to see also. One should go clad in a suit somewhat like their own, the warp of tawny and the woof of green, and then with painted or well-tanned face he might lie out on a sunny bank till they appeared.

We hear a thrasher sing for half an hour steadily, a very rich singer, and heard one fourth of a mile off very distinctly. This is first heard commonly at planting time. He sings as if conscious of his power.

May 4, 1860. P. M. To Great Meadows by boat. . . . Walking over the river meadows to examine the pools and see how much dried up they are, I notice, as usual, the track of the musquash, some five inches wide always, and always exactly in the lowest part of the muddy hollows connecting one pool with another, winding as they wind, as if loath to raise itself above the lowest mud. At first he swam there, and now as the water goes down he follows it stead-

ily, and at length travels on the bare mud, but
as low and close to the water as he can get.
Thus he first traces the channel of the future
brook and river, and deepens it by dragging his
belly along it. He lays out and engineers its
road. As our roads are said to follow the
track of the cow, so rivers in another period
follow the trail of the musquash. They are
perfect rats to look at, and swim fast against
the stream. When I am walking on a high
bank, I often see one swimming along within
half a dozen rods, and land openly, as if regardless of us. Probably, being under water at
first, he did not notice us.

Looking across the peninsula toward Ball's
Hill, I am struck by the bright blue of the
river (a deeper blue than the sky) contrasting
with the fresh yellow-green of the meadow (that
is, of coarse sedges just starting), and between
them a darker or greener green, next the edge
of the river, especially where that small sand-
bar island is, the green of that early rank river-
grass. This is the first painting or coloring in
the meadows. These several colors are, as it
were, daubed on, as on china-ware, or as distinct and simple as in a child's painting. I was
struck by the amount and variety of color after
so much brown.

As I stood there I heard a thumping sound,

which I referred to P——, three fourths of a
mile off over the meadow. But it was a pigeon
woodpecker excavating its nest inside a maple
within a rod of me. Though I had just landed
and made a noise with my boat, he was too
busy to hear me, but now he hears my tread,
and I see him put out his head and then withdraw it warily, and keep still while I stay there.

DAYS AND NIGHTS IN CONCORD

[The time of year is August and September.]

I DO not remember any page which will tell me how to spend this afternoon. I do not so much want to know how to economize time as how to spend it; by what means to grow rich. How to extract its honey from the flower of the world — that is *my* every-day business. I am as busy as a bee about it. Do I not impregnate and intermix the flowers, produce rarer and finer varieties, by transferring my eyes from one to another? It is with flowers I would deal. The art of spending a day! If it is possible that we may be addressed, it behooves us to be attentive. So by the dawning or radiance of beauty are we advertised where are the honey and the fruit of thought, of discourse and of action. The discoveries which we make abroad are special and particular; those which we make at home are general and significant. My profession is to be always on the alert, to find God in nature, to know his lurking-places, to attend all the oratorios, the operas in nature. Shall I not have words as

fresh as my thought? Shall I use any other
man's word? A genuine thought or feeling
can find expression for itself if it have to invent
hieroglyphics. It has the universe for tpye-
metal.

Since I perambulated the "bounds of the
town," I find that I have in some degree confined myself (my vision and my walks). On
whatever side I look off, I am reminded of the
mean and narrow-minded men whom I have
lately met there. What can be uglier than a
country occupied by groveling, coarse, and low-
lived men? — no scenery can redeem it. Hornets, hyenas, and baboons are not so great a
curse to a country as men of a similar character.
It is a charmed circle which I have drawn about
my abode, having walked, not with God, but
the devil. I am too well aware when I have
crossed this line. . . .

The Price-Farm road is one of those everlasting roads which the sun delights to shine
along in an August afternoon, playing truant;
which seem to stretch themselves with terrene
jest as the weary traveler travels them on; where
there are three white sandy furrows (*liræ*), —
two for the wheels and one between them for
the horse, with endless green grass borders between, and room on each side for blueberries
and birches; where the walls indulge in freaks,

not always parallel to the ruts, and golden-rod yellows all the path, which some elms began to border and shade over, but left off in despair, it was so long ; from no point of which can you be said to be at any definite distance from a town. . . .

Old Cato says well, *Patrem familias vendacem, non emacem esse oportet.* These Latin terminations express, better than any English I know, the greediness, as it were, and tenacity of purpose with which the husbandman and householder is required to be a seller and not a buyer. With mastiff-like tenacity these lipped words collect in the sense, with a certain greed. Here comes a laborer from his dinner, to resume his work at clearing out a ditch, notwithstanding the rain, remembering, as Cato says, *Per ferias potuisse fossas veteres tergeri.* One would think I were come to see if the steward of my farm had done his duty.

The prevailing conspicuous flowers at present [August 21] are the early golden-rods, tansy, the life-everlastings, fleabane (though not for its flower), yarrow (rather dry), hard-hack and meadow - sweet (both getting dry), also Mayweed, purple eupatorium, clethra, rhexia, thoroughwort, *Polygala sanguinea*, prunella and dogsbane (getting stale), touch-me-not (less observed), Canada snapdragon by roadsides,

purple gerardia, horsemint, veronica, marsh
speedwell, tall crowfoot (still in flower), also
the epilobium and cow-wheat.

Half an hour before sunset I was at Tupelo
cliff, when, looking up from my botanizing (I
had been examining the *Ranunculus filiformis*,
Conium maculatum, *Sium latifolium*, and the
obtuse *Galium* on the muddy shore), I saw the
seal of evening on the river. There was a
quiet beauty on the landscape at that hour
which my senses were prepared to appreciate.
When I have walked all day in vain under the
torrid sun, and the world has been all trivial,
as well field and wood as highway, then at eve
the sun goes down westward, and the dews begin to purify the air and make it transparent,
and the lakes and rivers acquire a glassy stillness, reflecting the skies, the reflex of the day.
Thus, long after feeding, the diviner faculties
begin to be fed, to feel their oats, their nutri-
ment, and are not oppressed by the body's load.
Every sound is music now. How rich, like what
we like to read of South American primitive
forests, is the scenery of this river; what luxuriance of weeds, what depths of mud, along its
sides! These old ante-historic, geologic, ante-
diluvian rocks, which only primitive wading-
birds still lingering among us are worthy to
tread! The season which we seem to live in

anticipation of is arrived. With what sober joy I stand to let the water drip, and feel my fresh vigor, who have been bathing in the same tub which the muskrat uses, — such a medicinal bath as only nature furnishes! A fish leaps, and the dimple he makes is observed now. Methinks that for a great part of the time, as much as is possible, I walk as one possessing the advantages of human culture, fresh from the society of men, but turned loose into the woods, the only man in nature, walking and meditating to a great extent, as if man and his customs and institutions were not. The cat-bird or the jay is sure of your whole ear now; each noise is like a stain on pure glass.

The rivers now, — these great blue subterra-nean heavens reflecting the supernal skies and red-tinged clouds — what unanimity between the water and the sky, — one only a little denser element than the other, — the grossest part of heaven! Think of a mirror on so large a scale! Standing on distant hills you see the heavens reflected, the evening sky, in some low lake or river in the valley, as perfectly as in any mirror that could be. Does it not prove how intimate heaven is with earth? We commonly sacrifice to supper this serene and sacred hour. Our customs turn the hour of sunset to a trivial time, as to the meeting of two roads,— one com-

ing from the noon, the other leading to the
night. It might be well if our repasts were
taken out-of-doors, in view of the sunset and the
rising stars; if there were two persons whose
pulses beat together; if men cared for the
cosmos or beauty of the world; if men were
social in a rare or high sense; if they associated
on rare or high levels; if we took with our tea
a draught of the dew-freighted, transparent
evening air; if with our bread and butter we
took a slice of the red western sky; if the
smoking, steaming urn was the vapor on a
thousand lakes and rivers and meads. The air
of the valleys at this hour is the distilled essence
of all those fragrances which during the day
have been filling and have been dispersed in the
atmosphere, — the fine fragrances, perchance,
which have floated in the upper atmospheres,
now settled to these low vales. I talked of
buying Conantum once, but for want of money
we did not come to terms. But I have farmed
it, in my own fashion, every year since.

I find three or four ordinary laborers to-day
putting up the necessary out-door fixtures for a
magnetic telegraph. They carry along a basket of simple implements, like traveling tinkers;
and with a little rude soldering and twisting
and straightening of wire, the work is done, —
as if you might set your hired man with the

poorest head and hands, with the greatest lati-
tude of ignorance and bungling, to this work.
All great inventions stoop thus low to succeed,
for the understanding is but little above the
feet. They preserve so low a tone, they are
simple almost to coarseness and commonplace-
ness. Some one had told them what he wanted,
and sent them forth with a coil of wire to make
a magnetic telegraph. It seems not so wonderful an invention as a common cart or plough.

The buckwheat already cut [September 4]
lies in red piles in the field. In the Marlboro'
road I saw a purple streak like a stain on the
red pine leaves and sand under my feet, which
I was surprised to find was made by a dense
mass of purple fleas, like snow-fleas. And now
we leave the road and go through the woods and
swamps toward Boon's Pond, crossing two or
three roads, and by Potter's house in Stow,
still on the east side of the river. Beyond Potter's, we struck into the extensive wooded plain,
where the ponds are found in Stow, Sudbury,
and Marlboro'; part of it is called Boon's
Plain. Boon is said to have lived on or under
Bailey's Hill, at the west of the pond, and was
killed by the Indians, between Boon's and
White's pond, as he was driving his ox-cart.
The oxen ran off to the Marlboro' garrison-
house ; his remains have been searched for.

There were two hen-hawks that soared and cir-
cled for our entertainment when we were in the
woods on this plain, crossing each other's orbits
from time to time, alternating like the squirrels
in their cylinder, till, alarmed by our imitation
of a hawk's shrill cry, they gradually inflated
themselves, made themselves more aerial, and
rose higher and higher into the heavens, and
were at length lost to sight; yet all the while
earnestly looking, scanning the surface of the
earth for a stray mouse or rabbit. We saw a
mass of sunflowers in a farmer's patch; such
is the destiny of this large coarse flower, the
farmers gather it like pumpkins. We noticed
a potato-field yellow with wild radish. Knight's
new dam has so raised the Assabet as to make
a permanent freshet, as it were, the fluviatile
trees standing dead for fish-hawk perches, and
the water stagnant for weeds to grow in. You
have only to dam up a running stream to give
it the aspect of a dead stream, and in some
degree restore its primitive wild appearance.
Tracts are thus made inaccessible to man and
at the same time more fertile, — the last gasp
of wildness before it yields to the civilization
of the factory; to cheer the eyes of the factory
people and educate them, — a little wilderness
above the factory.

As I looked back up the stream, I saw the

ripples sparkling in the sun, reminding me of the sparkling icy fleets which I saw last winter; and I thought how one corresponded to the other, — ice waves to water ones; the erect ice flakes were the waves stereotyped. It was the same sight, the same reflection of the sun sparkling from a myriad slanting surfaces; at a distance, a rippled water surface or a crystallized frozen one. We climbed the high hills on the west side of the river, in the east and southeast part of Stow. I observed that the walnut-trees conformed in their branches to the slope of the hill, being just as high from the ground on the upper side as the lower. I saw what I thought a small red dog in the road, which cantered along over the bridge, and then turned into the woods; this decided me, this turning into the woods, that it was a fox, the dog of the woods. A few oaks stand in the pastures, still great ornaments. I do not see any young ones springing up to supply their places, and will there be any a hundred years hence? We are a young people and have not learned by experience the consequences of cutting off the forest. I love to see the yellow knots and their lengthened stain on the dry, unpainted pitch-pine boards on barns and other buildings, as the Dugan house. The indestructible yellow fat, it fats my eyes to see it, worthy for art to imitate, telling of branches in the forest once.

From Strawberry Hill we caught the first, and but a very slight, glimpse of Nagog Pond, by standing on the wall. That is enough to relate of a hill, methinks, — that its elevation gives you the first sight of some distant lake. The horizon is remarkably blue with mist; looking from this hill over Acton, successive valleys filled with this mist appear, and are divided by darker lines of wooded hills. The shadows of the elms are deepened, as if the whole atmosphere were permeated by floods of ether, that give a velvet softness to the whole landscape; the hills float in it; a blue veil is drawn over the earth. Anursnack Hill had an exceedingly rich, empurpled look, telling of the juice of the wild grape and poke-berries. Noticed a large field of sunflowers for hens, in full bloom at Temple's, now — at six P. M. — facing the east. The larches in the front yards have turned red; their fall has come; the Roman wormwood (*Ambrosia artemisiæfolia*) is beginning to yellow-green my shoes, intermingled with the blue-curls in the sand of grain-fields. Perchance some poet likened this yellow dust to the ambrosia of the gods.

Do not the songs of birds and the fireflies go with the grass, whose greenness is the best symptom and evidence of the earth's health or youth? Perhaps a history of the year would be a history of the grass, or of a leaf, regarding the grass-blades as leaves. Plants soon cease to grow for the year, unless they may have a fall growth, which is a kind of second spring. In the feelings of the man, too, the year is already past, and he looks forward to the coming winter. It is a season of withering; of dust and heat; a season of small fruits and trivial experiences. But there is an aftermath, and some spring flowers bloom again. May my life be not destitute of its Indian Summer! I hear the locust still; some farmers are sowing their winter rye; I see the fields smoothly rolled. I see others ploughing steep, rocky, and bushy fields for rolling. How beautiful the sprout-land! When you look down on it, the light green of the maples shaded off with the darker red, enlivening the scene yet more. Surely this earth is fit to be inhabited, and many enterprises may be undertaken with hope, where so many young plants are pushing up. Shall man then despair? Is he not a sprout-land, too, after never so many searings and witherings? If you witness growth and luxuriance, it is all the same as if you grew luxuriantly. The woodbine is red on the rocks. The poke is a very rich and striking plant, cardinal in its rank, as in its color. The downy seeds of the groundsel are taking their flight; the calyx has dismissed them and quite curled back, having done its part.

When I got into Lincoln Road [September 11] I perceived a singular sweet scent in the air; but, though I smelled everything around, I could not detect it. It was one of the sweet scents which go to make up the autumn, which fed and dilated my sense of smell. I felt the better for it. Methinks that I possess the sense of smell in greater perfection than usual. How autumnal is the scent of wild grapes, now by the roadside! The cross-leaved polygala emits its fragrance as at will; you must not hold it too near, but on all sides and at all distances. The pendulous, drooping barberries are pretty well reddened. I am glad when the berries look fair and plump.

Windy autumnal weather is very exciting and bracing, clear and cold after a rain. The winds roars loudly in the woods, the ground is strewn with leaves, especially under the apple-trees. The surface of the river reflecting the sun is dazzlingly bright; the outlines of the hills are remarkably distinct and firm, their surfaces bare and hard, not clothed with a thick air. I notice one red maple, far brighter than the blossom of any tree in summer. What can be handsomer for a picture than our river scenery now? First, this smoothly shorn meadow on the west side of the stream, looking from the first Conantum cliff, with all the swaths distinct, sprinkled with apple-trees casting heavy shadows black as ink [9 A. M.], such as can be seen only in this clear air, this strong light, — one cow wandering restlessly about in it and lowing; then the blue river, scarcely darker than, and not to be distinguished from, the sky, its waves driven southward (or up the stream), by the wind, making it appear to flow that way, bordered by willows and button-bushes; then the narrow meadow beyond, with varied lights and shades from its waving grass, each grass-blade bending south before the wintry blast, as if looking for aid in that direction; then the hill, rising sixty feet to a terrace-like plain covered with shrub-oaks, maples, and other trees, each variously tinted, clad all in a livery of gay colors, every bush a feather in its cap; and further in the rear the wood-crowned cliffs, some two hundred feet high, whose gray rocks project here and there from amid the bushes, with an orchard on the slope, and the distant Lincoln Hills in the horizon. What honest, homely, earth-loving houses they used to live in, so low you can put your hands on the eaves behind! — the broad chimney, built for comfort, no alto or basso relievo! The air is of crystal purity, — both air and water so transparent, the fisherman tries in vain to deceive the fish with his baits. Walden plainly can never be spoiled by the wood-chopper; for, do what you will to the shore, there will still remain this crystal well. The intense brilliancy of the red, ripe maples, scattered here and there in the midst of the green oaks and hickories on its hilly shores, is quite charming. Alternating with yellow birches and poplars and green oaks, they remind one of a line of soldiers, red-coats and riflemen in green, mixed together.

From Ball's Hill [September 26], the meadows, now smoothly shorn, have a quite imposing appearance, so spacious and level. There is a shadow on the sides of the hills surrounding (it is a cloudy day), and where the meadow meets them it is darkest. Now the sun in the west is coming out, and lights up the river a mile off so that it shines with a white light, like a burnished silver mirror. The poplar-tree on Miss Ripley's hill seems quite important to the scene. The patches of sunlight on the meadow look lividly yellow, as if flames were traversing it. It is a day for fishermen. The farmers are gathering in their corn. The climbing hemp-weed (*Mikania scandens*) and the button-bushes and the pickerel-weed are sere and flat with frost. We fell into the path printed by the feet of the calves. The note of the yellow-hammer is heard from the edges of the fields.

Sitting by the spruce swamp in Conant's woods, I am reminded that this is a perfect day to visit the swamp, with its damp, mistling, mildewy air, so solemnly still. There are the spectre-like black spruces hanging with usnea lichens, and in the rear rise the dark green pines and oaks on the hillside, touched here and there with livelier tints where a maple or birch may shine, — this luxuriant vegetation standing heavy, dark, sombre, like mould in a cellar. . . .

Has one moon gone by unnoticed? It is peculiarly favorable to reflection, — a cold and dewy light in which the vapors of the day are condensed, and though the air is obscured by darkness it is more clear. Lunacy must be a cold excitement, not such insanity as a torrid sun on the brain would produce. But the moon is not to be judged alone by the quantity of light she sends us, but also by her influence on the thoughts. No thinker can afford to overlook her influence any more than the astronomer can. Has not the poet his spring-tides and his neap-tides, in which the ocean within him overflows its shores and bathes the dry land, — the former sometimes combining with the winds of heaven to produce those memorable high tides which leave their mark for ages, when all Broad Street is submerged and incalculable damage done the common shipping of the mind? I come out into the moonlit night where men are not, as if into a scenery, *anciently* deserted by men; the life of men is like a dream. It is three thousand years since night has had possession. Go forth and hear the crickets chirp at midnight. Hear if their dynasty is not an ancient one and well founded. I feel the antiquity of the night; she merely repossesses herself of her realms, as if her dynasty were uninterrupted, or she had underlaid the day. No sounds but the steady creaking of crickets, and the occasional crowing of cocks. I go by the farmer's houses and barns, standing there in the dim light under the trees, as if they lay at an immense distance, or under a veil. The farmer and his oxen are all asleep, not even a watch-dog is awake. The human slumbers; there is less of man in the world. To appreciate the moonlight, you must stand in the shade and see where a few rods or a few feet distant it falls in between the trees. It is a "milder day," made for some inhabitants whom you do not see. I am obliged to sleep enough the next night to make up for it (after being out) — *Endymionis somnum dormire* — to sleep an Endymion's sleep, as the ancients expressed it.

The fog on the lowlands (on the Corner Road) is never still. It now advances and envelops me as I stand to write these words before sunrise, then clears away with ever noiseless step. It covers the meadows like a web, — I hear the clock strike three. The light of Orion's belt seems to show traces of the blue day through which it came to us. The sky at least is lighter on that side than in the west, even about the moon. Even by night the sky is blue and not black, for we see through the veil of night into the distant atmosphere. I see to the plains of the sun where the sunbeams are reveling. The crickets' song by the causeway is not so loud at this hour as at evening, and the moon is getting low. I hear a wagon cross on one of the bridges leading into the town. I smell the ripe apples many rods off beyond the bridge. Will not my townsmen consider me a benefactor if I conquer some realms from the night, if I can show them that there is some beauty awake while they are asleep; if I add to the domains of poetry; if I report to the gazettes anything transpiring in our midst worthy of man's attention? I will say nothing here to the disparagement of Day, for he is not here to defend himself.

I hear the farmer harnessing his horse and starting for the distant market, but no man harnesses himself and starts for worthier enterprises. One cock-crow tells the whole story of the farmer's life. I see the little glow-worms deep in the grass by the brookside. The moon shines dim and red, a solitary whip-poor-will sings, the clock strikes four, a few dogs bark, a few more wagons start for market, their faint rattling is heard in the distance. I hear my owl without a name, the murmur of the slow approaching freight-train as far off perchance as Waltham, and one early bird. The round red moon is disappearing in the west. I detect a whiteness in the east. Some dark, massive clouds have come over from the west within the hour, as if attracted by the approaching sun, and have arranged themselves raywise across the eastern portal as if to bar his coming. They have moved, suddenly and almost unobservedly, quite across the sky (which before was clear) from west to east. No trumpet was heard which marshaled and advanced the dark masses of the west's forces thus rapidly against the coming day. Column after column the mighty west sent forth across the sky while men slept, but all in vain.

The eastern horizon is now grown dun-colored, showing where the advanced guard of the night are already skirmishing with the vanguard of the sun, — a lurid light tinging the atmosphere there, — while a dark-columned cloud hangs imminent over the broad portal untouched by the glare. Some bird flies over, making a noise like the barking of a puppy (it was a cuckoo). It is yet so dark that I have dropped my pencil and cannot find it. The sound of the cars is like that of a rushing wind; they come on slowly; I thought at first a morning wind was rising.

The whip-poor-wills now begin to sing in earnest, about half an hour before sunrise, as if making haste to improve the short time that is left them. As far as my observation goes they sing for several hours in the early part of the night, are silent commonly at midnight, — though you may meet them sitting on a rock or flitting silent about, — then sing again at just before sunrise. It grows more and more red in the east (a fine-grained red under the overhanging cloud), and lighter too, and the threatening clouds are falling off to southward of the sun's passage, shrunken and defeated, leaving his path comparatively clear. The increased light shows more distinctly the river and the fog. The light now (five o'clock) reveals a thin film of vapor like a gossamer veil cast over the lower hills beneath the cliffs, and stretching to the river, thicker in the ravines, thinnest on the even slopes. The distant meadows to the north

beyond Conant's grove, full of fog, appear like
a vast lake, out of which rise Anursnack and
Ponkawtasset like wooded islands. And all
the farms and houses of Concord are at the
bottom of that sea. So I forget them, and
my thought sails triumphantly over them. I
thought of nothing but the surface of a lake, a
summer sea over which to sail; no more would
the voyager on the Dead Sea who had not the
Testament think of Sodom and Gomorrah and
cities of the plain. I only wished to get off to
one of the low isles I saw in the midst of the
sea (it may have been the top of Holbrook's
elm) and spend the whole summer day there.
Meanwhile the redness in the east had diminished and was less deep. And next the red
was become a sort of yellowish or fawn-colored
light, and the sun now set fire to the edges of
the broken cloud which had hung over the horizon, and they glowed like burning turf.

It is remarkable that animals are often obviously, manifestly related to the plants which
they feed upon or live among, as caterpillars,
butterflies, tree-toads, partridges, chewinks. I
noticed a yellow spider on a golden-rod, — as
if every condition might have its expression in
some form of animated being. I have seen the
small mulleins in the fields for a day or two as
big as a ninepence; rattlesnake grass is ripe; a

stalk of purple eupatorium, eight feet, eight inches high, with a large convex corymb (hemispherical) of many stories, fourteen inches wide, and the width of the plant, from tip of leaf to tip of leaf, two feet, the diameter of its stalk one inch at the ground. Is not disease the rule of existence? There is not a lily-pad floating in the river but has been riddled by insects. Almost every tree and shrub has its gall, oftentimes esteemed its chief ornament, and hardly to be distinguished from its fruit. If misery loves company, misery has company enough. Now at midsummer find me a perfect leaf or fruit. The difference is not great between some fruits in which the worm is always present and those gall-fruits which were produced by the insect. The prunella leaves have turned a delicate claret or lake color by the roadside [September 1]. I am interested in these revolutions as much as in those of kingdoms. Is there not tragedy enough in the autumn? The pines are dead and leaning red against the shore of Walden Pond (which is going down at last), as if the ice had heaved them over. Thus by its rising it keeps an open shore. I found the succory on the railroad. May not this and the tree primrose, and other plants, be distributed from Boston on the rays of the railroads? The feathery-tailed fruit of

the fertile flowers of the clematis are conspicuous now. The shorn meadows looked of a living green as we came home at eve, even greener
than in spring. This reminds me of the
"*fenum cordum*," the aftermath, "*sicilimenta
de pratis*," the second mowing of the meadow,
in Cato. I now begin to pick wild apples.

I walk often in drizzly weather, for then the
small weeds (especially if they stand on bare
ground), covered with rain-drops like beads,
appear more beautiful than ever, — the hyperi-
cums, for instance. They are equally beautiful when covered with dew, fresh and adorned,
almost spirited away in a robe of dew-drops.
The air is filled with mist, yet a transparent
mist, a principle in it which you might call flavor, which ripens fruits. This haziness seems
to confine and concentrate the sunlight, as if
you lived in a halo, — it is August. Some
farmers have begun to thresh and to winnow
their oats. Not only the prunella turns lake,
but the *Hypericum virginicum* in the hollows by
the roadside, a handsome blush, a part of the
autumnal tints. Ripe leaves acquire red blood.
Red colors touch our blood and excite us as well
as cows and geese. We brushed against the
Polygonum arcuatum, with its spikes of reddish white flowers, — a slender and tender plant
which loves the middle of dry and sandy, not

much traveled roads, — to find that the very stones bloom, that there are flowers we rudely brush against which only the microscope reveals. The dense fog came into my chamber early, freighted with light, and woke me. It was one of those thick fogs which last well into the day. The farmers' simple enterprises! They improve this season, which is the dryest, their haying being done, and their harvest not begun, to do these jobs, — burn brush, build walls, dig ditches, cut turf, also topping corn and digging potatoes. Sometimes I smell these smokes several miles off, and, by their odor, know it is not a burning building, but withered leaves and the rubbish of the woods and swamps. Methinks the scent is a more oracular and trustworthy inquisition than the eye. When I criticise my own writing I go to the scent, as it were. It reveals what is concealed from the other senses. By it I detect earthiness.

The jays scream on the right and left as we go by, flitting and screaming from pine to pine. I hear no lark sing at evening as in the spring, only a few distressed notes from the robin. I saw a pigeon - place on George Heywood's cleared lot, with the six dead trees set up for the pigeons to alight on, and the brush-house close by to conceal the man. I was rather startled to find such a thing going now in Concord. The pigeons on the trees looked like fabulous birds, with their long tails and their pointed breasts. I could hardly believe they were alive and not some wooden birds used for decoys, they sat so still, and even when they moved their necks I thought it was the effect of art. I scare up the great bittern in the meadow by the Heywood brook near the ivy. He rises buoyantly as he flies against the wind, and sweeps south over the willow, surveying. I see ducks or teal flying silent, swift, and straight, the wild creatures! The partridge and the rabbit, they still are sure to thrive like true natives of the soil, whatever revolutions occur. If the forest is cut off, many bushes spring up which afford them concealment. In these cooler, windier, crystal days the note of the jay sounds a little more native.

I found on the shores of the pond that singular willow-herb in blossom, though its petals were gone. It grows up two feet from a large woody horizontal root, and drops over to the sand again, meeting which, it puts a myriad rootlets from the side of its stem, fastens itself and curves upward again to the air, thus spanning or looping itself along. The bark, just above the ground, thickens into a singular cellular or spongy substance, which at length appears to crack nearer the earth, giving that part of the plant a winged or somewhat four-sided appearance. The caducous *polygala* is faded in cool places almost white; knot-grass or door-grass (*Polygonum aviculare*) is still in bloom. I saw the lambkill in flower (a few fresh blossoms), beautiful bright flowers, as of a new spring with it, while the seed-vessels, apparently of this year, hung dry below. The ripening grapes begin to fill the air with their fragrance.

I hear the red-wing blackbirds and meadow-larks again by the river-side [October 5], as if it were a new spring. They appear to have come to bid farewell. The birds seem to depart at the coming of the frost, which kills the vegetation and directly or indirectly the insects on which they feed. As we sailed up the river, there was a pretty good-sized pickerel poised directly over the sandy bottom close to the shore, and motionless as a shadow. It is wonderful how they resist the slight current, and remain thus stationary for hours. He no doubt saw us plainly on the bridge, — in the sunny water, his whole form distinct and his shadow, — motionless as the steel-trap which does not spring till the fox's foot has touched it. In this drought you see the nests of the bream on the dry shore. The prinos berries are quite red, the dog-wood by the Corner Road has lost every leaf, its branches of dry greenish berries hanging straight down from the bare stout twigs, as if their peduncles were broken. It has assumed its winter aspect, — a Mithridatic look. The black birch is straw-colored, the witch-hazel is now in bloom. The little conical burs of the agrimony stick to my clothes; the pale lobelia still blooms freshly, and the rough hawk-weed holds up its globes of yellowish fuzzy seeds, as well as the panicled. The reclining sun, falling on the willows and on the water, produces a rare soft light I do not often see, — a greenish yellow. The milk-weed seeds are in the air; I see one in the river which a minnow occasionally jostles. The butternuts have shed nearly all their leaves, and their nuts are seen black against the sky. The white-ash has got its autumnal mulberry hue. It contrasts strangely with the other shade-trees on the village street. It is with leaves as with fruits, and woods, and animals, and men, — when they are mature their different characters appear. The elms are generally of a dirty or brownish yellow now. Some of the white pines have reached the acme of their fall; the same is the state of the pitch-pines. The shrub-oaks are almost uniformly of a deep red.

The reach of the river between Bedford and

Carlisle, seen from a distance, has a singularly ethereal, celestial, or elysian look. It is of a light sky blue, alternating with smoother white streaks, where the surface reflects the light differently, like a milk-pan full of the milk of Valhalla, partially skimmed; more gloriously and heavenly fair and pure than the sky itself. We have names for the rivers of Hell, but none for the rivers of Heaven, unless the milky way may be one. It is such a smooth and shining blue, like a panoply of sky-blue plates.

Some men, methinks, have found only their hands and feet. At least, I have seen some who appeared never to have found their heads, but used them only instinctively. What shall we say of those timid folks who carry the principle of thinking nothing, and doing nothing, and being nothing, to such an extreme? As if in the absence of thought, that vast yearning of their natures for something to fill the vacuum made the least traditionary expression and shadow of a thought to be clung to with instinctive tenacity. They atone for their producing nothing by a brutish respect for something.

INDEX

ACRE, an, as long measure, 75.
Acton (Mass.), 166, 447.
Agriculture, the task of Americans, 281–283.
Agrimony, the, 463.
Alphonse, Jean, and Falls of Montmorenci, 47; quoted, 112.
America, superiorities of, 269–275.
American, money in Quebec, 29; the, and government, 102.
Anacreon, quoted, 133, 135.
Andropogons or Beard-Grasses, 313–317.
Anemone, the, 419.
Ange Gardien Parish, 51; church of, 57.
Angler's Souvenir, the, 146.
Animals, related to plants on which they feed, 457.
Anursnack, 423; Hill, 447, 457.
Apple, history of the tree, 356–367; the wild, 367–369; the crab-, 369–371; growth of the wild, 371–378; cropped by cattle, 372–376; the fruit and flavor of the, 378–385; beauty of the, 385–387; naming of the, 387–389; last gleaning of the, 389–392; the frozen-, thawed, 392–394; dying out of the wild, 394–396.
Apple-howling, 366.
Arpent, the, 75.
Arrow-headiferous sands of Concord, 420.
Ashburnham (Mass.), 3; with a better house than any in Canada, 124.
Ash-trees, 7.
Aspen leaves, the green of, 420.
Assabet, the, 166, 445.
Audubon, John James, reading, 127; 134, note; 138, note.
Autumn foliage, brightness of, 305–308; weather and landscape, 449–452; the tragedy of, 458.
AUTUMNAL TINTS, 305–355.

Bailey's Hill, 444.
Ball's Hill, 426, 436, 451.
Bartram, William, quoted, 244.
Bathing feet in brooks, 172; at sunset, 442.
Bayfield's chart, Captain, 114, 116.
Beach-plums, inland, 246.
Beard-Grasses, Andropogons or, 313–317.
Beauport (Que.), and le Chemin de, 37; getting lodgings in, 43–46; church in, 85; Seigniory of, 119.
Beaupré, Seigniory of the Côte de, 50.
Bedford (Mass.), 463.
"Behold, how spring appearing," 135.
Bellows Falls (Vt.), 6.
Birch, yellow, 7; black, 463.
Birds and mountains, 182.
Bittern, booming of the, 137; the great, 461.
Blueberries, and milk, supper of, 177; 411.
Bluebird, the, 136.
Bobolink, the, 139.
Bodæus, quoted, 389.
Bolton (Mass.), 168.
Bonsecours Market (Montreal), 13.
Books on natural history, reading, 127–129.
Boon's Pond, 444.
Boots, Canadian, 63.
Boston (Mass.), 3, 8, .0.
Boucher, quoted, 113.
Boucherville (Que.), 24.
Bouchette, Topographical Description of the Canadas, quoted, 50, 52, 78, 79, 110, 114, 117.
Bout de l'Isle, 24.
Boylston (Mass.), 170.
Brand's Popular Antiquities quoted, 365.
Bravery of science, the, 131, 132.
Buckwheat, 444.
Burlington (Vt.), 8, 123.

Burton, Sir Richard Francis, 279, 280.
Butterfly, beauty of the, 417, 418; a blue, 430.
Butternut-tree, 7, 463.

Cabs, Montreal, 22; Quebec, 86.
Caddice-worms, 208.
Caen, Emery de, quoted, 64.
Caleche, the (see Cabs), 86.
Canada, apparently older than the United States, 100; population of, 101; the French in, a nation of peasants, 102.
Canada East, 49.
Canadense, Iter, and the word, 125.
Canadian, French, 11; horses, 41; women, 42; atmosphere, 42; love of neighborhood, 52, 53; houses, 54, 73; clothes, 55; salutations, 58; vegetables and trees, 59; boots, 63; tenures, 78, 79.
Cap aux Oyes, 115.
Cane, a straight and twisted, 225, 226.
Cape Diamond, 26, 50; signal-gun on, 105; the view from, 109.
Cape Rouge, 26, 118.
Cape Rosier, 114.
Cape Tourmente, 50, 110, 119.
Carlisle (Mass.), 464.
Carlisle Bridge, 426.
Cartier, Jacques, 9; and the St. Lawrence, 111, 112; quoted, 120, 121; 122.
Catbird, the, 412.
Cato Major, quoted, 440.
Cattle show, men at, 225.
Cemetery of fallen leaves, 331.
Chaleur, the Bay of, 112.
Chalmers, Dr., in criticism of Coleridge, 398.
Chambly (Que.), 13.
Champlain, Samuel, quoted, 9; whales in map of, 9, 113.
Charlesbourg (Que.), 110.
Charlevoix, quoted, 65, 113.
Chateau Richer, church of, 57; 60; lodgings at, 73, 85.
Chaucer, Geoffrey, quoted, 195, 196.
Chaudière River, the, 26; Falls of the, 86, 87.
Cheap men, 36.
Cherry-stones, transported by birds, 230.
Chewink, the, 429.
Chickadee, the, 134, 423.
Chien, La Rivière au, 69.
Chipping-sparrow, the fork-tailed, 410, 411.

Churches, Catholic and Protestant, 15–17; roadside, 57.
Claire Fontaine, La, 32.
Clams, moving, 420.
Clothes, bad-weather, 34; Canadian, 55.
Clouds, the moon and, 405.
Colors, names and joy of, 335–337; in a May landscape, 436.
Conant's woods, 452.
Conantum, 414, 431, 433, 443.
Concord (Mass.), 3, 6, 8; History of, quoted, 141; 163, 183, 186, 420, 457.
Concord River, the, 141, 170.
Connecticut River, 6, 177, 180, 181.
Coureurs de bois, and *de risques,* 53.
Creeper, the, 412, 429, 431.
Crickets, the creaking of, 133.
Crook-neck squash seeds, Quebec, 108.
Crosses, roadside, 56.
Crow, the, 134; not imported from Europe, 139; 430.
Crystalline botany, 155, 156.
Culm, bloom in the, 310.
Cyanometer, a, 414, 430.

Darby, William, quoted, 116.
Daybreak, 454–457.
DAYS AND NIGHTS IN CONCORD, 438–464.
Dogs in harness, 36, 37.
Dog-wood, 463.
Door-grass, 462.
Drake, Sir Francis, quoted, 400.
Dubartas, quoted, translation of Sylvester, 404.
Ducks, 135.

"Each summer sound," verse, 138.
East Main, Labrador and, health in the words, 128.
Easterbrooks Country, the, 367, 372.
Edda, the Prose, quoted, 358.
Eggs, a master in cooking, 76.
Elm, the, 322, 323, 338, 339, 463.
Emerson, George B., quoted, 245.
English and French in the New World, 83, 84.
Entomology, the study of, 132, 133.
Evelyn, John, quoted, 381.
Everlasting, fragrant, 429.
Ex Oriente Lux; ex Occidente Frux, 271.
Experiences, the paucity of men's, 295, 296.
Eyes, the sight of different men's, 350–354.

Fairhaven Bay, 426.
Fairhaven Hill, 411, 424.
Fallen Leaves, 324–602.
Falls, a drug of, 72.
Finch, the, 139 ; the to-wee, 412.
Fish, spearing, 147, 149–151.
Fisher, the pickerel, 220, 221.
Fishes, described in Massachusetts Report, 146.
Fish-hawk, the, 136.
Fitchburg (Mass.), 3.
Fitzwilliam (N. H.), 4.
Fleas, purple, 444.
Flicker, the, 137, 412, 423.
Flowers, conspicuous August, 440.
Fog, 454, 460.
Foreign country, quickly in a, 38.
Forests, nations preserved by, 281.
Fortifications, ancient and modern, 95, 96.
Fox, the, 144 ; mistaken for a dog, 446.
French, difficulties in talking, 43–45, 57 ; strange, 62 ; pure, 65 ; in the New World, English and, 83, 84 ; in Canada, 101, 102 ; the, spoken in Quebec streets, 107.
Frogs, peeping, 412, 413, 414, 424, 425 ; 419.
Froissart, good place to read, 28.
Frost-smoke, 203.
Fruits at the Isles of Richelieu, 19.
Fur Countries, inspiring neighborhood of the, 130.

Garget, Poke or, 311–313.
Geese, first flock of, 135.
Gesner, Konrad von, quoted, 391.
Goldfinch, the, 139.
Gosse, P. A., " Canadian Naturalist," 113.
Government, too much, 102.
Grass, a year's history of the, 448.
Great Brook, 167.
Great Fields, the, 315.
Great Meadows, 435.
Great River, the, or St. Lawrence, 110, 111, 113.
Green Mountains, the, 6, 7, 124, 177, 180.
Grey, the traveler, quoted, 116, 117.
Grippling for apples, 379.
Groton (Mass.), 170, 186.
Groundsel, the, 449.
Gulls, 135.
Gun, a signal, 105.
Guyot, Arnold, 115 ; quoted, 116, 270.

Harvard (Mass.), 185, 186.

Hawk, the, 134 ; and nest and eggs, 415.
Hawk-weed, 463.
Head, Sir Francis, quoted, 58, 271.
Heights of Abraham, 26.
Hen-hawk, the, 431, 445.
Herrick, Robert, 366.
Hickory, the, 324.
Highlanders in Quebec, 30–32, 33, 34, 98.
" His steady sails he never furls," 134.
Hoar-frost, 155, 156.
Hochelaga, 14, 120, 121, 123.
Holden Swamp, 430.
Homer, quoted, 221.
Hoosac Mountains, 180.
Hop, culture of the, 167.
Horses, Canadian, 41.
Hortus siccus, nature in winter a, 218, 219.
House, the perfect, 187.
Houses, Canadian, 54, 73 ; American compared with Canadian, 124.
Huckleberry bird, the, 412, 423.
Humboldt, Alex. von, 114, 115, 429.
Hunt House, the old, 247.
Hypericum, the, 459.

" I see the civil sun drying earth's tears," verse, 147.
Ice, the booming of, 215.
Ice formations in a river-bank, 157, 158.
Ignorance, Society for the Diffusion of Useful, 293.
Imitations of Charette drivers, Yankee, 123.
" In two years' time 't had thus," verse, 372.
Indian Summer, the, of life, 448.
Indigo bird, the, 429.
Indoors, living, 254–256.
Inn, inscription on wall of Swedish, 173.
Invertebrate Animals, Mass. Report on, quoted, 159.

Jay, the, 134, 243, 244, 429, 460.
Jesuit Relations, quoted, 119.
Jesuits' Barracks, the, in Quebec, 29.
Joel, the prophet, quoted, 395, 396.
Jonson, Ben, quoted, 277.
Josselyn, John, quoted, 1.

Kalm, Swedish traveler, quoted, 26, 37, 48, 81 ; on sea-plants near Quebec, 115.

Keene (N. H.) Street, 4; heads like, 5.
Kent, the Duke of, property of, 46.
Khaled, quoted, 410.
Killington Peak, 6.
Knot-grass, 462.
Knowledge, the slow growth of, 161; Society for the Diffusion of Useful, 293; true, 294.
Kossuth, the excitement about, 427, 428.

Labrador and East Main, health in the words, 128.
Lachine Railroad Depot, the, 123.
Lake, a woodland, in winter, 213, 214.
Lake Champlain, 7–9.
Lake St. Peter, 119, 121.
Lalemant, Hierosme, quoted, 27.
Lambkill, the, 462.
Lancaster (Mass.), 168, 170, 183.
LANDLORD, THE, 187–198.
Landlord, qualities of the, 188–198.
La Prairie (Que.), 12, 13, 22, 123.
Lark, the, 134, 136.
Lead, rain of, 32.
Leaves, Fallen, 324–332; Scarlet Oak, 341–344.
Lincoln (Mass.), 346, 347; Road, the, 449.
Linnæus, quoted, 272.
Longueil (Que.), 24.
Lord Sydenham steamer, the, 89, 118.
Lorette (Que.), 110.
Loudon, John Claudius, quoted, 241, 245, 358, 381.
Ludlow (Vt.), 6.

McCulloch's Geographical Dictionary, quoted, 61.
McTaggart, John, quoted, 116.
MacTavish, Simon, 121.
Map, drawing, on kitchen table, 74; of Canada, inspecting a, 118.
Maple, the red and sugar, 7; the Red, 317–322, 325; the Sugar, 320, 332–341.
Matane, Paps of, 114.
Marañon, the river, 116.
Marlborough (Mass.), 262; road, the, 444.
Meadow-larks, 462.
Merrimack River, the, 181.
Michaux, André, quoted, 269.
Michaux, François André, quoted, 271; 320, 370.
Midnight, exploring the, 397.
Milk-weed seeds, 463.

Miller, a crabbed, 85.
Milne, Alexander, quoted, 236, 237.
Mingan settlements, the, in Labrador, 114.
Mississippi, discovery of the, 111, 112; extent of the, 116; a panorama of the, 274.
Monadnock, 4, 175, 178, 180.
Montcalm, Wolfe and, monument to, 90, 91.
Montmorenci County, 76, 77; the habitans of, 79–84.
Montmorenci, Falls of, 36, 46–48.
Montreal (Que.), 10, 13; described, 17–19; the mixed population of, 21; from Quebec to, 120; and its surroundings, beautiful view of, 122; the name of, 122.
MOONLIGHT, NIGHT AND, 397–409.
Moonlight, reading by, 178; 423, 424; influence of, 452.
Moonshine, 399.
Moore, Thomas, 122.
Morning, winter, early, 200–203; landscape, early, 422.
Morton, Thomas, 1.
Mount Holly (Vt.), 6.
Mount Royal (Montreal), 13.
Mountains, the use of, 181, 182; and plain, influence of the, 185, 186.
Mouse-ear, the, 431.
Musketaquid, Prairie, or Concord River, 141.
Musk-rat, the, 141–144.
Musquash, track of the, 435.
Mussel, the, 159.
Myrtle bird, the, 414.

Nagog Pond, 447.
Names, poetry in, 24; of places, French, 70, 71; men's, 289–291; of colors, 335, 336.
Nashua River, the, 170, 185.
NATURAL HISTORY OF MASSACHUSETTS, 127–162.
Natural history, reading books of, 127, 129.
Nature, health to be found in, 129; man's work the most natural, compared with that of, 146; the hand of, upon her children, 153; different methods of work, 154; the civilized look of, 172; the winter purity of, 204; a *hortus siccus* in, 218, 219; men's relation to, 296; finding God in, 438.
Nawshawtuck Hill, 384.
New Liverpool Cove, 26.
New things to be seen near home, 259.

Niebuhr, Barthold Georg, quoted, 356.

Niepce, Joseph Nicéphore, quoted, 292.

NIGHT AND MOONLIGHT, 397–409.

Night, on Wachusett, 179; the senses in the, 403; out of doors, 453, 454.

Nobscot Hill, 372, 374.

Norumbega, 111.

"Not unconcerned Wachusett rears his head," verse, 176.

Notre Dame (Montreal), 13; a visit to, 14–17.

Notre Dame des Anges, Seigniory of, 119.

Nurse-plants, 236.

Nut-hatch, the, 134.

Nuttall, Thomas, quoted, 136, 137, 138, note, 411.

Oak, succeeding pine, and *vice versa*, 227, 229, 231; The Scarlet, 341–350; leaves, Scarlet, 341–344.

Ogilby, America of 1670, quoted, 113.

"Old Marlborough Road, The," verse, 263.

Orinoco, the river, 115.

Orleans, Isle of, 51, 61.

Orsinora, 111.

Ortelius, *Theatrum Orbis Terrarum*, 111.

Ossian, quoted, 408.

Ottawa River, the, 50, 116, 122.

Oui, the repeated, 75.

Palladius, quoted, 361, 378.

Partridge, the, 461.

Patent office, seeds sent by the, 248, 249.

Peetweet, the, 419.

Penobscot Indians, use of Musk-rat skins by, 143.

Perch, the, 151.

Philip's War, King, 183.

Phœbe, the, 138.

Pickerel, a motionless, 462.

Pickerel fisher, the, 220, 221.

Pies, no, in Quebec, 106.

Pigeons, 460, 461.

Pilots, all men, 422.

Pinbéna, the, 59.

Pine, oak succeeding, and *vice versa*, 227, 229, 231; family, a, 297–299; white and pitch, 463.

Pine-cone, stripped by squirrels, 240.

Pine-warbler, the, 427.

Plain and mountain, life of the, 185, 186.

Plants on Cape Diamond, Quebec, 33; and animals which feed on them, 457.

Plate, the river, 115.

Plattsburg (N. Y.), 8.

Plicipennes, 208.

Pliny, the Elder, quoted, 359.

Plover, the, 138.

Point Levi, by ferry to, 86; a night at, 88; 110.

Pointe aux Trembles, 24, 25.

Poke or Garget, the, 311–313, 448.

Polygala, the, 462.

Polygonum arcuatum, 459.

Pommettes, 48.

Ponkawtasset, 457.

Potherie, quoted, 65.

Prairie River, Musketaquid or, 141.

Price Farm road, the, 439.

Princeton (Mass.), 175.

Prinos berries, the, 462.

Purana, the, quoted, 402.

Purple Grasses, The, 308–317.

Quail, a white, 134, note.

Quebec (Que.), 3, 24, 25; approach to, 26; harbor and population of, 27; mediævalism of, 28, 31; the citadel, 33–36; 95–100; fine view of, 61; reëntering, through St. John's Gate, 86; lights in the lower town, 88; landing again at, 89; walk round the Upper Town, 89–94; the walls and gates, 91, 92; artillery barracks, 92; mounted guns, 94; restaurateurs, 105, 106; scenery of, 108–110; origin of word, 109; departure from, 118.

Rabbit, the, 461.

Rainbow in Falls of the Chaudière, 87.

Raleigh, Sir Walter, quoted, 404.

Redwing blackbirds, 462.

Redwings, 431.

Reports, Mass., of slight value, 160.

Return of Spring, verse, 135.

Rhexia, 309.

Richelieu, Isles of, 119.

Richelieu or St. John's River, 10.

Richelieu Rapids, the, 25.

Richter, Jean Paul, quoted, 406.

River, the flow of a, 217.

River-bank, ice formations in a, 157, 158.

Rivers of Hell and Heaven, names for, 464.

Rivière du Sud, the, 114.

Rivière more meandering than River, 70.

Roberval, Sieur de, 118, 119.
Robin, the, 134; a white, 134, note; 414, 430.
Robin Hood Ballads, quoted, 184, 254.
Rock-Maple, the, 325.
Rouse's Point (N. Y.), 9.
Rowlandson, Mrs., 183.

St. Anne, the Falls of, 49; Church of *La Bonne*, 60; lodgings in village of, 61–63; interior of the church of *La Bonne*, 63, 64; Falls of, described, 65–69.
St. Charles River, the, 87.
St. Helen's Island (Montreal), 13.
St. John's (Que.), 10–12.
St. John's River, 10.
St. Lawrence River, 13, 14; cottages along the, 25, 26; banks of the, above Quebec, 49, 50; breadth of, 61; or Great River, 111–118; old maps of, 111, 114; compared with other rivers, 111, 114–117.
St. Maurice River, 116.
Saguenay River, 112, 116.
Salutations, Canadian, 58.
Sault a la Puce, Rivière du, 60, 71.
Sault Norman, 13.
Sault St. Louis, 13.
Saunter, derivation of the word, 251, 252.
Scarlet Oak, The, 341–350.
Scent, autumn, 449; more trustworthy than sight, 460.
School-house, a Canadian, 57.
Science, the bravery of, 131, 132.
Scotchman dissatisfied with Canada, a, 93.
Scriptures, Hebrew, inadequacy of, regarding winter, 223, 224.
Sea-plants near Quebec, 115.
Seeds, the transportation of, by wind, 228; by birds, 229–231; by squirrels, 233–244; the vitality of, 245–248.
Seeing, individual, 350–354.
Selenites, 397.
Seven Islands, the, 114.
Shadows, the coming of, in spring, 433, 434.
Sheep, a load of, 23.
Shirley (Mass.), 170.
Shrub-oaks, 463.
Sign-language, 75, 76.
Sillery (Que.), 26.
Silliman, Benjamin, quoted, 121.
Skating, 216.
Smoke, winter morning, 201; seen

from a hilltop, 212; the smell of, 460.
Snake, the, 152.
Snipe-shooting grounds, 60.
Snow, 221, 222; not recognized in Hebrew Scriptures, 223.
Snow-bird, the, 134.
Society, health not to be found in, 129.
Soldiers, English, in Canada, 11, 19–21; in Quebec, 29–33, 98, 99.
Solomon, quoted, 357.
"Sometimes I hear the veery's clarion," verse, 138.
Song-sparrow, the, 135.
Sounds, winter morning, 200, 202.
Sorel River, 9, 10.
Sparrow, the white-throated, 428; the field, 429.
Spaulding's Farm, 297.
Spearing fish, 149–151.
Speech, country, 168.
Spending a day, the art of, 438.
Spirit, worshiping a bad, 417, 418.
Spring, on the Concord River, 147–

Squash, the large yellow, 249.
Squirrel, a red, burying nuts, 233, 234; with nuts under snow, 239; pine-cones stripped by the, 240; with filled cheek-pouches, 243.
Stars, the, 403–405.
Sterling (Mass.), 172, 183.
Stillriver Village (Mass.), 185.
Stillwater (Mass.), 184.
Stillwater, the, 172, 174.
Stow (Mass.), 166, 444, 446.
Strawberry Hill, 447.
Succession of Forest Trees, The, 225–250.
Sudbury (Mass.), 372, 425, 426, 444.
Sugar-Maple, The, 332–341.
Sunday, keeping, 427.
Sunflowers, 447.
Sunrise, 456, 457.
Sunset, a remarkable, 302–304; on the river, 441.
Supper, an interruption of sunsets, 442, 443.
Swamp, a day to visit the, 452.

Tamias, the steward squirrel, 243.
Tavern, the gods' interest in the, 187; compared with the church, the, 198.
Telegraph, workers on the, 443, 444.
Tenures, Canadian, 78.
"The needles of the pine," verse, 163.

"The river swelleth more and more," verse, 148.
"The sluggish smoke curls up from some deep dell," verse, 201.
Theophrastus, 359.
Thomson, James, quoted, 305.
Thoreau, Henry David, leaves Concord for Canada, 25th September, 1850, 3; traveling outfit of, 38-41; leaves Quebec for Montreal on return trip, 118; leaves Montreal for Boston, 123; total expense of Canada excursion, 125; walk from Concord to Wachusett and back, 163-186; observation of a red squirrel, 233, 234; experience with government squash-seed, 249.
"Thou dusky spirit of the wood," verse, 139.
Thought, the absence of, 464.
Thrasher, the brown, 423, 429, 435.
Three Rivers (Que.), 25, 115.
Three-o'clock courage, 255.
Toad, ring of the, 415, 416, 425.
Tortoise, colors on a, 419.
Trappers, 142.
Traverse, the, 114.
Traveling outfit, the best, 38-41.
Trees, Canadian, 59; the suggestions of, 154; the natural planting of, 227-248; a town's need of, 334, 337-341; for seasons, 339.
Tree-tops, things seen and found on, 300, 301.
Troy (N. H.), 4.
Tupelo Cliff, 441.
Turtle, the snapping, 152.

"Upon the lofty Elm-tree sprays," verse, 138.

Val Cartier (Que.), 110.
Vanessa antiopa, 430.
Varennes, the church of, 121.
Veery, the, 138.
Vegetation, the type of all growth, 157.
Vergennes (Vt.), 8.
Vermin generated by men, 421.
Village, a continuous, 51, 52; the, 261; trees in a, 337-341.
Violet, the first, 411.
Virgil, reading, 169, 176.

Wachusett, a view of, 169; range, the, 170; ascent of, 174; birds or vegetation on summit of, 175; night on, 178; an observatory, 180.

Walden (Mass.), 428.
Walden Pond, 458.
Walls, Quebec and other, 91.
WALK TO WACHUSETT, A, 163-186.
Walkers, the order of, 253.
WALKING, 251-304.
Walks, not on beaten paths, 262; the direction of, 265-268; adventurous, 350; by night, 401; in drizzly weather, 459.
Waltham (Mass.), 455.
Warblers, 430, 431, 432.
Watatic, 168, 181.
"We pronounce thee happy, Cicada," verse, 133.
Wealth, true, 416, 417.
West, walking towards the, 266-269; general tendency towards the, 269-275.
Westmoreland, etymology of, 6.
Whales in the St. Lawrence, 112, 113.
"When Winter fringes every bough," verse, 215.
"Where they once dug for money," verse, 263.
Whip-poor-will, the first, 425; singing before sunrise, 455, 456.
White-ash, the, 465.
White's Pond, 444.
Whitney, Peter, quoted, 383.
"Whoa," the crying of, to mankind, 288.
WILD APPLES, 356-396.
Wildness, the necessity of, 275-289; in literature, 283-285; in domestic animals, 287-289.
William Henry (Que.), 25.
Willow, Golden, leaves, 327.
Willow Bay, 415.
Willow-herb, the, 461.
WINTER WALK, A, 199-224.
Winter, warmth in, 205; the woods in, 206, 207; nature a *hortus siccus* in, 218, 219; as represented in the almanac, 222; ignored in Hebrew Revelation, 223; evening, 224.
Witch-hazel, 463.
"With frontier strength ye stand your ground," verse, 163.
"Within the circuit of this plodding life," 127.
Wolfe and Montcalm, monument to, 90, 91.
Wolfe's Cove, 26.
Women, Canadian, 42.
Woodbine, 3, 4, 338, 448.
Wood-chopper, writer to be represented as a, 222.

Woodchucks, 432, 433, 435.
Woodman, hut and work of, 210–212.
Woodpecker, the, 412, 429; the pigeon, 414, 437.
Wood-thrush, the, 429.

Woods in winter, the, 206, 207.
Wordsworth, reading, 176.
Wormwood, the Roman, 447.

YANKEE IN CANADA, A, 1–125.
"Yorrick," the, 138, note.

31